God and Conflict

God and Conflict

A Search for Peace in a Time of Crisis

Philip M. Hellmich

Spirit of Peace Press Petaluma

God and Conflict is a superb modern-day spiritual quest book. We live Hellmich's adventures on both the path of service and self-realization as he allows us all the way in to the most intimate dimensions of the quest. He takes us to the heart of his personal growth and transformation without compromising the raw truthfulness of the authentic seeker. God and Conflict is sure to inspire all those who want to help heal a traumatized world and surrender to the equal rigors of the spiritual path.

— James O'Dea
Internationally renowned peacebuilder and social healer
Author of *Creative Stress* and the recently published *Cultivating Peace*
Former president and extended faculty, Institute of Noetic Sciences
Former director, Washington DC office, Amnesty International

This is a brave, passionate book written from a broken heart that dared to engage in Sacred Activism.

— Andrew Harvey
Author, *The Hope a Guide to Sacred Activism*

Philip Hellmich is living the balance so many of us are yearning for, between cultivating the inner life and activating a path of service in the world. *God and Conflict* is a beautifully written love song to the paradoxical truth of the human experience as we struggle to show up for our sacred assignment: to be passionate peacemakers in this beautiful, broken world.

— Mirabai Starr
Translator, *Dark Night of the Soul and The Interior Castle*
Author, *Mother of God Similar to Fire and God of Love*

God and Conflict is an engaging book about an engaged life. From its provocative title to its closing observation that "inner peace is a global responsibility," it lets the reader into one of the most vibrant minds in the contemporary movement to discover what Rabbi Michael Lerner and others are calling spiritual activism: the life, of which Gandhi's is the supreme example, grounded in inner realization and extended to the widest reach of social action. It is in this movement that the ancient debate between the active and the contemplative life is turned from an "eitheror" to a "both-and." We desperately need that blend in an age plagued by alienation and violence, dogged by apathy on the one hand and raw protest on the other. Fortunately God and Conflict is a good read, because everyone who's interested in peace should read it.

— Michael Nagler
President, Metta Center for Nonviolence
Author, *The Search for a Nonviolent Future: A Promise of Peace for Ourselves, Our Families, and Our World*

A passionate account of one man's search for himself and his God, and the inspiration and guidance he found along the way that led him to discover how to make peace, profoundly, in his heart, and in the world. *God and Conflict* opens the way for deep exploration — of what is asked of each of us if we are:

- to declare peace with the same intensity as we have for so long declared war;
- to make a decision for peace in our every day lives, and live it; and
- to stand steadily for peace in these turbulent times that are cracking the foundations of the world as we know it.

This book tracks Philip Hellmich's journey as he charts the course to his north star, and we find him shining brightly, lighting the path for others to follow.

— Susan Collin Marks
Author, *Watching the Wind; Conflict Resolution during South Africa's Transition to Democracy*
Senior vice president, Search for Common Ground

Absolutely remarkable! Hellmich stirs every aspect of one's being throughout this courageous journey in book form. His transparency and openness to the very raw nature of life's utmost tragedies and triumphant sources of healing and peace make this a page-turner of the heart. It truly highlights the concept that even in our darkest hour, we can rest assured in the knowledge that we can rebound strong, brilliant and far more beautiful beings than before.

— Kimmie Weeks
Founder and executive director, Youth Action International
Awarded by Liberian President Ellen Johnson Sirleaf: Knight Grand Commander in the Humane Order of African Redemption (Liberia's highest honor)

God and Conflict is a very personal story about Philip Hellmich's journey where he struggles to make sense out of the Heaven and Hell that is found here on Earth. His time in Sierra Leone, West Africa and his firsthand accounts of war, tragedy, suffering and loss give us a peak into the Hell realms of Earth that push us beyond the mind to find meaning, understanding and inner peace. His experiences with Yoga, Kriya Yoga, Divine Mother and internal realms of love and bliss add more insight regarding this confusing mystery of duality. Philip's journey is shared by many, and his unique story of Sierra Leone is especially moving. His desire to help create a more loving and peaceful world is very sincere. He offers ancient wisdom and contemporary insights for anyone wanting to create more harmony, peace and love in their lives and worldwide.

— Ronald L Mann, PhD
Bestselling author and transformational coach

In *God and Conflict,* Philip Hellmich invites us to recognize conflict as a natural part of finding essence and truth, not only for us as individuals, but also in our organizations and businesses, societies, and in the world. An engaging storyteller, Hellmich beautifully weaves together his personal journey toward inner peace with stories of struggle, love, and humanity in conflict-ridden areas of the world where he has lived and served. He invites us to look beyond pain into healing, beyond separation and isolation into an experience of connection and oneness. Ultimately, he helps us see that somewhere within conflict there is a signpost pointing the way toward a new path — a path that, rather than serving one over the other, can serve all. *God and Conflict* is an important and insightful read for anyone committed to making a significant difference in the world.

— Alan Seale
Director, Center for Transformational Presence
Author, Create *A World That Works*

International peace and peacebuilding can only emerge from a profound movement of peace within ourselves, Philip Hellmich tells us. By sharing his personal story, and that of the people in Sierra Leone, he shows what this dynamic might look like for each us in a time when multiculturalism and globalization are inevitable.

— Dr. Kurt Johnson
Cofounder, Interspiritual Dialogue

It is hard for me to put into words how moved I was by *God and Conflict*. At first I expected it was about the horror of the violence witnessed in Africa, but it is so much more. Being a veteran of the Vietnam War, and coming from and being a subject of violence in youth and yet Love in youth, I resonated with Hellmich's spiritual journey of healing and transformation. In my own path, the only place I could turn was Jesus in my Catholic upbringing, not understanding and yet knowing there has to be more. *God and Conflict* is so heartfelt and so deep. It reminds me of the words of Pope John Paul talking about the free market: "Without high spiritual and moral values, it will destroy itself from within." I am sure he meant civilization without high spiritual and moral values will destroy itself. *God and Conflict* makes the universal teachings of Catholicism and other spiritual traditions all the more relevant for today.

— John Marqua
Founder of Abundance of Health, L.L.C.
CW2 1st Infantry Division, Vietnam, 1968–1969

I have long believed that the way to a more peaceful world is to experience how others live, love, and struggle, so we can discover our common humanity. Not everyone can do the travel that this requires. Philip Hellmich's book makes it easy to experience something of the cultures he encountered on his travels. Through Philip's deep questioning and hard-won awareness, the reader gets a heart-centered view of those who appear different from us. I highly recommend this book.

— Dianne Eppler Adams
Spiritual mentor
Bestselling author, *Conscious Footsteps: Finding Spirit in Everyday Matters*

I was humbled...... blasted into gratitude for the challenges I face today, which pale in comparison to the incomprehensible suffering and monumental courage shown by the extraordinary human beings Philip (I include him in that group) writes about. *God and Conflict* spoke directly to me and my personal journey. It is a toolbox filled with brilliant answers to achieving what each and every human being is ultimately searching for — Dignity, Respect, Security, and Love. Hellmich hit the nail squarely on the head here, proving that the way to solve the world's problems is to begin to work on your own. Certainly easier said than done, but this book clearly shows how to do it and proves beyond a shadow of a doubt that we are never alone — even in the darkest times of our lives. I feel blessed, reinspired, and grateful to have read it and intend to read it again and again.

— Peter Ressler
Coauthor, with Monika Mitchell, of *Conversations with Wall Street: The Inside Story of the Financial Armageddon and How to Prevent the Next One*

Philip Hellmich is one of the rare individuals who brings together his spiritual practice and his work in peacebuilding. He has devoted most of his adult years both to deepening his spiritual life and to enhancing understanding of the causes of conflict in regions around the world. Most peace activists focus on the political or economic causes of conflict. Philip has been able to see more deeply into the hidden, less visible aspects of war and has sought to draw attention to the spiritual resources that can help in healing and reconciliation. Philip's book is an important read for all of those seeking to use the spiritual principles inherent in all religious traditions to bring about a more peaceful and compassionate world.

— Dena Merriam
Founder and convener, the Global Peace Initiative of Women

For the 200,000 individuals who have served in the Peace Corps since its creation a half century ago, Philip M. Hellmich's *God and Conflict* is a story that will resonate deeply: being a Peace Corps Volunteer in Sierra Leone launches him on a journey of life-long discovery rooted in an enduring connection to the people and place where he served. Philip's inspiring journey chronicles the power of community and spirituality, even amidst the harsh reality of war. As a true child of Sargent Shriver, the founder of the Peace Corps, Philip learns that peace — internal and international — must be waged to be won. Philip's journey demonstrates that peace requires trust in the human spirit and the recognition of our common humanity. *God and Conflict* eloquently reaffirms that mindful service has enormous potential to develop empathy, tolerance, compassion, and love — the prerequisites for the peace we seek.

— Kevin F. F. Quigley
President, National Peace Corps Association

"In writing the book, I have sought to bridge the worlds of inner and outer peacebuilding" (Appendix Two). Author Philip Hellmich does this effectively in *God and Conflict.*

This book is an autobiography of a Peacebuilder, whose path continually reveals that personal and planetary Peace are inseparable.

Through his exceptionally honest and compelling story, Philip takes the reader intimately into conflicts on the front lines of Peacebuilding, and into the crucible of his personal relationship with God. He openly shares his personal inquiries, agonies, and spiritual explorations, as well as the wisdom from teachers, mentors, friends along his Soul's evolving path of unitive consciousness.

This book is a significant gift to all who seek to transform one's own personal conflicts, and to live and serve more integratively upon each unique Peacebuilding path.

The author concludes his autobiography with this gift of wisdom: "In essence, we all become instruments of Her peace in a grand symphony of peace that is emerging around the world."

— Avon Mattison
President & cofounder, Pathways To Peace
International peacebuilding and strategic planning consultant

Philip Hellmich has seen the hell caused by war, and he sincerely cares about the urgent need humanity has for peace. In *God and Conflict,* he takes us on a journey through the horrors of war and guides us through pragmatic steps each of us can take to bring about peace in ourselves and the world.

— David Fabricius
Internationally renowned business speaker for elite groups
Former military special forces instructor
Founder, Men of the Code

Sometimes it seems like the world is getting crazier and crazier. At other times we can see wonderful signs that humanity is evolving. In *God and Conflict,* Philip Hellmich builds a bridge between these two different experiences of reality, and he helps us to understand the core spiritual issues that underlie the terrible things that humans can do to one another. This book also shows us the powerful connections that exist among people, even in the most difficult situations. Through one man's deeply moving and inspiring journey, we can see a roadmap of our own potential for inner peace and for becoming peacebuilders in the world. Hellmich is a master storyteller and spiritual teacher all rolled into one. This riveting book helps to move us from horror to hope, from conflict to compassion, and from paralysis to possibility. Once you pick it up, you won't be able to put it down.

— Judi Neal, PhD
Director, Tyson Center for Faith and Spirituality in the Workplace
Sam M. Walton College of Business
University of Arkansas

God and Conflict shows us what it means to be spiritual in the midst of the worldly conflicts — whether on the fiery streets of civil war in West Africa or the searing emotional battles of family members or lovers locked at cross-purposes. Conflict becomes the illuminated path in Hellmich's hands, vulnerability his trusted companion...this is work worthy of respect.

— China Galland
Author, *Longing for Darkness, Tara and the Black Madonna*
Faculty, Center for Art, Religion, and Education, Graduate Theological Union, Berkeley, California

God and Conflict

A Search for Peace in a Time of Crisis

Philip M. Hellmich

Spirit of Peace Press
Petaluma, California
www.spiritofpeacepress.com

Ordering Information:

Quantity sales. Special discounts are available on quantity purchases by corporations, associations, and others. For details, contact the publisher at www.spiritofpeacepress.com.

EBook and Kindle editions available.

Cover design by Thomas Christian Wolfe (www.wolfestudios.com)
Interior design and typography by Jelehla Ziemba (www.zwordart.com)
Editing by Vanessa Arrington; Structural editing by Jenny Bird

Set in 11-point Adobe Jenson Pro with ITC Tiepolo, Post Antiqua, and Optima
Printed in the United States of America

ISBN 978-0-615-62590-4

Dedicated to

The Divine Mother

Paramahansa Yogananda

and

The People of Sierra Leone, West Africa

Love and compassion are the moral fabric of world peace.[1]

—His Holiness the 14th Dalai Lama

Philip Hellmich with "Sparky" — Kagbere, Sierra Leone 1985

Contents

Foreword

It is not news that our world is in crisis — environmental, economic, political, and conflict over resources; the list goes on and on. It is clear there is a need for collective as well as individual action guided by discriminating wisdom and skillful, creative intelligence. We need to awaken together and go beyond partisanship, isms and schisms and explore new ways to solve these problems. If we cannot pull together, we will be pulled apart.

All of the major spiritual traditions of our world offer contemplative practices — such as prayer and meditation, yoga, attitude transformation techniques and the like — which systematically guide an individual into the deeper inner realms where self-realization, innate wisdom-awareness and profound intuition can be accessed, cultivated, and further developed. Yet, as a spiritual teacher, I am often asked: "How do I bridge the gap between my meditation-cushion and yoga-mat experiences in confronting and striving to meet the seemingly overwhelming challenges facing the world today?" I always say that integration is our greatest spiritual challenge today, bringing deep spirituality into every nook and cranny of our daily lives. This means going deep inside ourselves and finding the water table or universal level, that united state which we all share, and then coming forth from that/there into the world.

This centering and penetration to the vital core can allow us to be in the world but not entirely *of* it, and remain uncaught up with the dream-like enticements and values of worldliness and immature egocentricism which lead to so much mischief along with even nastier trouble. I believe that each of us must find and express fully our own true vocation in this way — our true work, gift, and raison d'être — and thus gift ourselves through that avenue to the better world, present and future, that we all long for. There is simply no easy answer or simplistic one-size-fits-all way to do so, though some people might very well offer some.

One of my friends likes to tell her students and mentees: "The only way to eat an elephant is one bite at a time." For the journey of a thousand miles begins beneath ones feet. A Zen master of old, when he overheard two monks arguing about whether to eat their tofu with chopsticks or a spoon, shouted: "The only way to eat is with your mouth! The rest is detail." Like those argumentative monks, we too often get lost in the details and lose sight of the bigger picture. We need to make at least a single step in a new direction, perhaps even the right direction, and start being a provider, steward and guardian rather than just one more avaricious consumer.

I've found the uniquely efficacious antidote to ignorance, confusion and delusion is awakened awareness-wisdom — the ability to see things clearly and just as they are, not as we would like them to be or as *we* are, with all our projections and interpretations. This human capacity for insight and discernment can act as a panacea in helping us understand both causation and the ultimate nature of reality, directly relieving us of *weltschmerz*, the felt pain and sorrow of the human condition. When oneself becomes clear, everything becomes clearer: this is the truth. Turning the searchlight, the spotlight, inwards for some time — through contemplative practice, through re-mindfulness and awareness — definitely goes a long way in helping to rebalance our extreme modern outer-directedness. This is a jewel beyond price, in the palm of your own hand, and it is freely available.

Philip Hellmich has taken on the timeless and yet so timely challenge of applying that contemplative nowness-awareness called *mindfulness* and applying it compassionately to one of the harshest realities seen in modern times — deadly conflict that involves children as weapons of war. This is an awesome undertaking, audacious, ambitious and I believe quite significant. I myself have worked in refugee camps in Asia and on strife-torn borders, and I assure that such situations are hell on earth worse than can be imagined or grasped from afar, and the children often bear the worst of it. This can make me see red, and I'm usually a pretty equanimous guy.

I have sat in circles with Philip several times at retreat-like conference gatherings with the Global Peace Initiative of Women in California and also the Aspen Grove Project and inter-spiritual dialogue meetings in Colorado. What has stood out is his deep commitment to his meditation practice and a passion for trying to link the wisdom from that tradition with altruistic compassion in action Bodhisattva-activities as unselfish service in daily life and the world at large. Like myself and the many who are awakening together today, Philip thinks globally while acting locally, beginning within himself.

In *God and Conflict* Philip reveals the roots of his passion as stemming from a profound wounding that came from being exposed to the impact of Westernization and deadly violence on loved ones in Sierra Leone, West Africa. It is difficult to face such realities, and, at the same time, it is imperative that the world wake up to how our unconscious pursuit of happiness is impacting the lives of millions, if not billions, of people around the world.

As Philip reveals, the combination of witnessing the suffering of others and diving deeper into a meditation practice takes him into the heart of questions that have haunted humanity from the dawn of time, including how can any God allow such atrocities? If we don't work to better comprehend what's involved in the notion implied by the placeholder words we use for Higher Power, how can we meaningfully begin to see our way through such existential questions?

Philip takes us on a journey that is raw, powerful and transparent. He shares glimpses of the invisible hand that guides him without getting side tracked by spiritual phenomena. While Philip fully commits himself to one spiritual tradition, he consistently honors the universal wisdom of all traditions.

What lifts *God and Conflict* is that it takes the reader through the shadows and then focuses on the power of transformation. It reveals the tremendous positivity that is arising from the hearts and souls of men, women and youth around the world. Philip artfully highlights the parallels between the inner search for peace and the emerging practices of peacebuilding across what he and colleagues call the peace continuum from inner to international levels. He has looked into the very heart of the maelstrom and integrated both the terror and the joy, embraces it fully, and is a better man and spiritually centered and motivated social activist for it.

God and Conflict is a real gift, especially for any spiritual seeker wanting to bridge his or her practice with practical action in the world today. Enjoy meeting Philip and his numerous friends around the world. I have.

Lama Surya Das

Author, *Awakening the Buddha Within: Tibetan Wisdom for the Western World*
Founder, Dzogchen Center and Dzogchen Retreats

Valentine's Day
February 2012

Acknowledgements

Let me start by apologizing to anyone that I do not directly mention who has contributed to this book and my journey in exploring inner and outer peace. There have been many people who have touched and influenced my life and I am forever grateful for the friendships and teachers along the way.

First, I would like to thank Paramahansa Yogananda and the line of gurus, monks and nuns associated with Self-Realization Fellowship and the Yogoda Satsanga Society of India. I am eternally grateful for Yogananda's teaching of *Kriya Yoga* thereby providing a scientific method for having a direct relationship with God. My gratitude for the introduction to God as the Divine Mother is beyond words. I also am grateful for the guidance to daily honor the saints of all religions and to see the underlying wisdom of all religions.

I want to thank my parents, Richard and Phyllis Hellmich, who created a household rich in love and mutual respect. My parents were able to raise a family of ten children and inspire each of us to put ourselves through college and, more importantly, to be supportive of one another throughout our lives. My parents also had room in their hearts to adopt another son who has since become a brother. I also want to thank my siblings, their spouses and children for their part in cocreating the family, a continued source of nurturing and blessings.

My immediate family prepared me to embrace the people of Kagbere and Masongbo, Sierra Leone as extended family. I am forever grateful for the kindness and generosity given to me by the people of Sierra Leone, especially A.K. Sesay and his wife Tendy and daughter Josephine; and, the Conteh family — Pa Conteh, Adama, Bokarie, and Moses, along with their cousin Sanpha Mansaray.

I am also grateful for the United States Peace Corps and all the staff for providing the opportunity to live with and learn from the people of Sierra Leone. The Peace Corps' greatest impact is what Volunteers learn from people of other cultures and what we then do with those insights after our Peace Corps service.

I honor the life and courage of Mariatu Kamara, who endured the atrocities of Sierra Leone. Even as a young woman, Mariatu has influenced our world deeply toward peace and understanding. She is an example of the resilience of the people of Sierra Leone and their determination to create a culture of peace. (More information is available at her website www.mariatufoundation.com, including ordering information for her award-winning book, *The Bite of the Mango*.)

I want to thank Mickey Singer for his direct wisdom over the years. On several occasions Mickey challenged my perceptions of reality, thereby helping me break free of those limitations. I also am grateful for all of the people at the Temple of the Universe for creating an environment that was instrumental in my initial spiritual explorations. Also, I want to thank James O'Dea for his friendship and mentorship over the years. I was fortunate to meet James early in my journey after the Peace Corps and am delighted to be working with him now.

I also want to thank the staff of the Florida School of Massage for providing one of the most valuable and supportive educational experiences this lifetime. I highly recommend the Florida School of Massage to anyone wanting to discover themselves in new ways while also picking up practical tools that will be useful whether or not you choose to practice massage therapy.

Of course, I want to thank Dr. Rick Levy for his friendship and mentorship over the years. Rick has been patient in helping me move through several layers of pain that at times seemed insurmountable. Rick's insights and humor provided encouragement to keep on keeping on and reassurance that it was possible to experience states of inner peace and joy. Plus, Rick literally traveled to the ends of the world with me in the name of peacebuilding.

I also want to thank all of the people who I worked with while at Search for Common Ground, especially John Marks, Susan Collin Marks, Frances Fortune, Michael Shipler, Shawn Dunning, Lisa Shochat, Serena Rix Tripathee, Sanjaya Tripathee, Jane Shaw, Shannon Howard, Sheldon Himelfarb, John Langlois and many others. The people in Search for Common Ground provided the opportunity to contribute toward the peacebuilding process in Sierra Leone and to learn first-hand inspiring ways of transforming conflict. There are numerous heroes in Search for Common Ground, people who are bravely and creatively working for peace in some of the most difficult environments on the planet.

Also, I want to thank Dena Merriam and all of her colleagues at the Global Peace Initiative of Women (GPIW). Dena has been a dear friend, and I am grateful to participate in the GPIW contemplative dialogues. I am especially grateful that Dena provided the first opportunity for me to visit India this lifetime!

Also, I want to thank Stephen Dinan, Devaa Haley Mitchell, Emily Hine, and the rest of the team at The Shift Network for inviting me to explore the Peace Continuum with them in an environment that openly embraces the spiritual and scientific dimensions of peacebuilding.

There are many friends along the way who I would like to thank, including Patrick Collins, Kristen Boehme, Sister Jenna, Lama Surya Das, Emma Farr Rawlings, Lori Warmington, Michael Fuller, Michael Abdo, Adam Bucko, Kurt Johnson, Rev. Diane Berke, Judi Neal, Peter Ressler, Monika Mitchell Ressler, Mike Kelleher, Brian Richmond, Dan Smith, Lael Hagen, Kerri James, Carrie Cento, Peggy Digles, Mary Fukuyama, Ed Boucher, Ellen Brown, Lisa Tatum, Bill Moeller, Nanni Thestrup, Sandra de Castro Buffington, Michael Dunne, Susan Mills, Flynn Bucy, Claudia Sobrevila, Dana Verkouteren, and many more. I am rich with friends and I have come to see the one Friend behind all friendships.

I want to extend a special thanks to Molly Rowan Leach for her guidance and coaching in taking this book to publication and in helping me create the beginning of a social media presence. I also want to thank Vanessa Arrington for generously doing the first round of editing and for encouraging me to publish this book. I also want to thank Jenny Bird for the structural editing, Jelehla Ziemba for the final copyediting and interior layout, and Thomas Christian Wolfe for the cover design.

Introduction

There can never be peace between nations until there is first known that true peace which is within the souls of men.[2]

— Black Elk

There is a common belief that global peace first starts with inner peace. This theme has been described by great sages throughout the centuries. Yet how does one find that inner peace in the midst of crisis, and how can that peace translate into practical approaches to day-to-day challenges, let alone address the seemingly overwhelming complex global problems such as climate change and violent conflicts where children are used as weapons of war?

This book is an exploration of these questions through a personal journey that includes living for four years in the bush of Sierra Leone, West Africa with subsistence farmers, an experience that changed my life and perspective of the world forever. The people of Sierra Leone and their way of life started my inner exploration and questioning about "the pursuit of happiness" through consumerism and its impact on the world.

The devastating war in Sierra Leone drove me to seek the elusive peace that supposedly existed in my own soul and to ask the age-old question of how could God allow such suffering to happen. These questions led me to numerous spiritual teachers, an ancient yoga meditation tradition, and trips to India and Nepal, along with mystical experiences in divine love.

Meanwhile, I was privileged to work on tangible peacebuilding projects in war-torn African countries with colleagues who were pioneers on how to *transform conflict* across entire societies. Participating in a peacebuilding project in Sierra Leone was beyond an answer to a prayer — it was a dream come true to be able to help people I loved.

By diving inward through meditation while working on practical peacebuilding projects, I began to see parallels between the inner and outer peacebuilding processes. I could see intersections between science, spirituality, and peacebuilding in how they relate to energy and consciousness across a *peace continuum* from inner to international levels.

I also came to see conflict as a natural part of the human experience and an integral part of a spiritual path and societal evolution. How we deal with conflict across the continuum of inner, interpersonal, family, community, national, and international levels, as well as with the environment, determines how we evolve individually and as a species.

At the heart of all of these conflicts is the human soul and its relationship with God/Spirit/Universe, whatever word works for you. On this journey, my concept and experience of God has been evolving — and continues to evolve. It is my intention to share these insights and unresolved questions through transparent and often-revealing struggles that I have encountered on the inner, interpersonal, and international levels.

Section One

From Africa to Yoga

Love during a Coup d'état

There are few questions that have haunted the hearts, minds, and souls of men, women, and children more than: *how can there be a God that would allow the terrible suffering seen in wars, let alone a God that would permit religions to send millions of people to kill one another in the name of God?*

Meanwhile, mystics of all religions throughout the centuries have written about a divine love so intoxicating that it could only be described through poetry.

Reconciling this vast conflict between a God of love and the horrors of war has been attempted time and time again by scholars and theologians. Yet, it is through the breaking of the heart a thousand times over and the relentless pursuit of the one Beloved that eventually one experiences a glimpse of peace as one's own true essence.

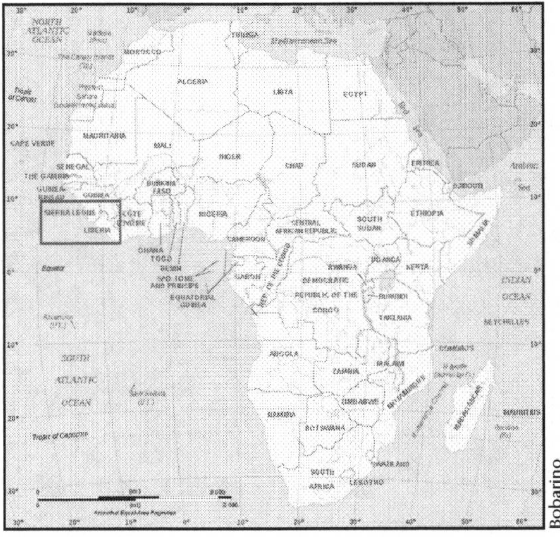

Bobarino

This has been my journey, one that seems so unlikely given that I was born and raised in rural Indiana; and that through a series of circumstances, my spiritual awakening came through falling in love with people in one of the poorest countries of Africa. While living in utter poverty, my African friends were rich in qualities of the human spirit, such as generosity, compassion, tolerance, and perseverance. When their world was shattered by a war fueled in part by a global economy, my heart was initiated into the excruciating path of seeking peace in a time of crisis.

One of the most dramatic instances of encountering the contrast between a taste of divine love and outer destruction came in April 2000.

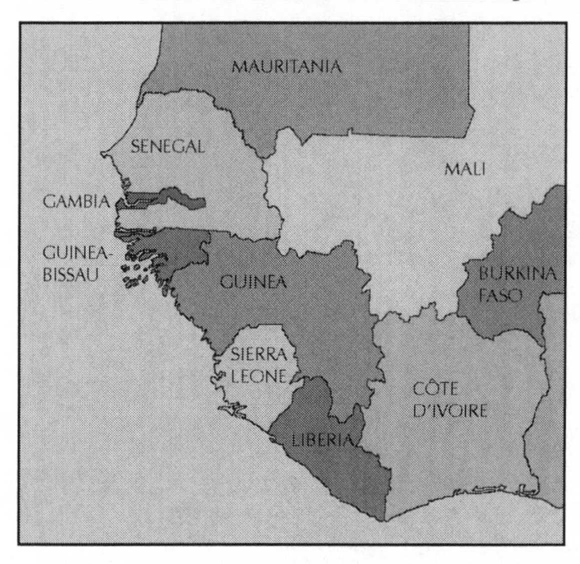

I was in Monrovia, Liberia, a West African coastal country about the size of Tennessee. Liberia was recovering from one of Africa's bloodiest civil wars; between 1989 and 1996, an estimated two hundred thousand people died, over a million people were displaced as refugees, and thousands of children were used as weapons of war. The people of Liberia wanted to rebuild their country, but their president was Charles Taylor, a man who would later stand trial at the Special Court for Sierra Leone for committing horrendous war crimes and crimes against humanity during the civil war in neighboring Sierra Leone.

Taylor had won the Liberian national elections in 1997 with people chanting, "He killed my father, he killed my mother, and I will vote for him." Liberians knew if Taylor lost the elections he would return to fighting. People in the United States and other Western countries did not understand the desperate act of electing a known mass murderer as president as an interim step toward peace.

Sitting in an air-conditioned office, I talked with three older, dark-brown Liberian men, all of whom had lived through the horrors of the war and were now part of Talking Drum Studio, a project that produced radio programs to promote peace and reconciliation. These men were wise and practical in designing insightful and entertaining radio shows that pushed the boundaries of ethnic healing and government accountability without drawing the fire of Charles Taylor.

I had gotten to know these African men over the previous three years during several visits to Liberia. Based in Washington, DC, my role with them had suddenly changed a few weeks earlier to that of being their supervisor after three colleagues had left our organization, Search for Common Ground, a nonprofit dedicated to transforming how the world deals with conflict. My colleagues had ill-advisedly joined Mondal Media, a dot-com company that would go belly up a few months later. (The company's collapse inspired all three colleagues to eventually return to peacebuilding work via various U.S. agencies.)

I was feeling a bit anxious with the new responsibilities, especially since we were starting a new Talking Drum Studio program in neighboring Sierra Leone, a country in the midst of a tenuous peace agreement. I had just flown to Monrovia from Freetown, Sierra Leone five days earlier. In Freetown, I had been overseeing the construction of the new radio studio and had hired the first staff for Search for Common Ground.

My colleagues in Liberia were quite proud that they had been the inspiration for the new program in Sierra Leone. They talked about the fledgling Sierra Leone studio like parents watching over a newborn child. They also were protective of me, knowing I was not as adept in navigating deadly conflict as they were.

I was scheduled to fly back to Freetown in a few hours. One of the Liberian men, Joe, was a stout and serious man with a childlike smile that he would occasionally reveal. Joe kept telling me it was safe to go back to Sierra Leone; that there was nothing to worry about. As Joe talked, I reflected on a war story he had once told me of hiding in the bottom of a latrine for a week to avoid being killed by a roaming band of militia. I trusted Joe, though I was not keen on ever having to face what he had to endure.

As I was about to leave for the airport, the phone rang. It was John, one of my colleagues who had recently left Search for Common Ground. John was born and raised in Louisiana and lived several years in Liberia. He had a keen sense of politics and strategic thinking, along with a demented sense of humor from years of being exposed to war. John was relieved to catch me before the flight, as his contacts in the U.S. State Department had told him a coup attempt was imminent in Freetown. John advised me to stay in Monrovia and to wait it out. Being he had been evacuated twice from Liberia due to armed conflict, I listened.

Instead of going to the airport, a staff driver took me back to a hotel. The signs of war's aftermath were still apparent in the streets of Monrovia even three years after a peaceful election. Phone and electrical wires had been stripped from poles; people carried water on their heads, as the city water system had been destroyed. The streets were lined with open sewers as people walked to and from, many carrying small pans on their heads with items to sell. Most people, various shades of brown and dark black skin, wore tattered T-shirts and pants from the United States.

As we crossed a bridge, I gazed at a young man wearing only torn shorts. He was covered in dirt and had knots in his hair. His eyes were red and wide open, giving him a crazed look. He was talking to himself out loud, stumbling and nearly falling with each step. The staff driver looked at me and said in a thick Liberian accent, "Former child soldier. Many of them have gone crazy."

A range of memories flashed through my mind, scenes of small remote bush villages in Sierra Leone where I had lived. I thought about my friends there, especially the young children and wondered if they were still alive. It was all so utterly absurd. How could the people I loved and a country that seemed so peaceful go through such horrific violence? When I left Sierra Leone in 1989, after four years with the Peace Corps, I had no idea that everything would fall apart, and that thousands of children, some as young as eight years of age, would be turned into killing machines.

We arrived at a gate with armed guards. Barbed wire and broken glass lined the top of a cement wall surrounding a series of buildings. One wall had sprayed painted on it "No Pee Pee here." Monrovia was renowned for people toileting anywhere, especially the beaches. The sound of a diesel generator filled the air, providing electricity for the hotel that was frequented largely by Western expatriates, wealthy West African businessmen, and young sex workers.

Thinking about Sierra Leone possibly returning into violence, about my friends in the villages, of Joe having hid in a latrine for a week to avoid being killed, my head began to spin. Would the violence ever stop? Would we ever get Talking Drum Studio up and running in Sierra Leone?

Once inside a bedroom in the hotel, I tried to relax by taking a shower. I marveled at the site of running water, aware that most people of Liberia and Sierra Leone did not have such a luxury. I kept the shower brief, thinking back to the young girls in the villages where I had lived and how they carried water on their heads, water that was often contaminated with giardia and/or amoebic dysentery; it was the lack of safe drinking water that inspired me to start a water well project while in the Peace Corps.

Feeling overwhelmed by the possibility of war erupting again, I did the only thing I knew to do: I prayed and then meditated.

As I sat in silence, I practiced a breathing and meditation technique. Slowly, I began to unwind, and my mind started to calm down. Several minutes into it, I sensed a presence, a familiar one. I was surprised She was there, and I could feel a tingling sensation go up my spine and settle in my heart. Tears began to form in my eyes as I mentally called to Her. The response was almost immediate, as a flood of love came pouring through me, saturating every cell of my being. All fears disappeared and I had a profound feeling that everything was all right. The intoxicating love went on for over an hour. Exhausted from the immense energy and my mind cleansed of all thoughts, I finally passed out and fell into a deep sleep.

When I awoke the next morning, the staff in the hotel was talking about a coup attempt in Sierra Leone. I later learned that the house I would have stayed in was caught in the crossfire. CNN was filled with news about the fighting in Freetown and I knew my family back in Indiana would be concerned and that I needed to send a message to them. The good news was that the coup attempt failed, and the United Nations, British, and Sierra Leonean troops held control of Freetown and a large portion of Sierra Leone, which meant a possible stop to the violence. We would be able to set up a new Talking Drum Studio.

While I felt completely safe and relieved for the people of Sierra Leone, the dramatic contrast between the deep ecstatic experience of love and the harsh realities of war was hard to reconcile. The experience, and many others that were to come, provided an intimate exposure to the dualistic nature of the human existence — deep pain and suffering, an instinctive response to do something about the pain of others, and a growing, almost haunting, awareness of a transcendent state of being underlying it all. My heart was being ripped open, bringing me deeper into my own humanity and allowing something to flow through, something that would drive me nearly mad and into ever-deeper searching for meaning and peace.

Homegrown in Indiana

Growing up as one of ten children in all-white Greensburg, Indiana in the 1960s and 70s, I knew little to nothing about Africa, international peacebuilding, or meditation, let alone God as Cosmic Consciousness or the Divine Mother.

My parents married while in high school. Their relationship had started in part as a way of healing for my father, who had lost two brothers during his childhood — one due to an allergic reaction during a tonsillitis operation and the other in a motorcycle accident. My mother became the love of his life, filling a void left by his brothers and his father, who had become estranged.

My parents embarked on their marriage and new family with a sense of innocence. As my mom often said, "We were so young. We thought it was fun; it was one big adventure!" They strived to give us children a good life. My father worked in a couple different factories and took a turn at selling insurance. My mother stayed home to provide guidance and care, and later babysat for other children. She had motherhood down pat. She said, "I knew if I kept your clothes clean and you did your homework, other kids would not laugh at you for being poor." My mother also could stretch a pound of hamburger to feed us, kind of like Christ with the loaves of bread!

I was the fifth-born, and only planned, child, at least so I was told by my parents. Being in the middle, I was a bridge between the "big ones" and the "little ones," a natural mediator. The ten of us had been born within the span of eighteen years, which meant we were close in age and provided constant companionship for one another. One of my fondest memories growing up came during early childhood when six brothers and I shared the same bedroom. I remember my parents being on the front porch, drinking Tab diet soft drinks, talking with the neighbors, Mary Ann and Dean. As my brothers and I were falling asleep, I listened to the sound of my parents' voices and trains passing in the distance. To this day, any time I hear a train at night, I am taken back to the feeling of safety and love of being surrounded by my brothers.

We eventually moved into a bigger house where there were only two kids to a bedroom. Still, we did almost everything together. My older brothers always had the younger ones' backs, keeping bullies away from us. They also paved the way by excelling in athletics and academics, setting an example the rest of us followed. Their reputations, and that of my parents, were helpful, given that we lived in a small town of about 8,000 people where everyone knew each other. It was very common for people to say, "You're a Hellmich, are you Dick and Phyllis's kids?" or, "Are you Rick's, or Vickie's, or Tom's brother?" In being part of the Hellmich family, people gave us the benefit of the doubt.

My grandfather also had been a well-known person in the community, having owned several restaurants, building them up and then selling them. He had owned Leo's Ranch, A&W Root Beer, The Wind Drift, along with a bakery, beauty salon, and gas station. My father worked in the restaurants while in high school, frying chicken, and my mother, prior to getting married, worked as a car hop.

My grandfather and grandmother worked hard and did their best, though they struggled with the deaths of their sons David and Bobby. After losing Bobby, openly her favorite son, my grandmother said in front of my father, "I have lost everything." My grandfather, who was partial to my father, was by nature an emotionally closed man with an inability to express love. After Bobby's death, he became even more distant from my father, which added an extra sense of loss for my father, as Bobby had been his best friend and constant companion.

As a result of my grandparents' pain, my parents banded together stronger and there was a sense of *team* between them, and among all the family. We all worked hard together and did everything we could to help one another succeed.

To help make ends meet, all the boys had paper routes, delivering the Indianapolis Star in the early morning hours. It was a way to buy books, clothes, and special foods, such as Chef Boyardee ravioli and Cap'n Crunch, foods we all craved but that our parents could not afford to buy for everyone.

To help feed the family, we had an acre garden at my grandparent's home in the country — five miles out of town. We grew green beans, corn, potatoes, onions, and tomatoes, much of it frozen, canned, or stored in a cool place over the winter. At the time, we kids did not enjoy working the garden or delivering newspapers. I would later see how the paper routes provided a sense of discipline, of getting up early in the morning — something I would later apply in meditation practice — and how gardening is a meditative hobby that provides a connection with the Earth.

Besides a connection with the land as a source of food, our spiritual life growing up was based on Catholicism. We each went to St. Mary's Catholic elementary school through sixth grade, the same school where my father and his brother Bobby had gone. We attended mass every morning before classes and also once on the weekends, usually after delivering the Sunday newspapers, when my parents would drive us because the papers were so large.

Once while at mass in first grade, I thought I saw something floating behind one of the altar boys. It was a misty white, almost transparent figure, which I took to be an angel. I wondered if it was my uncle Bobby or David. When I told the nuns and later my mother, they just nodded their heads, not knowing what to make of it.

The only other mystical experience I encountered was something that was so intuitive and commonplace that I did not realize it was unusual. When falling asleep at night, I would focus my eyes upward in a certain way so I could see a golden ring. When the bright light would appear, I would feel a deep sense of peace and could drift off to sleep. Sometime around the age of seven or eight, I realized the golden ring had stopped appearing and I could not get it to come back. I later learned through studying meditation that children prior to the age of seven are much closer to their spiritual essence and often able to see beings from other dimensions — angels, divas, etc. Many young children also are able to close their eyes and look upward to see different colored lights, including the *spiritual eye*, which has a golden ring surrounding a field of blue with a white star in the middle, each color corresponding to a different level of consciousness.

My brother Steve and I said our prayers every night before bed. We would get on our knees and say, "Now I lay me down to sleep, pray the lord my soul to keep. If I die before I wake, pray the lord my soul to take. God bless, Nanny and Pappy (our grandparents), Mom, Dad, Ricky, Vickie...." We would run through the entire family and then add "everyone. Amen."

The Catholic Church also gave us a sense of God being some old white man in the clouds, one who would send us to hell if we were bad. In third grade, I was chewing gum when the nun stopped the class to say, "Someone is chewing gum. I will not punish him but He will," pointing her finger to the sky, to God. I swallowed the gum and made sure I added it to the list of other significant sins for the next confession with the priest.

When I hit puberty, I had a heck of a time when the hormones started to rage. I kept thinking *if I masturbate one more time, I will go blind or, even worse, to hell!* When I got glasses in high school, I thought for sure I had brought it on myself.

The main pastimes for absorbing all our youthful and adolescent energies were sports. Whether on formal teams or pickup games in the neighborhood, we were always playing football, basketball, or some homemade variation.

Outside of sports, my brother Steve and I also loved to fish. We would catch night crawlers (worms) in the evenings and keep them in the refrigerator in cardboard milk cartons. We also saved money from our paper route to buy fishing gear. We were thrilled when we graduated from cane poles to the advanced *Zebco 33* reels with monofilament line and artificial lures. The biggest fish I ever caught, completely by accident, was a five-pound largemouth bass. On July 3, 1976, a date imprinted in my memory, I cast an artificial lure into a pond, only to get it stuck in moss floating on the surface. A bass hit the lure and I jumped back pulling the fish out of the water. My brother Steve surprised me by arranging for the fish to be mounted on the wall as a Christmas present.

Besides the bass on the wall, we did eat some of the fish. However, fishing was largely a time to be with my brothers in nature — nature being farm ponds surrounded by a few trees and miles of corn and soy bean fields.

The wholesome pastimes and hard work of academics, sports, and paper routes paid off — all my siblings and I put ourselves through college, and a few through graduate schools. We earned scholarships and grants, while taking out student loans and working summer jobs in the factories or painting houses and barns.

While in college, I stopped going to church and became more interested in books, women, and beer than God. The only mystical-like experience during college happened while traveling through Europe with my brother, Dave, his fiancé Linda, and my sister Vickie. I became haunted by a photograph by David Hamilton of a woman with long dark hair, wearing a see-through white gown, sitting on a beach, looking into the distance. Everywhere I turned, I saw the image. One night while in a hotel room in Paris, Vickie told me I talked in my sleep in a foreign language. I had no memory of the dream. Yet, when I got to Greece, I visited beaches on the nights of full moons and just looked out to sea, and even slept a few times on the beach. There was something stirring inside that I did not comprehend at the time and I wondered if it had anything to do with my Uncle David.

The night before he died, my uncle David told his mother he had had a dream of a beautiful woman in a white dress coming to him with white horses, telling him she was going to take him for a ride. David was happy and calm when he went into the operation, never to awake again. We all assumed the woman was there to carry him to the other side.

I could not tell for sure if the image of the woman in Europe had anything to do with Uncle David. I did, however, have my Uncle Bobby come back into my life in an unusual way during college. My brother Steve and I collected and wore bowling shirts. My favorite shirt was from the bowling team of a local factory, Delta Faucet. The shirt had the name "Bob" on it, and I wore it the first day working at a summer job at Indiana Beach, a resort in northern Indiana known as the Riviera of the Midwest. Everyone at the resort thought my name was Bob. When they found out I was from a family of ten, it reminded them of *The Waltons*, so I became "Phil Bob."

At first, my mother refused to call me Phil Bob, but over time it grew on her and my siblings all became "Bobs" — Rick Bob, Vickie Bob, Tom Bob, etc. I consciously took the name Phil Bob as a way to carry my Uncle Bobby with me. It was my way of coming to terms with this hidden part of the family legacy, something that made us emotionally sensitive to loss and farewells.

Toward the end of college, two friends signed up for the Peace Corps. It sounded like a good idea — a nice way to travel and possibly do some good. My brother Tom, while in medical school, had spent a semester in Liberia, West Africa and came back with exotic stories, including the thirty-six-hour bus ride that broke down at night, allowing him to hear drums being played in a distant village. Tom's stories sparked my interest in the Peace Corps and West Africa.

There was a mistake in the Peace Corps' placement process, and I was called one evening and asked over the phone where I wanted to go. Most people did not have a chance to choose the country assignment, but I jumped on the opportunity. I picked a health and rural development program in Sierra Leone because one of my college friends had been assigned to it and because it was next to Liberia. After I was accepted, my college friend dropped out to pursue dancing in New York. I often thought back to how she had redirected my life.

The entire family gathered for my send-off at the Indianapolis airport. We all cried, a lot. When I landed at the first stop in Philadelphia for a few days of training, I was greeted at the airport by a Hari Krishna devotee dressed in an orange-pink outfit. He said something about Krishna while pointing to a book and handing me a flower. I must have looked like a naïve and gullible country boy, because he picked me out from a crowd of people. I walked on by him, not realizing that Africa was about to prepare me for a life-long exploration of a yoga meditation tradition from India.

Africa ~ Not in Indiana Anymore

Stepping off the plane on the night of May 2, 1985 at Lungi Airport in Sierra Leone, I was hit with a wave of hot, humid air and unusual smells. One of the other volunteers in our group said the obvious, "We are not in Kansas anymore."

We were swarmed by people at the airport, all black, very black-skinned people. Some were so black their skin looked blue. Seeing so many black people was new for me and would be something that would become second nature very quickly.

Our first few days in Sierra Leone were filled with a barrage of sights, smells, and sounds. The first night, another volunteer and I shared a hotel room. We were concerned about mosquitoes and malaria, so we lit Chinese coils to drive away the mosquitoes. Instead of lighting one coil, we accidentally lit four. With the windows closed, we nearly fumigated ourselves.

On the second night, the Sierra Leonean national dance troop did a dynamic performance of traditional dance and music! It rocked us to no end, vibrating through our bodies, calling us out to dance and filling us with what I came to know as a powerful aliveness, primal vitality, and playfulness that permeated the people and culture.

We then headed to a nearby village for two months of training where we learned how to speak Krio, which was similar to Pidgin English, and to build latrines and teach basic public health messages. Some strong friendships were formed with the other volunteers, ones that would endure for decades. At the end of the training, we were assigned communities where we would live and serve.

Kagbere was to be my home for two years. (At the time, I had no idea I would stay an additional two years in another village called Masongbo.) Kagbere was a small remote bush village of the Loko tribe in the northern part of Sierra Leone. There were over fifteen tribes in Sierra Leone; Loko was a smaller one. Kagbere was known by Sierra Leonean public health workers as "in the pocket," five miles off a main road into a vast, lush, hilly bush, or forest. "Main road" seemed like an overstatement, as it was a dirt road that flooded in the rainy season and became impassable except by four-wheel drive vehicles, motorcycles, or foot.

Needless to say, Kagbere, Sierra Leone was dramatically different from Greensburg, Indiana. Even though they were both small, rural farm communities, they were worlds apart, literally and figuratively. It reminded me of the way the late-night Monty Python show my brothers and I used to watch would transition to another scene with John Cleese saying, "And now for something completely different."

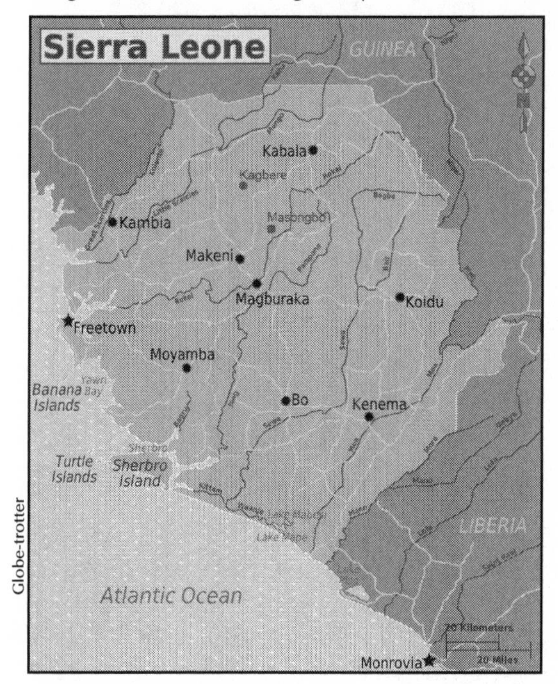

Globe-trotter

The most striking differences were that Kagbere had no running water or electricity, and I was the only white person for several miles, whereas in Greensburg there were only white people. There were no TVs or newspapers, and the nearest telephone was two days' travel, more than 120 miles away. Communication was limited to a town crier, a young man who walked through the village at night or early morning calling out announcements of village events. The only other source of news was word of mouth or the BBC World Service shortwave radio broadcasts.

There were thirty houses and huts in Kagbere, which translated into 300 people. The population was determined by counting the houses and multiplying by ten, which made sense given my own family. However, the houses and/or huts were much smaller, and most were made out of mud walls, some with tin roofs and many with grass thatch. Except for the tin roofing, nails, and door hinges, the houses and huts were made from local materials — Earth, cow dung, sticks, vines (called bush rope), and lumber from trees.

There was a seamless continuity between natural environment and homes. The mud walls appeared to rise out of the Earth the same way the trees did. The bush was only twenty yards away from any house. The latrine I used was a mud-and-stick structure with grass thatch. There was a dirt floor with a hole over a deep pit.

The latrine was located right next to the bush, which meant I had to look out for snakes, scorpions, spiders, and driver ants — one- to two-inch–thick lines of ants that meander through the bush. If disturbed, driver ants scatter and attack whoever or whatever bothered them. The ants were so respected in Sierra Leone that if they came through a house, everyone left until the ants moved on. In Nigeria, physicians have been known to use driver ants to suture cuts because of the strong and relentless bites — they have the ants bite the site of a wound and then pinch off the heads, leaving the pincers in place like stitches.

Large spiders, the size of my hand, lizards, and, once in a while, a scorpion would come into the house from the bush. Chickens and sheep, which roamed freely through the village, also would come in from time to time. When the neighbor's rooster kept waking me up well before sunrise, I purchased it and had it cooked for dinner.

The saying that it takes a village to raise a child holds true in terms of taking care of a Peace Corps Volunteer. Everyone in Kagbere was concerned that I had left my family to be with them. It was inconceivable to be so far from family and community. People often came by just to "keep time" — to be together. They did not want me to feel lonely. There was little that needed to be said, and often all that was said was "*kusheh*," which was "hello"... over and over and over again.

People also talked about Mr. Dean, a Peace Corps Volunteer who had lived in the area in the 1960s. I called him the ghost of Mr. Dean because many people talked about him as if he had left only yesterday. Ironically, people called me Mr. Bob, short for Phil Bob. It was an interesting reminder of my uncle Bobby.

The elementary school headmaster, A.K. Sesay, was my neighbor, and he and I could engage in more in-depth conversations. A.K. helped me understand the dynamics of the community and over time we became very close friends. He arranged for his wife, Tendy, to cook for me in exchange for rice and other ingredients for his family's meals. Every day I ate rice with one of four or five palm-oil–based sauces on it.

A.K. and Tendy with three daughters Josephine (left), Juliet (held) and Yebu (right) and nephew Sparky (far left)

A.K.'s eldest of three daughters, Josephine, was about eight years old when I arrived, and she fetched water for me to drink. She also washed my clothes on rocks at a nearby stream. In return, I paid for her school fees, which was equivalent to a few dollars a semester. Meanwhile, the chief of the village, who had been raised by missionaries, knew many Western people liked hot water. He arranged for one of his fourteen wives to heat a bucket of water each night for bathing.

During the day, people went to their farms — growing rice in the rainy season and cassava and vegetables in the dry season. People lived largely on what they grew, and worked the farms with hand tools, much different farming than the John Deere tractors and vast tracts of corn and soy beans in Indiana. It was physically demanding work and people's bodies were lean and muscular. Most women had a baby wrapped to their backs throughout the day, whether working on the farms, fetching water, or firewood, washing clothes on rocks or cooking over three-stone fires.

It became apparent that I was incredibly wealthy simply because I was from America and I had a motorcycle, several pairs of shoes, and numerous shirts and pants. I also could afford to buy rice in the "hungry season," when crop yields were gone, and other supplies that went beyond people's means. My friends in Kagbere lived on less than a dollar a day.

For all its lack of Western conveniences, Kagbere and much of Sierra Leone were rich in social connections. There were frequently three or four generations of family members living together in the same huts. The elderly were respected for their wisdom and life experiences and were often available to help take care of the younger ones.

I often marveled at how each person seemed to know his or her place in their family and village. This was in part because of the education provided by the "secret spiritual societies," traditions that were hundreds of years old and that existed right alongside Christianity and Islam. The secret societies initiated young boys and girls into adulthood, teaching them about their roles and responsibilities in the community and their relationship with the spiritual realms of ancestors and nature. These societies were strictly off-limits to outsiders and initiation rituals would last for weeks, as the young boys or girls would be taken into a sacred part of the bush. I remember going to sleep at night, listening to the drumming and singing, wondering about their practices. Each initiation ended with a large community celebration, welcoming the new men and women back into the village.

Besides the traditional secret spiritual societies, there also was a small missionary church and makeshift mosque in Kagbere. The traditional spiritual ways and modern religions seemed to coexist peacefully, side by side. God was an integral part of everyday life for my friends in Kagbere as well with people all across Sierra Leone. Whenever greeting someone and asking how they were ("How di bodi?"), a typical response would be "I tell God tanki" (I tell God thanks) or "*alhamdulillah*," which is Arabic for "I tell God thanks."

Young girls after a Bundu secret society initiation
Kagbere, Sierra Leone

When referring to anything in the future, such as I will see you tomorrow, people would say, "by God in power" or "*inshallah*," another Arabic term meaning "God willing." Another expression was "E de to God," meaning it is all up to God whether something will happen or not. When asking people why something occurred, whether about a crop yield or someone being ill, people would respond by saying "na God," meaning it was God. Everything was by the grace of God, which drove me crazy, as it seemed to be turning over free will and self-responsibility to some concept of God.

One of the most humorous stories I had heard along this line happened forty miles north of Kagbere at a ferry crossing on the Little Scarcies River on the road to the Outamba-Kilimi National Park. A farm tractor, which was rare in Sierra Leone, came down a steep hill and raced onto the ferry with excess speed. Instead of stopping, the tractor rolled off the ferry and plummeted to the bottom of the river.

When the driver was asked why he did not stop, he said the tractor did not have brakes. When asked why he came down the ramp without brakes, he said it was up to God to stop the tractor. While this story was an extreme example, it was commonplace to give everything over to God.

One of the most endearing expressions about God was around palm wine, the local alcoholic beverage that was tapped from palm trees. Palm wine that came straight from the tree was said to be "from God to man," whereas palm wine sold in urban areas was known to be mixed with water as a way of being able to sell more. The water, of course, was often contaminated and would cause "runny belly," or diarrhea.

Besides my fascination with palm wine and questions about God's will and human responsibility, I noticed a deeper sense of spirituality in the village that was part of everyday life. As subsistence farmers, people followed the rhythms of their crops — hungry season, the time to plant when the previous crop yields were gone, and harvest season, when there was abundance. There were rainy seasons and dry seasons, and there were the cycles of the moon. On nights with a new moon in the rainy season, it was dark and people went to bed early. The only light at those times was from kerosene lamps, which people used sparingly. When the moon was full in the dry season, there was what A.K. called lots of "village electricity," or light, and children laughed and played throughout the night.

It was so beautiful to be in Kagbere on full moon nights. I would place a chair in front of the house and sit to watch the moon and greet people as they walked up and down the village. A.K., the chief, and other friends often joined me. I was so entranced with the moon — its bright, pale-blue light and ability to bring an entire community out to be with one another. It was in Kagbere that I first saw my moon shadow and those of other people. Like so much about village life, the moon awakened a deep, joyful connection with the Earth. My love affair with the moon became a source of humor as I would tell A.K. and others that she was my wife. They laughed and frequently asked about her.

Besides the moon, there were so many aspects of nature that were transforming me. When I first got to Kagbere, I was shocked by the sounds. With no TV, electrical devices, traffic, or sirens, and very little radio, I noticed the sounds of birds, of women beating rice with long poles, of children greeting me or laughing at me (I was their free source of entertainment). Then, there was a hum. I could not understand it at first as it was a very subtle buzzing sound, almost like a white noise that I thought was coming from inside my head. When I asked a missionary doctor in a hospital forty miles away about the hum, he prescribed Valium, thinking I was stressed by the remote bush life. The hum was ever-present … it was the Earth, something I had never noticed.

In the rainy season, I frequently hiked into the bush to go to streams with small waterfalls that formed natural Jacuzzis. I would sit for hours, enjoying the peacefulness of the bush and the soothing effects of the water. It also was nice to be alone, as people in Kagbere would not go to these spots because of the spirits in the bush. There were stories all across the country, and it turns out all of West Africa, about spirits in nature, especially around water. The most common water spirits tended to be female, some were called "Mami Water," or Mother Water. Many Mami Water stories were of beautiful women who would make love with men and lure them into a range of situations, some benevolent, others less so. Years later I learned these stories existed in Ghana and Nigeria, as well as deep in the Amazon with indigenous peoples.

It would have been easy to romanticize village life in Kagbere if not for the fact that Sierra Leone was, and still is, one of the poorest countries in the world, where one in every four children died before the age of five and women frequently died during childbirth. I remember the first time I heard death sweep through Kagbere. A woman began crying loudly at the far end of the village and then one by one, women across Kagbere joined in wailing openly. The wave of crying came where I lived and I too was drawn out to see what had happened. Everyone in the village moved toward the house where a young child had died. Infant and child mortality was no longer a statistic; it was hitting home.

Seeing dead children moved me. I thought back to my family and how the deaths of my uncles David and Bobby had impacted my grandparents and parents and rippled through my siblings and me. The deaths added an emotional depth to our family, imparting a readily accessible sadness around loss. It was hard to understand how people could deal with the frequency of children dying as well as women dying in childbirth.

I did not realize it, but I was falling in love with the people of Kagbere: A.K., the chief, their families, etc. I was transferring my love for my family into them. They were becoming my family, and I was being transformed by their lives' simplicity, beauty, and hardships.

This affection for my friends in Kagbere made it a little easier to be away from my family in Indiana during Christmas. Plus, it was a time of celebration there too. People who were born and raised in Kagbere and surrounding areas, and who had left for work elsewhere, returned in droves. Those living in Freetown chartered a bus and came back together for a week of family, community, and festivities. Some of the younger people came with rented speakers and musical equipment to put on dances in the village "court barrier," or common space. I was more into the traditional instruments — drums, gourd shakers with shells, and hollowed-out logs called *keles*. The music and dancing would start late in the evening and go until the next morning.

Adding to the festivities was the fact that it was the start of harvest season, so there was fresh "upland rice," — rice grown on hills instead of swamps — a favorite of all Sierra Leoneans.

A couple close Peace Corps friends came to visit, and we spent the holidays together in Kagbere. New Year's Eve completely surprised us. At midnight, a group of people played instruments and danced through the village, going from house to house singing, "Happy New Year, me no die-o. I tell God tanki me no die-o." The song was a reminder of the fragility of life and yet the ever-present aliveness, primal vitality, and joyfulness of the people.

Rotten Bellies — Done Poil

My Peace Corps friends and I often talked about the social and political realities of Sierra Leone. It infuriated us that so many young children died and that schools were underfunded when Sierra Leone had vast natural resources of diamonds and gold, along with one of the world's richest reserves of rutile, a mineral composed largely of titanium dioxide. Very few people in Sierra Leone benefited from the sale of these resources on the international market. Whenever I would go to Makeni, a nearby town where I bought supplies and drank beer with other volunteers, or to Freetown, I would see huge contrasts between rich and poor, as government officials and wealthy businessmen would drive expensive vehicles and live in huge houses with electricity supplied by generators. Most of my friends in Kagbere lived in mud-walled houses or huts. They also barely had sandals to wear — either Chinese- imported flip-flops or locally made "black powers," sandals with soles made out of old automobile tires and rubber laces from sliced inner tubes.

Decades of government corruption had all but destroyed the country's infrastructure, and teachers like A.K. often went months without payment, which seemed to upset my Peace Corps friends and me more than most people in Sierra Leone. There was a story of how Pa Siaka Stevens, a long-time president of Sierra Leone, had once caught a waiter stealing a bottle of wine at a dinner function. He stopped the event to ask his government colleagues what was wrong with the incident, and then answered his own question: "He got caught."

This attitude toward corruption seeped throughout the government and beyond, inspiring local expressions for corruption. A person would "eat" the money or other resources. If they were particularly greedy, they had a "rotten belly," which meant no matter how much they ate, they would want to eat more, as if they had worms or other common intestinal ailments. Siaka Stevens was one of the richest men in the world during his presidency — he had a rotten belly.

As salaries disappeared due to corruption, police, military personnel, and other government employees resorted to corruption out of necessity. Bribing was a way of life. When vehicles came to police or army checkpoints along a road, drivers would hold out a few *leones*, the local currency, and then go on their way.

When asked about the corruption and state of affairs in Sierra Leone, the typical responses from people in Kagbere and elsewhere were: "Tings done poil," (everything has spoiled); "white man good, black man bad;" or something to the effect that life was better when the English were there and most people wished they would come back.

It was so hard to hear these attitudes. I loved and respected my friends in Kagbere — their relationships with one another, nature, ways of life — and yet I could not fully comprehend the impact of British colonialism, slavery, missionaries, global economy, and decades of corruption. Traditional African life had been and still was being affected by Western influence.

Signs of Westernization were ever-present, often in bizarre ways. Throughout the country, even in the most remote villages, people wore T-shirts and other used clothing from the United States. I once hiked for a day, deep into the hills behind Kagbere to conduct a census of a small village. When my guide and I arrived, there was no one in the village. My guide looked around and came back laughing. Everyone was hiding. They had not seen a white person since the British left in the early 60s. Eventually they came out and, when they did, most people were wearing T-shirts and other clothes from the U.S.

Goodwill and The Salvation Army received so many donations of clothes in the U.S. that they could not sell them all, so they dumped the extra goods on the global market through companies called "junks." When the fashion trends changed in the United States, Sierra Leone and other countries got the hand-me-downs. The result was that the local textile industries could not compete with the flood of inexpensive clothing, and there was a surreal blending of cultures. I frequently saw people wearing clothes that looked utterly comical from my perspective, such as an elderly man who was unaware that his shirt read "baby on board" or a woman with a shirt that read "Cocaine," in Coca Cola's typeface.

Another inadvertent impact of Western influence was PL-480 rice, food provided by the U.S. at inexpensive prices or straight-out donated, only to be sold by government officials and businessmen. U.S. farmers received subsidies for growing

PL-480, and the prices undercut Sierra Leone farmers. Combined with inexpensive rice from Asia, Sierra Leone had gone from being self-sufficient in growing rice to becoming a major importer.

Yet, Sierra Leone's social tapestry appeared to be holding together under the strain of poverty, corruption, high infant mortality, and the onslaught of Western influences.

Water is Life — TWIT-TWAT

Seeing the impact of Westernization, infant mortality, and other challenges made me more thoughtful and intentional about my own work as a Peace Corps Volunteer. At first, everything moved very slowly and there was little to do, at least from my goal-oriented, Western perspective. There was a health center in Kagbere, and I worked with two Sierra Leonean healthcare workers. In the first six months we conducted a census and organized an immunization campaign.

The vaccines for the immunization campaign arrived by truck, and we kept them refrigerated so they would not spoil. The clinic had the only refrigerator for miles around and, given that there was no electricity, it ran on kerosene. We had a strict rule of opening the refrigerator only when needed as a way of conserving the kerosene and keeping the temperature cold enough to preserve the vaccines.

Immunization days were fun, though most young children in the surrounding area had never seen a white person so they would scream and run when they saw me. The parents would laugh and laugh, bringing the kids close to the strange "white man" only to have them scream in terror. Eventually, the kids would settle and slowly, very slowly, warm up to me.

The census and immunizations took a few days each, leaving long periods with little to do at the clinic. This meant I had lots of time to "keep time" with people in Kagbere. This was the tough part: accepting that *being* was *doing*, that there was a value in building relationships and learning about life in the village. This was where the theory of the Peace Corps — of building relationships across cultures — and its practical application hit the ground.

The first goal of the Peace Corps was to provide the person-power needed to do work — it was hit-or-miss, as there were so many variables that affected the compatibility of tasks with someone coming from the States. The second goal was for people of other cultures to learn about people of the United States and the third was for people of the United States to learn about people of other cultures. The idea was that the international exchange, the human-to-human connection, was essential. Most volunteers would say that they learned far more than what they offered in return, which felt true in my case too.

The Peace Corps also believed that the first goal, doing work, could not be accomplished unless carried out in a culturally appropriate way, which made the third goal of learning about people of other cultures even more essential. I almost missed this idea completely, and was fortunate that someone helped redirect me early on when I was tasked with how to address a shortage of clean water.

In the initial Peace Corps training in Sierra Leone, we were taught how to conduct a public health survey, to identify the most pressing health needs. This was not rocket science. Lack of clean drinking water was a huge problem. When I first arrived at the village, it was the end of the dry season, which meant people were digging a small pit near the swamp to collect water. Josephine brought me a bucket of water to drink. It was so cloudy and filled with swimming insects that I could not see the bottom. It took me a day to filter and treat the water before I could drink it, and I still got dysentery several times in the first few months. I went from 140 pounds down to 115. I was skin and bones!! I went from being a vegetarian to eating anything and everything with protein, including bush rat.

During the rainy season, I traveled to the nearest large town, Makeni, to explore water well options. I did not want to go through another dry season without clean drinking water. I had a vested interest in addressing this need.

There was one organization based in Makeni, the Integrated Agriculture Development Program (IADP) that had the technical capacity to dig a water well in Kagbere. Even though IADP was supported by the World Bank, the people of Kagbere needed to find the funding for them to create the well. After a couple trips to Catholic Relief Service (CRS) in Freetown, we received a $5,000 grant to build a well in Kagbere.

The day after landing the funding, I was drinking beer at a bar in Makeni with some other volunteers and a Canadian engineer. That conversation kept me from going down the road of creating yet another white elephant — a monument to good intentions gone astray. Sierra Leone was dotted with the remains of white elephants from years of international assistance.

The engineer worked with Plan International, an international aid organization, and had conducted a study of 121 of the IADP–World Bank wells. He found that ninety percent were not used after the first year. The reason: the IADP field staff asked the elders of the villages, the men, if they wanted a well. They said yes. When asked where to locate the wells, they invariably said in front of the chief's house.

The problems were twofold: the chief's house tended to be on a higher elevation than the traditional water sites, which meant the wells were anywhere from fifty to eighty feet deep. That style of well used a rope and bucket system. Meanwhile, the women and children, who did the work of fetching water, did not like looking down into the well or pulling up a heavy bucket of water.

The other problem was cultural: There was an important social aspect for the women and children in collecting water that could not take place near the men, let alone in front of the chief's house. Thus, the women and children would still go to the traditional site at the edge of a dried swamp so they could have their time together.

The engineer solved the problems by designing wells to go at the traditional sites. I talked to CRS and they agreed to redirect the funding to build the same type of wells, but more of them at less cost. The CRS director had a distinct sense of humor after two decades of working in West Africa, initially as a Peace Corps Volunteer in Liberia. Every organization and project in Sierra Leone had an acronym, so he called the water project "Traditional Water Improvement Team, Together With Appropriate Technology," or TWIT-TWAT.

A water well at a traditional site where women and children collected water

Another volunteer, two Sierra Leonean health workers, and I were part of TWIT-TWAT. Instead of building one IADP well, we built seventeen TWIT-TWAT wells in fifteen villages over a three-year period. The wells required a lot of community participation, which was great for instilling a sense of ownership. If a village did not do the preparation work for a well — digging a ten-foot by ten-foot pit down to the water table (anywhere from eight to sixteen feet deep) and collecting sand and stones for the cement — we skipped those villages. The villages that were organized and worked hard received the wells. Given there were no other options for assistance with clean water, most villages jumped at the opportunity.

The wells were shallow and lined with cement and covered with a slab with metal doors. When we tested the water, it was safe to drink, and people used the wells.

In the rainy season, people continued to use rainwater. This was one of my favorite parts about water: drinking rainwater that came straight off the roof! In the rainy season, the rains tended to come at night and be very heavy, often lasting for hours. They would pound the tin roof and make a loud and soothing sound. I had a small gutter set up so the rainwater from my roof would go into an old oil barrel. At times, I would move the gutter so I could shower right under the flow of water. The water was always cold, clear, and refreshing. Given that rainy nights were pitch black and everyone was in their houses asleep, showering naked in front of the house was not a problem.

There was a saying in Sierra Leone: Water is life! The water well project and rainwater brought home a new relationship with and appreciation for water.

Fishing: Landing the Big One

In the Peace Corps, we were encouraged to create secondary projects based on personal interests, perceived needs, and culturally appropriate opportunities. While that sounds good in theory, it was not even on my mind when a friend invited me to go fishing.

Peggy was a volunteer from the same training group. She lived in Masongbo village, fourteen miles from Makeni and about forty miles from Kagbere. Masongbo was near the Rokel River, and Peggy's boyfriend (and husband-to-be) was David, an American expatriate who loved to fish. Peggy had told me they were catching huge Nile perch, some as big as twenty pounds, from the Rokel River. Her stories awakened my childhood fantasies of catching "the big one" and, after several inquiries, she and David agreed to take me fishing with them.

My mind raced with imagination as we drove in David's four-wheel drive vehicle along a dirt road. We came to a small village, maybe ten houses, and parked. After greeting the village chief and asking permission to fish, which was the culturally proper thing to do, we started to hike along a foot path through the thick bush. Our guide was Pa Conteh, an elderly man and good friend of Peggy from Masongbo, and another young man from the area named Mohammed.

It took us nearly thirty minutes of walking before we reached the river. It was beautiful! So pristine — slow-moving water dotted with large boulders; the banks lined with large cottonwood, palm, and other trees. There were no roads or electrical lines, nothing but bush, river, and the exotic sounds of birds and other wildlife.

David showed me how to use his gear, which was far more sophisticated than the Zebco 33s in Indiana. We then spread out, Peggy, David and I fishing, with

Pa Conteh pointing out locations in the river. My enthusiasm quickly turned to frustration when my lure got stuck on a hidden fishing net. David had to stop fishing and help me free the lure. I felt somewhat embarrassed, as David was clearly an experienced fisherman and he was ready to fish.

Well, getting stuck once would have been fine, but I did it a few more times on submerged rocks and nets. I did not know how to use the gear, and I was creating headache after headache for David and Peggy. We even lost one of the lures that could not be recovered. Meanwhile, David landed a ten-pound Nile perch, and I just looked at the fish in amazement.

I finally got the hang of using the equipment, but the day was almost gone. As the sun started to set behind the palm trees, I finally gave up and put down the fishing rod. If not for Pa Conteh's intervention, my fishing fantasy would have been over and the next two years would have been much different. In a soft-spoken voice, Pa Conteh pointed to a red-and-white lure (made by the respected Rapala company) and said, "Try dat one." He smiled and encouraged me to keep fishing.

I cast the lure about thirty yards into the river and began to retrieve it. Almost immediately it got stuck. I flinched, dreading having to tell David and Peggy the news. Before I could say anything, the line started to take off. Damn, it was the big one!!!

For the life of me, I had never felt a fish pull so strongly! My heart started to race and Pa Conteh called David over to help. The line kept going out! I started to say every prayer that I knew from my childhood, "Oh God, please, let me land this one fish, please!!!"

David stood next to me and started coaching, telling me not to reel when the fish was running and let it take line. He showed me how to pull the rod back to draw the fish nearer and then to retrieve line when dropping the rod back toward the water. We checked the drag mechanism on the reel to make sure the tension was set so line could go out when the fish made a run.

Standing knee deep in the river, I battled what must have been a monster. After nearly ten minutes, which seemed like an eternity with my heart beating so fast, the fish came to the surface and shook its head out of the water. "Oh my God," was all I thought. I had never, ever seen a fish mouth that big! I was sure there was not a single fish that big in all of Indiana.

I intensified my prayers, thought about my brothers in Indiana, and did everything, everything David told me to do. We got the fish within ten feet, and it made another run into deeper waters. Being able to see the full length of the fish only increased my excitement and praying. After nearly twenty minutes, we finally brought the fish close to shore and Mohammed reached down and pulled it out of the water!

I was beyond euphoric. "Oh my gosh, it is huge!" was all I thought.

Pa Conteh came over and just smiled, saying "I bin tell you, try dat bait!"

The Nile perch was thirty-two inches long and weighed over twenty-five pounds! The best part: it looked similar to a large-mouth bass and we got pictures to send home to my brothers in Indiana!

I gave the fish to Pa Conteh, and he later gave me something much more precious in return, his family.

Hellmich and Conteh children with a Nile Perch

At the end of my two years of service, I decided to stay for a third and eventually a fourth year. I needed to move from Kagbere because another volunteer was coming to replace me. Pa Conteh agreed that I could live in Masongbo in the house where Peggy lived after she left. For the next two years, I lived with the Conteh family, continuing with the water wells and other projects, making periodic visits to see A.K. and others in Kagbere, and fishing with them during the dry season.

The Conteh Brothers

The most endearing part about living in Masongbo was the Conteh family, especially Pa Conteh, the Conteh brothers, and Adama.

Pa Conteh often would come and sit with me, telling stories about Peggy, David, and village happenings. He would bring mangos, bananas, coconuts, and other gifts, and we often ate together. I reveled in his elfish smile and shiny eyes, thinking about all he had seen during his life. His health started to decline, so he had his sons, Moses and Bokarie, take me fishing. Their cousin, Sanpha, later joined us and they became my fishing partners and, over time, dear friends.

The Rokel River was about a mile away from Masongbo via a small winding footpath through the bush. We would head out from the village about three hours before sunset. One of the Conteh brothers would lead the way and I would follow closely, navigating the fishing rod between the trees and brush. There was one small village, a cluster of three small huts in the middle of the bush. If people were there, we would stop and greet briefly, then continue to the river. As we neared the water, I could sense its slow, peaceful, moving presence.

There was such a deep calmness to being on the river, mixed with the childhood excitement of fishing. I marveled at the endless line of trees along the banks and loved it when a troop of monkeys would come by, jumping from tree to tree. There were few people at the river, which added to its exotic mystique.

There was a rhythm to fishing, of casting and retrieving lures, listening to the calls of birds, as the sun slowly set. With no electricity anywhere for miles, the planets and stars would emerge as the brightest lights, except on nights with a full moon.

There was one evening when the peacefulness of the river was disturbed by an overwhelming feeling of unease. I kept thinking about a crocodile that lived in a deep pool near where we were fishing. I had never seen the crocodile, only footprints in the sand. Bokarie was with me that night and when I asked him repeatedly about the crocodile he would laugh and tell me not to worry and to keep fishing.

Standing thigh-deep in the water, the feeling grew stronger, so I asked Bokarie how he knew it was okay to fish. He responded by saying, "Crocodile na Contehs, you na Conteh, and Contehs no de eat Contehs."

"Great, I thought, the family totem is going to keep me safe." So, I yelled to the river that I was "Kaibow Conteh and I was there to fish." Bokarie thought this was all the more funny as I was always quiet when fishing and the name "Kaibow" meant "real man" in Limba, his tribal language.

The feeling was still strong, so I finally asked Bokarie to take over fishing. Given there was no water well in Masongbo at that time, I needed to bathe in the river. With Venus as the brightest light in the sky, I took a stick and checked each rock to make sure it was a rock. I then stripped and slowly walked into the water. I stepped on one rock and it suddenly moved. My entire leg shot in pain and the next few seconds became a blur of terror. I lost all coherent thoughts and began to shriek, trying to get out of the water.

Bokarie began to yell, "Crocodile done get Phil Bob, Crocodile done get Phil Bob."

Crawling as fast as I could on all fours, I was out of the water, standing naked, breathing deeply. Bokarie came over and shouted, "*Na watin?*" ("What?") As I caught my breath, I said, "Electricity."

Bokarie fell to the rocks laughing. He kept laughing and laughing. Finally, I got him to quiet just enough to say, "Na electric catfish." I had stepped on a West African electric catfish, which I later learned could give out up to 400 volts of electricity. The shock had been so strong that I felt my knee and hip sockets were going to explode.

That night the walk back to Masongbo was extra enjoyable for Bokarie. He kept laughing, telling stories about how most people living along the river had accidently stepped on or picked up an electric catfish, always resulting in an outbreak of humor. When we reached the three small huts, Bokarie began telling the inhabitants something in Limba and then broke out, "eeee, eee, eee," imitating my shrieks of terror. The farmers all looked at me, smiled, and laughed.

When we got back to Masongbo, I ate quickly and headed to bed. As the moon rose, I feel asleep hearing young children run throughout the village making shrieking sounds.

Electric catfish and crocodiles aside, I caught over 125 pounds of Nile perch a month that first dry season. It was pretty easy, given I was the only person with a rod, reel, and artificial lures on the river. Adama Conteh loved it when I came back with fresh fish, as it was valuable food and would feed much of the Conteh family. It was every man's dream come true: go to a pristine river in an exotic location, fish with guy friends, come back with large fish, and be treated as heroes, with the women gladly cleaning the fish and preparing dinner. I thought I was in fishing heaven.

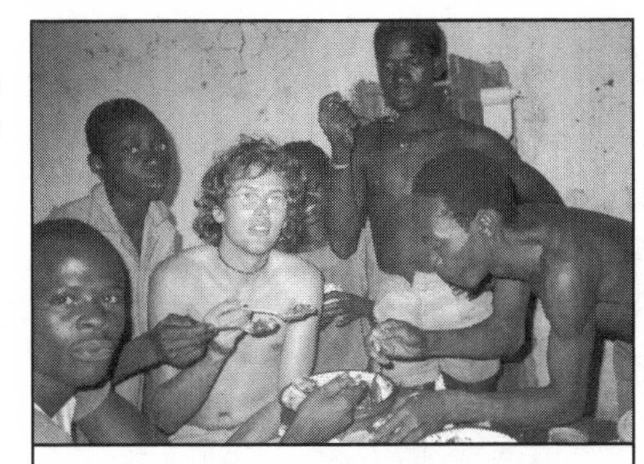

The Contehs and Hellmich ate together almost every night

Bokarie, Moses, and Sanpha also loved to fish, and we would take turns using the equipment; but generally, they encouraged me to fish — I was the guest in their home, plus I was catching food. They hinted that I should leave the equipment with them when I returned to America. But I knew they could not sustain using it, as I was stretched as a volunteer to buy new lures when I lost one on rocks or to a big fish.

In the evenings, Bokarie, Moses, Sanpha, and I would eat together, and Adama would often join us, breaking a taboo of women eating with men. We would laugh and tell stories about the fishing or they would update me about happenings in the village. After eating, they often tried to teach me how to drum, a futile effort given I took after my mother in having no sense of rhythm. I would try a few beats and then sit back and listen, as they jammed away on their homemade instruments. I loved it!

I was so drawn in by their music that they convinced me to go to church with them, something I had stopped doing after high school. But with the Contehs, they brought Catholic mass alive for me in new way, as they skillfully played drums, weaving together rhythms in a complex way, all the while singing the same hymns I had heard in grade school, but this time in an African dialect. What was most touching was the way, when the music stopped, they would reverently lower their heads, close their eyes, and pray. They had a much deeper sense of devotion than I had.

Adama Conteh (right) cooking over a three-stone fire in Masongbo

When Pa Conteh's health took a turn for the worse, and Adama asked me to take him to a traditional healer in a nearby village, I was glad to help. We rode together on the motorcycle, Pa Conteh with his fragile arms around me. When we got there, we laughed, and I made sure he had everything he needed. I then came back for Adama's sister, who joined Pa Conteh to cook and take care of him while the traditional healer practiced his trade.

This healer was the last stop, Pa Conteh said. He had tried Western missionary doctors; it did not work. Pa Conteh was getting old, and he knew it.

Still, I was not prepared when Sanpha found me a few weeks later shopping in Makeni. He looked at me and said, "Pa Conteh done die." I immediately went back to Masongbo.

When I went to see Pa Conteh's body, he had been dead for three days. The hot, humid weather had turned his vibrant face and twinkling eyes into a skull wrapped in dry brown skin. The pungent odor was so strong it was difficult to breathe. This was the first time I had smelled the decomposing body of a friend.

For the next couple of days, Conteh family members came from around the country. Whenever a woman arrived, she would openly wail for a few hours. I asked Adama why she was not wailing and she said, "I did that already," and then went on cooking.

The Conteh family conducted traditional rituals for Pa Conteh and an Italian Catholic missionary priest did a funeral service, reflecting the ever-present syncretism of traditional village life and Western influences. Unlike burials in the United States, where people were embalmed and placed in coffins, Pa Conteh's body was wrapped in a white piece of cloth and placed directly in the ground not far from the family's houses.

As I pondered Pa Conteh's body being consumed by the Earth, the village began a celebration. This caught me completely off guard, as I was still grieving. The entire village danced, sang, ate, and drank well into the next day. It was at that time that I noticed the music contained rhythms from nature — the calls of birds in the bush — and the dancing reflected movements of daily life such as pounding rice or making love.

The festivities for Pa Conteh highlighted the social sophistication of life in the village. There was a complex weaving together of relationships among family, community, nature, livelihood, spirituality, music, dance, life, and death. I was caught in that web, not fully understanding it, yet being transformed on profound levels. The social fabric provided a sense of connection and belonging far beyond anything I had ever experienced, even in my large, close-knit family and small hometown in Indiana.

With Pa Conteh dead, I took a more keen interest in the well-being of Adama and the brothers. I began to contemplate more deeply the impact of the fishing and the needs in their family and the village. On one hand, I was mixed, as Masongbo and surrounding villages were crawling with international and national development organizations. There was almost too much aid, much of it in competition with each other.

There was one day when two vehicles arrived at the same time, each from a different aid organization. Adama laughed as the elders did not know what to do, which group to meet with first. One had a white man from America, so that group finally won out. The elders nodded their head, said yes we need help, and agreed to whatever was proposed. Later, Adama told me they would be given tools for gardening, even though there was a blacksmith in the village who made the metal parts for all their tools while most men in Masongbo could carve the wooden handles.

In another nearby village, a volunteer told me the chief said no to an organization proposing a latrine project. When asked why, the chief said another organization had offered more cement and tin roofing materials. The chief would not take the aid unless they could make a better offer.

Part of the problem was that Masongbo was in the home chiefdom of His Honorable Dr. Major-General Joseph Momoh, the president of the country. That chiefdom also happened to be the poorest in the country, according to studies, qualifying it for more aid. Unlike Kagbere, which had little to no outside assistance, Masongbo had too much in ways that did more long-term harm than good, creating dependency and a lower self-image.

With all of this in mind, I knew the people working in those organizations were doing their best. It simply was not easy to do good.

What did infuriate me was that the paramount chief of that area was also a member of the national parliament. He was very wealthy and powerful and drove expensive vehicles. Yet he still had people from Masongbo and other villages work on his farms for free. Moses, Bokarie, and Sanpha would come back exhausted and upset, yet knowing they could not complain.

I looked for appropriate and sustainable ways to help the Contehs. When I heard about a training event where people could learn how to grow palm trees for oil production, I asked the Conteh brothers if they wanted to attend. We made an agreement that their oldest brother, the new head of the family, would pay for part of the training. They loved it! Bokarie, Moses, and Sanpha came back from the training very excited. They created an oil palm nursery and planted 250 trees over the course of two years.

Masongbo also did not have safe drinking water, so I discussed options with the Contehs and the chief. We agreed that if the village did all the work, I would arrange for the equipment and materials. Being detached from the outcome helped, as I was not driving the process. Sure enough, the village did the work, and together we built a well.

When it came to fishing, I realized my hobby was going contrary to everything else I was doing. After losing one more lure, and faced with having to drive 120 miles to replace it with more money than a Sierra Leonean teacher made in a month, I knew it was time to do something. Several Peace Corps friends recommended carving lures by hand, which was far beyond my know-how. I had never tied a fishing fly, let alone made a wooden lure that moved like a fish through the water. Still, I had to do something.

Moses (left) and Sanpha (right) painting fishing lures

I tried to carve a stick, but the Conteh brothers took it from me, afraid I would hurt myself. They carved all their own hand tools and knew the qualities of every tree in the bush. They were willing to help me, but were strangely unenthusiastic. It took a while to figure out their hesitancy: they were embarrassed to be seen trying to make a "white man's gadget," at which everyone expected them to fail.

I kept the Contehs engaged by continuing to try to carve sticks in front of them, so they would take them from me and do the work themselves. I made sure that whatever materials we used were locally available — sticks, pieces of wire, single hooks and monofilament line we could buy in the markets in Makeni, and old coins and pieces of metal for the nose that would make the lures dive. The only place I yielded was letting Sanpha use some of my shoulder-length hair to make paintbrushes. After all, I was easier to catch than a goat.

With a lot of back and forth, we eventually made lures that dove and danced in the water, just like the expensive Rapala "English baits." And we caught fish. Before long, the Contehs had a small business making and selling lures and giving workshops to other Peace Corps Volunteers and Sierra Leoneans. One day, when I was away from the village, calling my family in Indiana, Sanpha caught four Nile perch weighing 101 pounds total, all using lures and a tin-can fishing reel he had made himself. When I questioned Sanpha about the exact weight, he smiled and said, "UNICEF was here weighing babies, so they weighed the fish!"

Sanpha then said one of my favorite Sierra Leonean expressions, "I don't want to praise myself," and then he paused with a big smile, waiting for me to reply.

Playing my part in this expression, I laughed and said, "but," thus giving Sanpha permission to go ahead and praise himself.

"I've caught bigger fish than you!" Sanpha exclaimed. He then went on to tell me how he had caught the biggest fish while using baits and a fishing reel he had made himself. Sanpha was truly a brother, bragging and teasing in the same way my brothers and I did back in Indiana.

Enjoying Sanpha's playful confidence, I picked up a stick and asked him to teach me how to make a lure.

By this point, my official Peace Corps time was ending, and I was not sure whether to stay or leave. I did a two-month consulting assignment for the Peace Corps, reviewing sites for new volunteers. That was when I met my first Apple computer, and had a real shock — I did not have to retype everything!!

After that consultancy, I talked with the United Nations in Freetown about becoming a volunteer and continuing with the fishing project with the Contehs. The process was moving slowly, so I decided to go back to Masongbo to be with the Contehs for a few more months of fishing and one last adventure.

I bought three dugout canoes and proposed to Moses, Sanpha, Bokarie, Adama, and another sister that we go on a canoe trip down the Rokel River.

At first, Moses was hesitant. He said everyone in Masongbo would laugh at us. He agreed to join us when the local Peace Corps regional director wanted to come for the first couple days. Sedu was a "big man" in the Limba tribe, the same tribe as the Contehs, and was very respected by the Contehs.

We loaded the canoes with heavy pots, plates, spoons, and fresh food, including pumpkins, rice, palm oil, and onions. Given it was dry season, we took mosquito nets for sleeping. The first night it rained and we only caught one small fish. While Moses said everyone in Masongbo would be laughing, Sedu began to sing. The brothers joined in and the rain slowed.

The next morning, Moses and Sanpha went upstream toward the village. The rest of us went downstream. We agreed if we did not catch anything, we would go home. We did catch several large Nile perch, including one over twenty pounds! The people in the nearby village were so excited to see the Contehs fishing with homemade gear that they asked to buy lures.

Bokarie Conteh and Hellmich with a day's catch during a twelve-day canoe trip

Adama was happy because she had fresh fish to smoke and sell; she always wanted to be a market woman. Sanpha, Bokarie, and Moses were happy because they were making and selling lures. I was thrilled just to be in the bush, listening to the birds, watching monkeys swing from tree to tree, and fishing with my family. We went twelve days down the Rokel River together.

That was the last hurrah with the Contehs. In April, 1989, the Contehs, A.K., and a few other friends came together for a goodbye party. It was poignant, as I did not know when I would return.

When I left Sierra Leone, the movie *Rambo* was playing in Makeni and Freetown. As I watched young boys imitate Rambo on the streets, I had no idea of the hell that was going to be unleashed on the country and people I loved.

Reverse Culture Shock

Flying into Indianapolis, there was a joyous reunion at the airport with my family. My mother hugged me and cried, then gave me a huge kiss, saying it was good to have me home. Several siblings were there, as was my aunt and a couple cousins. It was a celebration.

My parents had kept a candle lit for me while I was in Sierra Leone. When we walked into the house, my parents ceremoniously blew out the candle. The family was together again; ever close-knit, with a strong sense of sentimentality.

Over the first few days and ensuing months, I started to realize how much I had changed by living with my family in Africa — the Contehs, A.K., and other friends in Sierra Leone. Without knowing it, I had taken on the rhythms of West African village life and was seeing my old life in Indiana through a new lens. While everything was ever-familiar — my parents' house, the town, family members, and friends — it was also completely different.

Nonetheless, little events could trigger flashbacks to Masongbo or Kagbere. For instance, my youngest brother stood at the freezer one day and held the door open for several minutes while looking for a Popsicle. I was back in Kagbere, at the health clinic where we preciously guarded the refrigerator, opening it only sparingly so we could keep vaccines and other medicines cool and protected from the West African heat. I could see the lines of mothers with their children, all smiling, hoping that the Western medicine would keep their kids from being the one of five that would die before the age of five.

And then there was the issue of water. Water was used endlessly in Indiana! The tap water would be left running, family members took long showers, and — the one that got me the most —golf courses and homes had sprinkler systems shooting safe drinking water over vast expanses of grass. I remember the first time Josephine brought a bucket of water for me to drink. She was a small, young girl with a bucket on her head, spilling only a few drops, carefully placing the bucket on the floor in my small hut. She shyly smiled, happy to help the strange white man from America. I looked at the water and could not see the bottom for the clouds of dirt and swimming insects.

I flashed back to entire villages where we built wells — women and children collected rocks and sand, while the men worked long hours digging a hole. How villages celebrated when the wells were finally completed and the first buckets of clear water were drawn. How the men and women talked about village laws to protect the wells and how to encourage the children to use the wells wisely. How refreshing it was to drink water that we, all of Kagbere and many other villages, had dug together.

I remembered the long nights of listening to the sound of rain pounding the roof, aware that water is life, and that the rain was filling my water drum for drinking water.

I went back to the streams, sitting for hours in the sacred spots of spirits, bathing in Jacuzzi-like pools, wondering if there was really something to nature, especially water, having spirits.

Flipping light switches was an old habit with a new blinding effect. In the village, we used kerosene lamps or moonlight. I remember how completely, utterly black the nights were when it rained and there was no moon, how I could not see my hand. But, with a flip of a switch in Indiana and all across America, there was light, everywhere. The moon, my love affair with the moon, was harder to maintain. I had to drive out of town to get away from the lines of streetlights so I could see her more pronouncedly and the shadows she cast.

In defiance of electricity, I followed the rhythms of the moon, nightly going out and looking. Each time I saw the moon, I thought about the Contehs in Masongbo and A.K. and his family in Kagbere. I visualized the villages going to bed early on new moon nights or up late into the morning on nights of a full moon.

In the evenings, I was confused by how my family could retire in front of the TV, sitting there, looking at it for hours. Cable television had come to Greensburg and there were dozens of channels. How could we focus on random sitcoms when we could be talking with each other?

And the level of violence on TV and in movies shocked me. Maybe, because I had been on a media fast for four years, I had forgotten what it was like to see people killed. Or had the level of violence gone up slowly and no one noticed, kind of like the old boiled frog story: If you throw a frog in boiling water, it will jump out quickly, but if you put it in cool water and heat the water slowly, it will sit there and boil to death.

The first time I saw someone killed in a movie I flinched. I thought, "Damn, that person is dead! I am sure his parents and other family members would be upset." I could see young kids dead from diseases, but from violence? What? My family would watch and not even flinch. They might say something about how it was a good movie, with twists and turns about the killer.

What?! Killing was entertaining? How could that be? Was I in some twilight zone?

Many other things stood out — for instance, my grandmother lived alone in a small house. My parents lived in a huge house with one younger brother and his high school friend, Kyle, living with us. There were retirement homes in town, where the elderly, including my grandmother, eventually would go. Why all the houses? Why were generations living so far apart? The Contehs had three or four generations, all living closely together in their huts, huts they built together, out of materials from the land. The elderly were an important and respected part of the family.

One way I dealt with my confusion and all of the abundance was to clean out my parents' attic. It was something they wanted done, and I had time on my hands. Heck, I was on African time. The attic had over twenty years of stuff from ten kids in numerous piles. I spent over a week, going through, organizing, and throwing out. Yes, taking things to Goodwill, and knowing much of it could end up in Sierra Leone or some other African country.

The abundance and waste was mind-boggling.

The amount of trash seemed absurd. I would see a plastic bottle go into the garbage and remember how people in Kagbere and all across Sierra Leone would use any old container for storage — kerosene, palm oil, etc. Recycling was a way of life, as nothing ever went unused.

When I would see the number of garbage bags on the street waiting to be picked up, I would multiply it by the 100 to 200 million houses across America and just think, "Wow, we use so much! Where in the hell does all that waste go, into the Earth? Where does all that material come from?"

Going to a gas station, I was amazed to see gas ready to be pumped. Sierra Leone would slow to a halt when "the boat" did not arrive — meaning the government did not have the foreign currency to pay for that shipment of fuel. I once waited a week in Makeni to get two gallons of gas, enough to last a couple months. Yet, there we were in Indiana, easily going and pumping as much gas as we wanted.

What also drove me bonkers were the advertisements. I had gone nearly four years without any ads, and with only looking in a mirror maybe once a week. The images on TV and on billboards, the advertisements on the radio, were all about youth, sex, and beauty. You must look this way, or, you must have this or that thing to be happy or to feel safe.

Advertisements were like a spell, cast out over mass media that got millions, tens of millions of people, to crave and want things...to go out and consume in droves, like herds of wild animals. It was like the entire country was hypnotized — more was better, more stuff was better, buy more, stay busy making more money, to buy more...store the extra stuff in the attic, garage, in a closet — or give it away and make room to buy more.

My childhood best friend put it this way, "It's great. When I see something I want, I can buy it now with a credit card and pay for it later. I don't have to wait." Instant gratification was the way of life. There was no going through hungry season to get to and celebrate harvest season.

The stories of people crowding department stores for the latest children's toys drove me crazy. Kids in Masongbo or Kagbere would take pieces of wire or sticks and make toy automobiles, or take an old bicycle rim and run with it, guiding it with a stick.

Meanwhile, nature was just one more commodity to use, to consume. Water, Earth, trees, all of it, commodities for mindless consumption. Farms were vast fields of the same crops, going on for miles, sprayed with chemicals, most of the grain to be feed to animals. There was little connection with the Earth, the life cycles...nature. It was no surprise that my hometown was in a county with one of the highest cancer rates per capita in the country. The amount of farm chemicals going into the land had to be reaching the water table.

Meanwhile, Super Wal-Mart, K-Mart, and other large, national chain stores were new to Greensburg and were offering much lower prices to buy more things. The result was that the small family-owned businesses, such as Gamble's Hardware, Batterton's Pharmacy, and Minear's Clothing Store, were going out of business. The town square was becoming a ghost town of a once-thriving community center. Even my cousin's dairy farm could not compete with the larger corporate farms and would eventually close a few years later. That farm had been in the family for four generations.

Greensburg was becoming part of a global economy that was driven by massive consumption at the lowest cost, the same economy that was impacting Sierra Leone. The livelihoods of people in Greensburg were becoming dependent upon the growth and success of the consumption machinery, including that of my father, whose factory was teetering on closing. While I wanted my family and friends in my hometown to have happy lives, it all seemed so far away from Kagbere and Masongbo, where there was such a close relationship between Earth, community, spirituality, work, food, and life.

Our interconnectedness and interdependence with nature and the rest of the world was so apparent, yet it was so clear that the American lifestyle was not sustainable. The Earth could not afford many other countries living like we did in the United States. In Sierra Leone, much of the work as a volunteer was on how to be sustainable — fishing lures, etc. If 250 to 300 million people were all consuming at an outrageous rate, unaware of its impact on nature and/or the rest of the world, it simply was not sustainable.

I found myself wondering about "the pursuit of happiness," a right of the American people stated in the Declaration of Independence. What would Thomas Jefferson say to a world accelerating to consume more and more at the peril of its own survival? How much did anyone need to be happy anyway? And, why was everyone in a hurry, going someplace, doing something? There was little time to "keep time." And when people did ask about Sierra Leone, they would say, "How was Africa?" And, a little later, they would change the subject to the latest episode of a TV show.

It also was telling that the U.S. dollar had written on it, "In God We Trust." Money was God and valued at the expense of connecting with one another and nature. In a subconscious way of protesting, I began to frequently say, "*inshallah*" and "by God in power." I was missing the ever-present way of affirming we were all bound together by something invisible.

Confused by the Western pursuit of happiness, I was the one who was unhappy... not knowing where I felt at home — the U.S. or Africa. I did not know whether to go back to Africa or stay in America.

My First Yogi

After a few months at home in Indiana, my brother Dave invited me to live with him and his family in Gainesville, Florida. It was a chance to reconnect with him and to get to know his daughters, my nieces. Dave also was an English literature major and wanted to support my ambitions to write about my experiences in Sierra Leone.

Writing was my way to come to terms with the reverse culture shock and to think through what was next — did I want to go back to Sierra Leone or stay in the U.S.?

Living with Dave and his family was physically comfortable; they went out of their way to have me be part of the family. He and his wife both were getting PhDs while working and raising three kids. They had busy and full lives. Meanwhile, I was still reacting to the abundance, wealth, and waste of America, and was living on West African time with no sense of urgency. I am sure I was more than they bargained for.

The writing I did was all focused on a concept I called the *ball of balance* to describe how the Earth has a delicate balance that is being threatened by Western consumption. Flashing between the U.S. and Sierra Leone, my intention was to provide a fresh perspective on the Western pursuit of happiness and its impact on the environment and people who lived thousands of miles away; all the while not providing a level of happiness that could be experienced through a deeper sense of community and connection with nature.

I had not intended to seek a spiritual path or a teacher while in Florida — the idea had not even entered my mind. It just happened.

Within the first few weeks, I went to an art festival and struck up a conversation with an artist. After hearing about my Africa experience and writing ambitions, she suggested I go to the Temple of the Universe.

The following Sunday, I found myself driving my brother's car into the countryside outside Gainesville to a wooded area. Several cars were parked along a gravel road, and people were walking toward a single-story, wood building nestled in trees and covered in Spanish moss.

The smell of incense and patchouli oil was in the air as I neared the door. Following the example, I took off my shoes, placed them at the door, and went inside. There were no chairs, just pillows on the floor. Everyone was sitting cross-legged with their eyes closed. On the walls were pictures of various people, most of them Indian-looking. The only photo I recognized was Christ. I later learned the images were of yogis and other illumined beings from many different spiritual traditions.

The room slowly filled, and then a thin man with a graying pony tail walked in, nodded to a photograph, sat down, and started to play an electric keyboard instrument. He began singing some strange song and everyone responded. Back and forth it went, with this guy calling out and everyone else responding, similar to some of the singing in Sierra Leone, where one person would lead.

After the chant, there was silence for several minutes. I noticed the thin guy, who I later learned was Mickey Singer, had a huge, almost exaggerated, smile on his face.

Mickey than began to talk, and I tried to listen without moving too much, but my legs were getting cramped and my butt sore. He mentioned something about when a yogi goes inward; there was a state of consciousness that was beyond desire. None of it made sense, yet, I was intrigued.

Following the service, everyone filed outside to a large open field. They joined hands in a circle, said a prayer, and then shared tea and cookies. There was a sense of community, in nature, centered on a spiritual connection. Even though it was all strange, my heart soaked it up, as it was the closest thing to Kagbere and Masongbo I had experienced since coming back to America.

The Temple of the Universe

Every Sunday I would go to the Temple and listen and then join in the community circle. I loved that the Temple was in the woods, kind of like a sacred part of the bush near Kagbere and Masongbo, where spiritual activities occurred.

I became friends with a young woman named Shimra, who helped me to begin to understand what in the world this guy, Mickey, was talking about. She also taught me a basic meditation technique: observing — witnessing — the breath coming in and out.

It helped that Shimra was cute, so I enjoyed being with her. She too was very critical of Western consumerism and its impact on the world, so we had that in common as well.

After I heard Mickey several times, I asked to meet with him in person. We set a time, and Shimra drove me out to see him.

The meeting was at Mickey's business near the Temple. It was a two-floor, cement-block building that housed some type of software company. Computers were still new to me, and I was just getting used to WordPerfect. The idea of creating a software program was beyond my imagination.

Shimra and I were late for the meeting, and Mickey immediately pointed it out. I was invited into his office, surprised to see a large wooden desk with lots of papers. Somehow I had expected this yogi to be unconcerned with time and worldly matters. On the contrary, Mickey was punctual and businesslike.

Mickey asked what he could do for me. I told him I had returned from four years in Africa and was writing about the experience. As I started to describe some of the reverse culture shock images and the ball of balance, Mickey asked, "What do you think people in the United States and Africa are seeking?"

"I don't know; happiness," I replied.

"Yes," Mickey said, "happiness outside of themselves. Everyone is looking in the wrong place. There is a state that exists inside that will satisfy all desires."

This made no sense and I asked, "But how can you say that when thousands of children in Sierra Leone die before the age of five? What about this massive consumerism in the United States? It's clear it cannot be sustained and it is affecting the rest of the world."

Mickey looked straight at me and said, "Who asked you how it should be?"

I became animated, "But it's just wrong! Thousands and thousands of children dying and people in the U.S. spending millions and billions of dollars on things they don't need, sucking up the world's resources for pleasure."

"Who asked you how it should be?" Mickey continued.

I went off even further, talking about Goodwill clothes being dumped on the markets, about excess grain from the U.S. flooding Africa, about illegal trade of diamonds and corruption in Sierra Leone....

Mickey looked at me and said, "If the planet Pluto was orbiting in a way that you did not like, what are you going to do about it?"

That comment lost me all together, and I became frustrated.

Mickey went on, "Look, there are billions of stars and planets in the Milky Way. There are billions of galaxies, all with billions of stars and planets. Science is discovering more and more galaxies all the time. All of them are guided by some intelligence and by natural laws."

"All you have to do is turn to that intelligence and it will guide you. It may even take you back to Africa in ways that you never imagined. That intelligence is much more creative than what you can ever come up with on your own."

"Your preferences, your judgments, your likes and dislikes, and all of your beliefs about how the world should be — they only separate you from that very subtle state of consciousness that is in you, that is in everything and that is manifesting everything."

"That state of 'super consciousness' is behind your thoughts. When you tap into it, the bliss and the love will overwhelm you and you will feel a connection with everything in the universe. There is nothing, nothing in the world you would trade for it, not all the money in the world or all the rice in Africa. If you were in that state of bliss 24/7, you wouldn't care if you were sweeping floors. That state of consciousness is what you and everyone is seeking."

At that point, I was in way over my head, plus I was pissed, as I just did not understand what he was saying. I was still upset with the disparities between West Africa and the United States and not ready to move beyond what I thought was right for the world.

Even Deeper Still ~ Massage School

Despite my resistance, Mickey sparked something, and I had no idea what it was. I kept going to the Temple on Sundays and became more restless as I listened, trying to understand. Meanwhile, it was clear that I was not going back to Sierra Leone anytime soon and that I needed to face the reality of staying in the States.

After several months of living with my brother's family, it was time to move out on my own. My judgments of Western lifestyles and confusion over reverse culture shock came across in moodiness and snide comments. It was much better to be on my own.

I found the bottom floor of a house to rent from a professor who taught cross-cultural and spiritual aspects of psychology. It was a nice match, as she, Mary, was open to my peculiar habits of relying primarily on a bicycle for getting around town and recycling almost everything. I would come back to the house with small pieces of wire, empty containers, and other items I found along the road.

Meanwhile, Shimra had introduced me to the Florida School of Massage. In discussing the ball of balance, she said they taught the same concept there. This at first confused me, so I went to visit the school. Sure enough, there were similarities, and I wanted to learn more. The school was known for its strong mind-body awareness approach and most instructors were either students or teachers of Vispassana meditation, as well as trained in Gestalt therapy.

I worked for several months painting houses and saved money to take a four-month massage certification program. Shimra also introduced me to Patrick, a Cornell University graduate who had entered massage school after the suicide of a close friend. Massage school was a way for him to heal. Patrick and I became close friends, and he moved into Mary's house with me.

Patrick got a kick out of the fact that he had dozens of kitchen utensils and I only had a Swiss army knife and two pots. I bought rice in twenty-pound bags and refused to plug in the refrigerator or accept free furniture. Being that Patrick was in a transition too, he was open to living a more spartan lifestyle. Knowing Patrick was a well-educated and thoughtful person helped me relax about going to massage school and overcome my family's inquiries about what the hell I was doing with my life — massage school and talking about yogis.

Neither Patrick, Mary, Shimra, nor I owned a TV, and one of our favorite activities was drumming and chanting. Mary had a wide selection of percussion instruments, as she was a big fan of *peace through music*. We often would break out into spontaneous sessions of drumming and playing other instruments. Mary taught us something called *toning*, which was a way of using the voice to allow deeper expressions of one's feelings and spirit. We would start playing, chanting, and toning, going off in many different directions, rising and falling tempos, and playing off of one another's leads. We would then go into silence or break out into laughter.

Mary, Patrick, Shimra, and I became a new community, and we loved going out into nature. Mary would take me canoeing on the rivers, or Patrick, Shimra and I would go for hikes on the prairies. The massage school itself was surrounded by trees and was in a process of moving to a new property with extended trails in the woods.

Massage school was a whole new adventure. There were a range of people, from doctors to high school dropouts, all there for different reasons, all treated with the same respect. Some people, like Patrick, were going through life transitions. Others wanted deeper self awareness and many wanted a new profession.

What I found was a safe and nurturing environment to explore new ideas and to process my own transition. The core concepts and principles of the school helped clarify my Peace Corps experience and were ones I would apply for years to come, without ever practicing massage professionally.

The first two concepts were simple: create a safe space for people to experience themselves in new ways, and meet people *where they are*.

In hindsight, I could see that my Peace Corps experience also had provided these things. Kagbere and Masongbo had provided a safe space for me to experience myself in new ways, and the Peace Corps in general was all about meeting people where they are — speaking the local language and living with people in their communities. It was not a parachuting-in type of approach — come in with ideas and leave. No, it was to stay, at least for two years.

In many ways, the Contehs and I applied these ideas with the fishing lures. We met each other where we were — love of fishing and need for food. By only using locally available materials, we stayed within the bounds of what was appropriate for their lives. Moses, Sanpha, Bokarie, and I all experienced ourselves in new ways; we had that trust with one another to do it.

In massage, these concepts were applied by speaking a language that was appropriate for the client — was it sports massage, talking about peak performance of muscles, or was the client more interested simply in reducing stress, or would the client want to get behind the root cause of a chronic back problem and want to explore the mind-body connection?

The practitioner was responsible for meeting the client where he or she was and then *holding the space* through the session.

On a practical level, this meant we had to learn the techniques of massage as well as communication skills. Even more important, we had to learn how to be *present*. This was a new concept and it was powerful to be exposed to people who were good at doing it.

Many of the instructors had an ability to focus and concentrate that I had never seen before. When talking with them, they would look straight at me without flinching or moving. This was so much different from the distracted and meandering conversation style I had lived with most of my life.

Marcela Martinez/Florida School of Massage

No, the instructors modeled being present, fully present. This is where the meditation came in. Many of them had taken ten-day Vispassana silent meditation retreats. Without preaching, they encouraged us to watch our thoughts while practicing massage or talking with a client, to be aware of when the mind wandered and to bring it back on the person's words or to where our hands were touching them.

Another concept was to learn the difference between imagination and observation. The exercise drove us crazy, as we would sit across from one another and say things like, " I observe you look nice" only to be told, no, that is an imagination. An observation is, "you are wearing a shirt." The differences were subtle, yet the intent was to become aware of how our minds would create judgments that we would take as reality and then go off into realms of interpretations and emotional reaction.

The ideas were simple: be present, let go of thoughts and judgments, meet people where they are, and provide the space for people to experience themselves in new ways.

Every day we had four hours of anatomy or communication and then four hours of practical learning of massage techniques. When on the table receiving a massage, the practitioner would invite the client to bring his or her awareness to the place where the hands were touching. They would meet the person at the point of contact and hold the space for the client to experience himself in new ways.

I was amazed to learn that the tissues of my body held vast memories of past experiences. When going into the pectorals, the muscles on the chest going to the shoulders, I would flash back to childhood scenes where I had a crush on the neighbor girl and how I was heartbroken when I figured out she thought I was too young for her. Massaging the tissues of my legs took me back to running cross-country. My entire body was one huge memory bank of past experiences, or as one student liked to say, "Issues turn into tissues."

With the practitioner being present and letting go of judgments, students receiving massages were allowed to "go even deeper still" into their own mind-body experience. It was very common for students, myself included, to break out into crying, while remembering some experience. The massage was facilitating the release of the old, stored-up emotions.

Another experience that took me totally by surprise was going into an almost trance-like state, where I was in a village, some village that seemed very familiar. It was evening and a full moon was rising. There was a person on a table, with a woman, like a priestess, next to him. Surrounding her was a circle of women, singing, and behind them a circle of men playing drums. The children of the village were running around on the outside, also singing.

The memory-like vision went on and on, lasting several minutes. Tears flowed, as I felt like I knew the scene and understood that the village was healing the person in the middle, using the energy of the moon and their collective energies, all channeled through music and ritual.

Meanwhile, through the weeks of receiving bodywork, I became aware of a haunting void and at times a deep sadness. When I saw the movie *Dances with Wolves*, I literally wept for hours afterward. I was so drawn into the Lakota lifestyle, the deep sense of community, living close with nature and a sense of spirituality that was interwoven with all aspects of life. The idea of those villages and that way of life being destroyed by mindless greed, consumption, and brutal war hurt, hurt deeply.

I did not know what to make of the sorrow stirred up by *Dances with Wolves*, or the village healing trance on the massage table, or all the other memories from my childhood and beyond that were triggered by massage. Living in Masongbo and Kagbere had introduced a whole new way of being and seeing the world. Sierra Leone had cracked me open. Massage school and Mickey's talks were taking me into those cracks, going inward into realms that were familiar, foreign, and at times scary.

Navajo Reservation

After graduating from massage school, it was time to move on. Patrick had returned to Ithaca, New York to work for Cornell University and start a private massage practice on the side. Shimra had moved to Hawaii to swim with dolphins and practice massage. Even though I was licensed to practice massage, I felt drawn back to the international work.

The first Persian Gulf War was underway, and stories were coming out of Sierra Leone that the war in neighboring Liberia had spilled over. It was clear that the American lifestyle and dependence on oil directly contributed to the Persian Gulf War, and that Sierra Leone was also impacted by the Western world, as diamonds were being used to buy weapons. The world was interdependent, and how we lived in the U.S. influenced the rest. I wanted to do something about it; I just did not know what.

A couple friends from Peace Corps Sierra Leone invited me to Washington, DC and encouraged me to apply for a job at the Peace Corps. I flew up for a visit and thought there were nice possibilities. On the return flight to Gainesville, I volunteered to be bumped off the flight and received a coupon for a free round-trip flight.

When I got back to Gainesville, I told Mary about the move and started packing. Another friend from Peace Corps Sierra Leone called; this one was living in New Mexico and teaching in an elementary school. She told me a school on the Navajo Reservation in Arizona had lost a teacher and desperately needed someone to finish out the school year; otherwise they would lose their federal grant. When I told her I had never taught, she laughed, "They need someone who can live in a remote, cross-cultural setting. Don't worry, I will give you the lesson plans; I had that job last year."

For some reason, the job on the Navajo reservation felt right, though I did not know why. It was only a six-month commitment and would provide an opportunity to see a whole new part of the world and to explore teaching while helping out a school in a pinch. With the free flight coupon in hand, the choice was easy.

Arriving in New Mexico and driving to Arizona, the first thing to stand out was the landscape — wide open spaces, to be seen for miles. It was incredible! Florida was flat with swamps. Arizona — I had never seen anything like it. I was mesmerized by the land!

The school was on top of a mesa, miles from any town. There was a small cluster of houses built by the U.S. government and then a few trailers for teachers a hundred yards from the school. I later learned from one of the teachers that Navajos liked to live spread apart from one another in hogans — houses made from trees and Earth. The U.S. government purposively built houses for the Navajos close together. Meanwhile, the neighboring Hopi reservations had U.S. government houses spread apart though the Hopis liked to live close together. The teacher suggested it was one more way for the U.S. government to disturb the Indians.

My friend who told me about the job dropped me off at the school and then drove back to New Mexico. One of the other teachers at the school also had been a Peace Corps Volunteer in Sierra Leone, so we developed a quick friendship.

My job was to teach reading and writing to troubled students in grades one through eight. The classes were small, maybe five or six students. What stood out was how reserved the kids and Navajo teachers were — friendly and respectful, yet almost cool at times. It was so different than Sierra Leone, where there was a friendly, outgoing, and inviting openness. Plus, the Navajo word for "white person," was *Billigana*, which translated into "he who is killed." Knowing the history of white conquest of the West, the name and reserved demeanor were understandable.

The teaching part went slowly, as I learned to take lesson plans and walk kids through them. But what most caught my attention was seeing how the students were bridging the different worlds. They were being prepared to take standardized government exams, which the school historically underperformed on compared to national standards. The low performances made sense, given the exams were based on mainstream-American history and culture. For instance, when asked about the oldest settlement in America, the students would answer Acoma, New Mexico or another nearby community that had been inhabited for well over 1,000 years. The "correct" answer was Jamestown, 1607.

I tried to apply the concepts from the Peace Corps and massage school — to show up, meet the kids where they were, and provide a safe space for them to experience themselves in new ways. I enjoyed the teaching and took on one student who was struggling and provided additional tutoring to help him graduate.

One afternoon, I took five of the older kids for a hike. The surrounding hills were beautiful, sparsely dotted with sage brush, large boulders, and wonderful views. As we walked along, they told stories about "skin walkers," people who could turn into wolves and who guarded the sacred sites. They pointed out a feather and said it was from an eagle. When I picked it up, they laughed and said it was a crow feather and that it was bad luck to touch it. I put it down and then took some soil and rubbed my hands together. They asked, "How did you know to do that?"

"Do what?" I replied.

"Clean your hands with Earth," one said.

"I don't know, just knew," I said.

As we walked, one by one the kids disappeared into the landscape. They reminded me so much of the Conteh brothers in their knowledge of the land. I thought about the white invaders and the natural advantage the Navajo warriors must have had and how I would be an easy target.

The kids eventually came out of hiding and we headed back to the indoor classroom, which was void of all signs of nature. The disconnect between school and the kids' everyday lives was so clear, especially as each young boy would write the same story: "I found a wild pony. I caught it, named it, and made it my own. Now I ride it."

I empathized with the students, as I did not feel at home in the Western way of life. My heart ached for the deeper sense of connection with nature and community that I experienced in Kagbere and Masongbo.

One of the Navajo teachers did share with me a story about the power of the land. He told me about a white man who had been introduced to him and his family. This man was terribly unhappy from years of working in a corporation. In a state of desperation, he came and stayed with the teacher's family for many months. He helped with farming and tending to the sheep, but mainly, he just lived close to the land. The teacher said, "The land and the quiet healed him. He came back to a place of peace and then returned to his life."

I was finding the land was having a similar effect on me. After class, I loved going hiking, especially to the site of an Anasazi ruin on top of a nearby hill. The Anasazis had lived there nearly two to three thousand years ago and were considered wise and peaceful people by the Navajos. This site had the remains of stone walls from houses and lots of pottery shards, many pieces with designs such as spirals.

I would sit at the site and look out into the distance. This was my solace; this is where I found some peace, as the Earth slowly worked on me. There was an expansive feeling that came from being able to see for so many miles. It also was easy to practice being present, as there was little sound, just the wind and then the hum of the Earth. It was so nice to hear the hum again. I had not heard the Earth since leaving Sierra Leone. I found myself dissolving into the whole experience, relaxing, feeling more peaceful than I had since returning from West Africa.

My experience in Sierra Leone helped me to imagine the way of life for the Anasazi people and then the Hopi and Navajos years later. Like my friends in Kagbere and Masongbo, the Anasazis' lives must have been shaped and influenced by the land. I thought about being in those communities, under the stars at night with electricity not even invented yet. I imagined how their lives must have been interwoven with community, cycles of crops, and seasons of nature. How their pottery, now in shards, may have stored fresh rain water for drinking. How there must have been a deep sense of spirituality, connecting them with ancestors and nature.

I wondered about the Anasazi people's concepts of God — was everything seen as part of God (Earth, sky, plants, animals, people...) and thus everything was considered sacred? Unlike Sierra Leone, they did not have the Christian and Muslim influence to blend with their traditional spiritual practices. Surely their idea of God was not an old white man in the sky.

I thought about their family and community ceremonies, and their rites of passage for young men and women. I wondered if the vision I had had of a village with circles of healing had any relation to the Anasazis or any other tribe in history.

I wondered if the Anasazis had hardships with subsistence farming, like the Contehs, or whether there was a high infant mortality rate.

I did not know at the time, and only years later would I learn from a yogi, that the land in Arizona and New Mexico was known for having a strong spiritual vibration, one associated with the feminine aspect of Spirit. All I knew was that I was dissolving and relaxing.

While sitting in the stillness, I would reflect on the Persian Gulf War and the war in Liberia spilling over into Sierra Leone. It seemed so absurd that the U.S. would go to war over natural resources, and yet that was exactly what brought settlers West. Were there no lessons learned? Did we, people in the U.S. and other Western countries, not see we were still being driven by the same type of worldview that killed millions of Native Americans? Just because we could not see the impact of our lifestyles on other people, did that make us innocent?

Meanwhile, the war in Liberia and Sierra Leone was of no concern to people in the U.S. whatsoever. Even though those countries had little "strategic importance," did that really make their plight less compelling than Kuwait or Iraq?

During the evenings, when not making out with the other former Peace Corps Volunteer, I would read books by the Dalai Lama, Jack Kornfield (a Vispassana meditation teacher and former Peace Corps Volunteer), and others. I was intrigued by their teachings, how everyone wants to be happy and wants to avoid suffering, and that these basic desires were motivating all of people's actions. They talked about developing compassion by recognizing the common desires of all humanity. They also mentioned states of deep peace that existed inside when the mind is calm. Was that the state Mickey was talking about?

It all seemed so simple.

If we are all seeking peace and happiness, then that commonality in itself should be enough for us to see and recognize our oneness with people around the world. If the desire for peace and happiness was driving consumption, then it made sense that no amount of material wealth would ever quench that thirst. Sure, there must be a balance to help alleviate causes of suffering — lack of water, food, and shelter — but how much was enough? If the Contehs could experience happiness from a sense of community and relationship with nature, then could they not have something to teach people in the United States? If sitting in beautiful natural environments helps to heal and awaken feelings of peace, could we, humanity, change our perception of nature to one of reverence instead of consumption?

The relationship between inner peace and international peace, or rather inner unrest and global conflict, was so clear.

While sitting at the Anasazi site, these thoughts would come and go, dissolving into the expansiveness of time and space. Slowly what emerged was an idea for an inner-peace–global-peace project, to collect and disseminate the wisdom from different cultures on how to find inner peace. (Later, I would further develop the ideas with others into the Peace Continuum from inner to international peace.)

Another Peace Corps Sierra Leone friend came to visit from Washington, DC. We went for a hike to the Anasazi ruin. As we sat there, I told him about the project idea. He looked, smiled, and said, "You can do that in Washington. You might be able to do it at the Peace Corps."

It was time to move to Washington, DC. The semester on the reservation and time with the land had provided clarity of purpose.

Dynamite

Fueled by the global context and carrying a very clear purpose, I left the Navajo reservation after the school semester was over and headed for Washington, DC, bound and determined "to do" the peace project. I started the journey by attending a ten-day Vipassana silent meditation retreat in upstate Massachusetts.

The idea of ten days of silence was at first intimidating. However, the retreat center had volunteer staff and instructors who made it easy to forget about everything and to focus on learning the techniques. It was another example of the concept of creating a safe space for someone to experience him/herself in a new way.

The days were divided into periods of meditation with breaks, starting early in the morning and going into the evening. The instructors provided guidance in two basic techniques, one building upon the other, and then we practiced and practiced and practiced. What I came to find was my mind was an absolute zoo, full of roaming thoughts, and that my body would habitually move and ache. The task at hand was to observe, simply observe, without going off on the thoughts or reacting to physical discomfort. When the thoughts and physical sensations would arise, we were encouraged to go back to the techniques with the breath as an anchor.

The ten days provided ample opportunity to experience *the witness*, the part of me that could observe thoughts, emotions, and physical sensations rise and pass away without reacting to or attaching to them. Mickey Singer had talked a lot about the witness and even suggested it was the soul, or superconsciousness. At the retreat center there was no reference to soul, spirit, or God. This particular meditation center was teaching a universal technique that could be used free of religious overtone and would provide scientifically proven results of focus and calmness.

By developing the witness, a person could free him/herself from unconscious patterns and reactions. Instead of going on automatic stimulus and reaction, the witness would allow the stimulation to come and thoughts to rise and pass away, providing time to reflect and respond. It was easy to imagine how meditation would be helpful for breaking unconscious patterns of behavior, including reactive tendencies that can lead to arguments or fighting.

Toward the end of the retreat, I noticed how intensely I could concentrate. Wherever I focused my attention, I could keep it on the object, whether it was a person talking, a cloud passing overhead, or a blade of grass.

I remembered how Mickey used to say, "Wherever you place your attention, that is where your energy and consciousness goes." That had not meant a whole lot to me, as energy and consciousness were vague concepts at that point. What I did notice was that my ability to concentrate was like a laser and, as a result, I was much more creative and productive.

When I returned to Washington, DC, I was highly disciplined and focused. My meditation practice was an hour in the morning and an hour at night, a dramatic increase from the ten-minutes a day prior to the retreat.

A couple weeks after the retreat there was an article in the *Washington Post* about the Peace Corps's thirtieth anniversary. It was a small piece next to a larger story about young girls spending thousands of dollars on expensive beauty-pageant dresses. The contrast between the Peace Corps and materialism was too much, so I wrote a letter to the editor about the need to redefine the pursuit of happiness. The letter was published in its entirety.

Along with the letter, everything seemed to move according to some divine plan. The former Catholic Relief Service director in Sierra Leone, the one who had funded the TWIT-TWAT water well project, worked at the Peace Corps headquarters and helped me secure a job supporting water and sanitation projects around the world. A few weeks later, I met a woman outside of the Peace Corps developing a peacebuilding project and she introduced me to James O'Dea, the director of Amnesty International. James was a tall, Irish man with a deep sense of justice and what I slowly came to realize was the heart of a poet and mystic. James and I quickly became friends, as I greatly valued his older-brother-like and wise qualities.

Meanwhile, I pitched my inner-peace–global-peace idea to the Peace Corps supervisors and it was run up the flagpole to the lawyers, who deemed it inappropriate because of separation of state and religion. I was not deterred. Though I kept working at the Peace Corps, I also started working with James and another friend to create a nonprofit organization that would celebrate the lives of people promoting peace.

James had introduced to me the need to celebrate the positive that was happening in the world. He often told me he was tired of being exposed to suffering day in and day out. While the human rights work was necessary, James felt the longer-term way of changing the world was to acknowledge and celebrate the positive potential of humanity.

Over the course of the next year, while I helped to look for funding to start the peace project, other friends introduced me to Sufism and shamans from Latin America. I began to attend workshops and to dabble in these traditions while continuing to meditate daily. What I did not realize was that the various practices were opening me on energetic levels, and that each of them had their own sophisticated systems for understanding consciousness and energy.

One Vispassana meditation practitioner in the DC area told me, "It is okay to have one foot in one canoe and the other in another canoe as long as the water is calm. As soon as there are waves, it becomes hard to find balance."

This was exactly what happened. I began to observe a wide range of emotions rising up. It took a while before I realized that I was a "psychic sponge," that I could feel the emotions of people around me. When a new supervisor at the Peace Corps arrived, this became a problem because she was going through menopause. Sitting near her, I would get hot flashes and find myself riding a wave of emotions. When I would leave work, I would feel better. I had no control over what I would pick up and experience.

To compound matters, the peace project and a romantic relationship both were hitting rocky times. Meanwhile, I had passed up opportunities to apply for new jobs at the Peace Corps, thinking I was moving on to the new nonprofit. As the waves of energies and emotional reactions kept coming, I did not know where to turn — Vispassana, Sufism, Quechuan shamanism or Umbanda, an Afro-Brazilian spiritual tradition with roots from West Africa. I entered a period where I did not know which way was up, and I was burning from excess energies and emotions much of the time.

To compound matters, the news from Sierra Leone was getting worse. The war was spreading to other parts of the country. I felt so far away from being able to do anything to help, as I was struggling myself.

Needing some type of break, I went on vacation to Florida to see Mickey. I arrived late yet again at his office. He was understanding and suggested we take a drive around the new office building, which was nearly completed. As Mickey drove, I told him how I had burned for the past couple years.

"I know," he said."

"No Mickey, I really burned," I stressed.

"I know," he replied. "You thought you knew what was going on, and you had to be blown out of that seat with dynamite."

Mickey then began to tell me about how his business had grown from a dozen to almost a thousand employees.

"I did not do any of it, all I did was follow the energy," Mickey said.

"What do you mean, 'follow the energy'?" I asked.

"You learn to follow energy, Shakti — She will guide you. That is the most important relationship you can have; it is the only relationship that matters. When She tells you to go left, you go left. When She tells you to go right, you go right.

"With this business, all I did was get out of the way; I learned to do nothing," Mickey said.

I still did not understand, as Mickey was the CEO and president. How could he do nothing?

"It is hard to do good in this world as long as you think you are the doer. Your ego and attachments get in the way, and you find yourself doing things for reasons that are more about you than what wants to emerge through you," Mickey said. "As soon as *you* touch anything, you're dead.

"You have to learn to let go and follow the energy. It will be much more creative than you ever will be. And, most importantly, you have to be detached to it looking the way you think it should or want it to look.

"Many people can have inspired visions, but then they spoil them through their own interpretations and attachments. This business, it could be gone tomorrow and it would not matter," Mickey said.

Years later, employees under Mickey were accused of illegal practices. The FBI walked into Mickey's office and ordered him out and started an investigation. Mickey simply went back to his ashram across the street, as if nothing had happened. Mickey was later cleared of wrongdoing, yet did not return to work at the company; instead, he started writing books and became the bestselling author of *The Untethered Soul.*

Picking a Spiritual Path

The situation in Washington, DC only intensified.

The fledgling peace-focused nonprofit folded, so I worked with colleagues at the Peace Corps to start a "peace in the Peace Corps" group to look at how the agency could expand its role in promoting peace in the world. The group met a few times and drew interest from a wide range of staff and former Volunteers, including a former acting director of the Peace Corps. There were several ideas for ways the Peace Corps could draw upon emerging practices in conflict resolution to better prepare volunteers for cross-cultural situations and for using former volunteers to help promote peace in countries where they once served as well as in the United States. The group was hamstrung, however, by the federal bureaucracy, and it proved difficult to introduce innovative ideas so broad in scope.

Meanwhile, I was struggling with my own inner peace as I was trying to get a handle on being around other people's energies. A few friends shared simple techniques of putting up an energetic boundary through visualization, and I began to practice them on a daily basis.

Other experiences proved difficult to understand, too. One friend asked if I could help edit the book of a shaman. As we worked on the project together, we both began to have strange phenomena happening, such as lots of coincidences and an excess of sexual energy. We suddenly had an overwhelmingly strong mutual attraction. Given she was married; we kept clear from acting on the strong desires.

At another time, I suddenly found myself wanting to drive to the countryside on a Saturday afternoon. With no clue on where I was going, I drove toward the Shenandoah Valley near Front Royal, Virginia. I looked for a place to camp and, as the sun started to set, I found myself at a public campground. When I arrived, I was asked at the front gate if I was there for the pagan ceremony. I replied, "Sure."

The next thing I knew, I was in the middle of a circle of nearly fifty people, all singing and playing drums around a fire. A very large, bare-chested man with a huge beard began conducting a healing ceremony on me.

When I later mentioned the story to James O'Dea he simply said, "You need a container. You are too wide open; you need a form for the formless."

The comment from James stayed with me. I wanted to simplify my life and focus on one spiritual tradition. By this point, I had done three ten-day silent meditation retreats, dabbled in Sufism, and been on several Shamanism workshops, including the Afro-Brazilian tradition which was my way of trying to understand the war in Sierra Leone from a spiritual perspective. I was confused about which path to follow.

I also was far off track with the inner-peace–global-peace idea, as I certainly did not have inner peace. I felt stuck and out of balance. So much for writing a book on the ball of balance!

Burnt out and disappointed by my venture to save the world, I decided to leave the Peace Corps.

It was a good time for a road trip, so I made another journey to Florida and had another conversation with Mickey. This time I asked, "I am trying to choose a spiritual path — Vispassana meditation or Sufism. What do you think?"

Ever calm, Mickey replied, "They both will get you there, they are both good paths."

That was not the answer I was looking for. What did he mean, "They are both good paths and will get me there?" I wanted to know "the" path to take.

When I pressed Mickey, he said, "Look, you have it all set up in dualism already. Take a step back and focus on the intention; the rest will take care of itself."

I was not sure what Mickey meant about having it "set up in dualism," though the concept of dualism would later become an important underpinning for understanding conflict.

I did as Mickey suggested. I prayed deeply for a path that would help me experience a sense of peace. I added a nuance of asking for a three-year curriculum. For some reason, that idea kept coming to mind — "all I need is a three-year curriculum." For weeks, I kept repeating the prayer, not sure who or what I was praying to.

I went to live with Patrick in Ithaca, New York, and he recommended reading *Autobiography of a Yogi*, by Paramahansa Yogananda (published by Self-Realization Fellowship/Yogoda Satsanga Society of India). Coincentally, my older sister in Ohio recommended the same book. As I read the book, Patrick pointed out, "Did you know the organization that publishes the book offers a three-year course by mail to learn *Kriya Yoga*?"

When Patrick mentioned the course, I nearly fell over.

I signed up for the lessons and slowly embarked on a spiritual journey I had not planned but that felt intuitively like a good way to go.

On the next trip to Florida, Mickey openly referred to Yogananda as Master. I also noticed there were photos of Yogananda in the Temple of the Universe and that *Autobiography of a Yogi* was one of the few books for sale there too.

"It took me years," Mickey said, "to realize that Master was pulling my strings."

Yoga ~ The Science of Soul Exploration

What joy awaits discovery in the silence behind the portals of your mind no human tongue can tell. But you must convince yourself; you must meditate and create that environment.[3]

— Paramahansa Yogananda

In theory, Yoga is simple. Yogananda once wrote, "Yoga is definite and scientific. Yoga means union of soul and God, through step-by-step methods with specific and known results. It raises the practice of religion above the differences of dogma." [4]

It surprised me to be drawn to this Kriya Yoga tradition because I was not seeking "God" or a guru; in fact I had knee-jerk reactions to both words. Rather, I just wanted inner peace and to understand how the inner dynamics related to the global context. I had all but put aside the inner-peace–global-peace project and was focused on grounding and centering myself.

While exploring Kriya Yoga, I lived in Ithaca, New York with Patrick for a while, then moved back to the DC area to work on an organic farm. The farming was perfect; it had me outside, in nature, close to the Earth. It was very grounding and healing.

In practice, I came to find Kriya Yoga to be highly sophisticated and requiring nothing less than a complete willingness to transform myself from the inside out, gradually, over a long period of time. It was not an instantaneous ticket to peace and bliss, even though there were glimpses of these states in meditation.

Kriya Yoga also satisfied my mind's need to understand what I was doing and why. I no longer had tolerance for religious dogma or performing rituals in foreign languages while not understanding what the heck I was doing. This Kriya Yoga tradition explained everything in terms of science and consciousness, which worked for me. It was adapted for the Western person in mind in that anyone could practice it, even busy business people and heads of households.

Consciousness, Energy, and the Soul

As I studied Kriya Yoga, I learned it was far more than *hatha yoga*, a system of physical postures and breathing control designed to prepare a person for meditation, as well as provide physical, emotional, and mental benefits. Kriya Yoga was a type of *raja yoga*, or royal yoga, a form of meditation that was a nondenominational "scientific method for attaining direct, personal relationship with God."

"God" was such a loaded word for me, as it brought up images of Catholic school and being told I was going to hell for chewing gum, and thoughts of wars throughout the ages fueled by religious differences. I was not interested in a God that would damn third graders for chewing gum or send millions of people into battle to fight people from other religions.

A basic premise of Kriya Yoga, at least in my limited understanding of it, was that God/Spirit (whatever word works for a person) was beyond creation and also was all of creation at the same time. When God created the universe, it was done through the vehicle of conscious energy manifesting as frequencies of vibrations from subtle to more dense, initially as ideas (the causal plane); then as light, in mental and emotional forms (the astral plane); and then the physical plane. The causal level of ideas carried the blueprints that then manifested as light and finally physical form.

Kriya Yoga was sounding more and more like quantum physics and other emerging theories of science that saw the universe as one big idea emerging from consciousness, and matter as energy or waves of light. Kriya Yoga also was like science in saying, "Do not believe what we say, experiment and see for yourself."

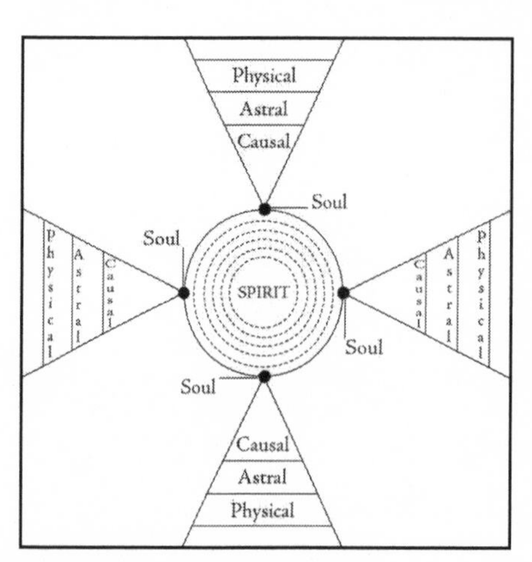

One of the first questions I had was: what is the soul? There was one diagram that helped me understand the soul, at least from a theoretical perspective.

This image showed the soul as the focal point in which Spirit/God manifested as an individual, giving birth to the three levels — causal, astral, and physical. As part of Spirit, the soul was made of the same essence (or image of God) — pure conscious energy.

A way to start experiencing the soul was to develop the witness. (Back to the witness!) The witness was consciousness; it was the awareness that there were thoughts, emotions, and physical sensations. When thinking about who was witnessing, it was like going down a rabbit hole, or like a cat chasing its tail in a mirror.

I began to realize that my mind, through thinking, could not know or experience the soul, let alone higher states of consciousness, or God. In fact, my mind and thoughts were keeping me from being aware of the consciousness that was manifesting through me. It was like figures on a movie screen thinking they were real, when in fact they were projections of light and shadow from a movie projector; or even better, it was like the movie *The Matrix,* with its alternate realities.

My thoughts were helping provide a framework for going inward into meditation, but inevitably the goal was to quiet the mind and its restless thoughts to allow one to directly experience ever-more-subtle states of consciousness. Over the years, my concept of God kept evolving and changing, as I slowly realized God was beyond the mind's comprehension. Arguing over God seemed utterly absurd, like waves on the ocean arguing who knew the ocean better or who was the chosen wave.

As a child, the soul seemed so mysterious and out of reach, something otherworldly that would be damned to hell if I were bad. Now, here it was — the soul was right under my own nose.

A student once asked Yogananda if there was a hell. He responded with laughter, "Where do you think you are now?" referring to being stuck in a state of delusion and feeling separate from the soul and God.

According to these Kriya Yoga teachings, the soul had the same qualities as Spirit — eternal peace, bliss, love, etc. In fact, peace was the first experience of the soul when meditating, and, going deeper into peace, opened one to joy, bliss, and then ecstasy.

Mickey said the challenge was that we, people, intuitively know these ecstatic states exist inside of us, but we identify so strongly with our thoughts, emotions, and physical body that we are not sensitive to or in *tune* with the subtle nature of our own soul, even though it is right there, behind our thoughts. We try to create *peak experiences* of pleasure, happiness and even ecstasy and joy largely through interacting with people and/or things outside of ourselves that get the energy moving in us — going from the lower *chakras,* or energy centers, to the higher ones. (For a thorough description of chakras and the flow of energy through them, refer to *Three Essays on Universal Law: The Laws of Karma, Will, and Love* by Michael A. Singer.)

I learned that the physical universe was made of duality (light and shadows, birth and death, health and illness, positive and negative...) and was guided by natural and subtle laws. Like an ocean, the waves of physical existence keep rising and falling, everything constantly changing. Therefore, most of us spend all our time and energy trying to rearrange the world to get it just the way we want it so we can have peak experiences. By design it was not possible to find eternal peace and bliss in this world, even though those states already existed in our soul, which, like Spirit, was changeless.

Kriya Yoga scientifically reverses the flow of energy and consciousness inward instead of going outward through the senses. Through deep practice and concentration, tremendous energy could be brought inward into stillness and higher states of consciousness. "Be still and know that I am God," was both a biblical quote and theme for this particular Kriya Yoga tradition. It was not that a person was God, just as a wave was not the ocean. Rather, over time, a person learns to identify with and experience the soul as his or her true nature and so eventually merges the soul back with the ocean of consciousness, or God, and then experiences the changing phenomenal universe without attachment.

The challenge was that the soul was trapped in three bodies: the causal, astral, and physical. The entrapment comes when the soul falsely identifies with the thoughts, emotions, and physical body, thinking that was who it was. That delusive state of the soul, known as the ego, fights and struggles to find happiness and to avoid suffering in this world of change, and gets more and more entangled. The ego's desires and fears become energetic patterns around the soul. When a person dies, the soul is freed from the physical body, yet remains bound in the energetic patterns of the desires and fears, keeping it stuck in its astral and causal bodies — like ocean water in three bottles. When the physical bottle breaks, the water is still stuck in the other two bodies, the astral and causal.

The astral plane is said to be experienced as light, often thought of as heaven. The desires and fears around the soul eventually bring a person back to be reborn in the physical world again and again and again. Kriya Yoga was a systematic way of freeing the soul from the cycles of death and rebirth and to merge fully back with God.

This overly simplistic understanding sounded so easy, yet was so hard to use in my everyday life.

Creating a Container — Daily Sanctuary

There was no immediate solution — *take a pill and be enlightened!* — even though many people tried doing just that in the 1960s. (One of my first books about yoga was the classic *Be Here Now,* about Richard Alpert, a scientist at Harvard who studied the effects of LSD on the human mind. Alpert went to India and met his guru, who showed him how to maintain higher states of consciousness without taking drugs. Alpert returned to the U.S. and became Ram Dass, a spiritual pioneer and legend.)

The three-year Kriya Yoga course by mail provided ample reading, with a gradual increase in meditation practices and insights on how to address challenges in daily life from a place of wisdom. The teachings were a road map; it was me who had to apply them and do the inner work. The metaphor that came to mind was reading cookbooks and then cooking.

I was determined to go for it, mainly because of how unhappy I was, and because of my questions about how the Western pursuit of happiness was contributing to environmental destruction and global unrest, including the war in Sierra Leone. Kriya Yoga, or meditation, became the container, the laboratory, for soul exploration.

My spiritual life became one of rhythms, just as in Africa, except this time around I used a daily practice of Kriya Yoga. Using Kriya Yoga techniques, I slowly began to learn how to control *prana*, or "life force energies," through intention and concentration. The idea was exactly what Mickey had mentioned, "Wherever you place your focus, that is where your energy and consciousness go." I was being taught, step by step, how to consciously move energy through the body by intention, and then inward through meditation.

Each morning I continued to meditate for an hour and then again in the evening for an hour before bed. Over time, I would increase the meditations in the morning to two hours.

On weekends, I would go to a center and meditate with a group of people, often for three and even up to eight hours. Going to a center — having a community — was a major part of creating my container. I was no longer on my own; rather, there was a group of fellow meditators, all studying and practicing the same tradition.

The people who attended the meditation center, which I called "yoga church," were from many walks of life — white, black, and yellow; Christian, Jewish, Buddhist, Muslim, and Hindu; North and South American, Asian, European, Caribbean, and even West African. The diversity appealed to me, as did the fellowship. We were all drawn together by a common calling.

During Christmas season, more than one hundred people would attend a day-long meditation to focus on the vibrations of Christ consciousness, a time when it was easy to feel deep peace. Kriya Yoga was bringing me back to my Christian roots by demystifying the Bible and providing practical methods to eventually commune with the consciousness that Christ embodied.

Once a year I would go on spiritual retreats, either a week at an ashram (meditation center/community) or to a gathering of over 5,000 yogis from over fifty countries, who all came for a week-long series of classes. It was during one of the retreats that I began to understand the significance of spiritual pilgrimages to Mecca, Jerusalem, Medjugorje (the Balkan town where Mother Mary appeared), and other places.

Initially I had been resistant to the word "guru." However, the first time I went on a pilgrimage to the place where Yogananda had lived, I was overwhelmed with a flood of unconditional love. My entire body vibrated, and I cried like a child. I simply dissolved into love and felt at home like I had never felt before.

The practice of Kriya Yoga had created a particular frequency in me, the same frequency that was supercharged in the place where my guru had lived. As I came closer to that physical location, the deep sense of reverence inside allowed that frequency to intensify. I could so easily empathize with devout Muslims going to Mecca; with Christian lovers of Mother Mary, such as my grandmother, going to Medjugorje. The places where great saints lived strongly maintain their vibrations, allowing people who deeply love those saints to tune in. Imagine tuning into a radio station and then getting closer to its source. Of course, when it comes to matters of spirit, the frequency is available anywhere — it is just easier to experience in places where great saints lived because of their vibration imprint.

These experiences of deep love kept me coming back for more. During a couple retreats, I considered becoming a monk, thinking I wanted out of the world of challenges and difficulties so I could focus on my spiritual practice, so I could stay in that place of unconditional love. An older monk, Brother S, recognized my dilemma and pointed out that the daily practice was "the refuge" and that I did not need to be a monk or go off into a cave to find God. In fact, he assured me that my problems would follow me into the ashram. Brother S also picked up on my passion for peacebuilding and encouraged me to keep following that interest, especially since our guru was a close friend of Mahatma Gandhi, who had asked to be initiated into Kriya Yoga.

Leaving One Community Behind

One part of Kriya Yoga that was challenging was leaving behind people and activities that took me away from or diluted my practice. There was one group of friends in the Washington, DC area that were like family. We had started to study Umbanda together, an Afro-Brazilian spiritual tradition. It started by having shaman-like healers come up from Brazil for weekend workshops, which led to our forming a study group, which led to trips to Brazil, which led to founding a temple that met weekly to perform ceremonies.

I loved their friendship, the community, the drumming and dancing. It was so much like Sierra Leone, and the tradition provided insights into the rich and sophisticated West African spiritual cosmology, which was also based on energy and consciousness. There also was the direct experience of exploring ancestors, spirits, and energies in nature.

During the ceremonies, specific songs and drumming would occur, and the advanced practitioners would *incorporate* the consciousness of a disembodied spirit. The spirit would then speak through the medium and provide messages for people, including prescriptions for special healing, such as lighting candles.

When I started practicing Kriya Yoga, my friends kept telling me I could do both Kriya Yoga and Umbanda. I struggled for a couple years, trying to balance the two traditions, primarily to maintain my friendships and to better understand Sierra Leone. However, I never felt relaxed with Umbanda or the idea of allowing spirits to use me as a medium. With Kriya Yoga, I felt a sense of peace. Eventually, I stopped attending the Umbanda ceremonies and other activities. While I respected my friends' spiritual path and continued to deeply love them, I needed to follow what was true to my own soul essence.

Though I maintained the friendships, it was never the same. My friends spent more time in Umbanda as it was becoming more important to their everyday lives. Meanwhile, I was diving deeper into Kriya Yoga and was developing new friendship with people in that tradition. My old friends eventually moved to Brazil to be close to the Umbanda temples there.

I later learned from one of the monks that it was common on a spiritual path to let go of friendships and behaviors, such as excessive drinking of alcohol, that no longer served a spiritual aspirant. This also felt like a natural part of life, as people go through life phases.

Section Two

Heaven and Hell on Earth

Africa Dream & Nightmare

While I worked on the organic farm near DC and practiced Kriya Yoga, I continued to explore different peace projects, including how former Peace Corps Volunteers could be mobilized to promote peace in the countries where they once served. I wanted to bridge the spiritual theories of peace and compassion with tangible projects in this world; the ideas, however, were not going anywhere. A friend suggested that, instead of trying to create a new project, I work for an organization that does peacebuilding. I called around and talked with a few people and then sent a resume to a nonprofit called Search for Common Ground (Search).

I then headed off to a Kriya Yoga retreat in Southern California to reflect one more time on whether or not to become a monk. During that retreat, one of the monks kept saying, "common ground," repeatedly.

When I returned to Washington, DC, I was interviewed for a job at Search for Common Ground. A few weeks later I was hired to support a new peacebuilding project in Liberia, West Africa. I was selected because of my experience living and working in Sierra Leone.

Search's mission was to transform the way the world deals with conflict, away from adversarial approaches and toward collaborative problem solving. I was in the media department, which was pioneering the use of radio and television to transform conflict. At the heart of the work was helping people rediscover their common humanity.

Based in Washington, DC, I quickly realized how fortunate I was to be working in the new job. I was part of a small team that was exploring a new frontier of peacebuilding — using media. One of my first tasks was to research people who had the combination of media, conflict resolution, and evaluation experience. I could not find anyone, which my supervisor expected.

My supervisor then brought in Ed Palmer as a consultant to our team. Ed had worked for over thirty years as a senior researcher for *Sesame Street* and had influenced U.S. legislation around issues of children and television education. Ed was a tall, soft-spoken man with white hair and a goatee. In listening to him, it was clear he was brilliant. Ed often said, "The next leading edge for media is how to resolve conflicts peacefully."

What I did not realize at the time, and only found out later, was that Ed had terminal cancer. He spent the last two years of his life helping our team develop methodologies to measure the impact of our radio programs, and he made trips to both Liberia and Burundi. Ed also helped design a children's television program in Macedonia, a country bordering Kosovo. That TV series helped promote interethnic understanding among young kids and adults alike.

Ed was a Buddhist meditation practitioner and we talked occasionally about how media shaped attitudes, behaviors, and, ultimately, consciousness. Seeing Ed's commitment to this work touched and inspired me.

Back to Sierra Leone

Working with the Liberia program, I had access to a lot of information about the war in Sierra Leone. Much of it was simply heartbreaking and surreal, the stories of villages being raided, mutilation of women and children, and hundreds of thousands of refugees. I kept wondering how the place could fall apart so badly.

Our country director in Liberia, John, had been a Peace Corps Volunteer and then a staff person for the Carter Center in Liberia. John was keen on West African politics. During our weekly phone calls and my visits to Liberia, John would go into detail about the politial dimensions of the wars in Liberia and Sierra Leone. He once pointed out the absurdity of how the war in Sierra Leone was sparked by a dispute between Samuel Doe, the former Liberian president, and Gaddafi of Libya. Doe had insulted Gaddafi at a meeting of the Organization of African Unity. Gaddafi did not reply, but swore revenge.

Gaddafi set up camps to train combatants on how to overthrow governments in Africa. Charles Taylor, who later became president of Liberia, and Foday Sanko of Sierra Leone were trained by Gaddafi, along with other people from both countries. While some of the recruits had legitimate concerns about the corruption in Liberia and Sierra Leone and wanted to help, Charles Taylor and Foday Sanko took the fighting down a path of diabolical horror, training thousands of child soldiers.

Charles Taylor also was angry at the government of Sierra Leone for sending troops to participate in a West African peacekeeping mission to stop the civil war in Liberia. The diamonds in Sierra Leone were another reason for Taylor to support Foday Sanko and the Revolutionary United Front (RUF) in Sierra Leone. Taylor and Sanko used the diamonds, along with clear-cut timber in Liberia, to buy weapons from Ukraine and other countries. The dissolution of the Soviet Union had resulted in a flood of weapons and mercenaries from Ukraine and other former Soviet-bloc countries into West Africa and other parts of the world.

Like it or not, Sierra Leone had become a pawn in a complex international power struggle fueled by a global economy and rapidly changing technology.

In early 1998, a West African peacekeeping mission in Sierra Leone, led by Nigerian troops, had pushed back RUF rebels to the eastern part of the country. In April, my supervisor asked me to go back to Sierra Leone on an assessment mission to see if Search could develop a radio project there. I flashed back to Mickey's prediction years earlier, about how spirit was much more creative than me and that, if I let go, it might bring me back to Africa in ways I could never imagine. It was happening!

Part of me did not want to see the horror that had happened to the people and country I loved. I moved past the hesitation and agreed to go, largely because I wanted to know if the Contehs, A.K., and other friends were alive, and I wanted to help in any way possible.

The trip to Sierra Leone was intense, to say the least. Because of the conflict, there were no major airlines flying directly to Sierra Leone. I also could not get a visa to Sierra Leone in the United States, so I had to fly to Liberia first. From there, I flew to Conakry, Guinea on a local airline to catch a flight to Freetown.

My flight from Conakry to Lungi Airport in Sierra Leone was canceled. One of the other passengers was a man wearing an expensive, Italian-looking suit. He organized a chartered fight, and I jumped on it. The small, twin-engine propeller plane held maybe twenty people. As we flew above the coastline, I looked down wondering if we were near a rebel-held area. I also marveled at the well-dressed man, who pulled out a huge wad of crisp, U.S. hundred-dollar bills to pay for the flight. When I asked him about what brought him to Sierra Leone, he said, "Business." I inquired further and he said, "Natural Resources."

Being completely naïve to the world of international business and conflict zones, I asked more questions. "Is it hard to do business when there is a war?"

"No," he replied. "For diamonds, it is easy. Oil and other natural resources, it can be harder, but you manage how much infrastructure you invest in."

The plane landed and there I was, back at Lungi Airport, nine years after having left the country. The airport was much different, in that there were scores of military personnel with automatic weapons that had live bullets — the joke when I was a Peace Corps Volunteer was that the army did not have bullets. Outside the airport were armored vehicles with large guns, and, on the tarmac, sat various types of helicopters and other military hardware.

The signs of war were readily apparent in Freetown, too. Many buildings were burned down, including the Ministry of Finance. There were military roadblocks throughout the city, reinforced with sand bags and machine guns. There were bullet holes in the walls of most buildings, and the hotel where I stayed had lots of young girls working as prostitutes.

John, Search's country director for Liberia, was already in Sierra Leone for the assessment mission. He met me at the hotel, and we made arrangements to go up to Makeni. He said there was a security risk because a BBC reporter had been killed in a rebel ambush earlier in the week on the same road, but past Makeni.

We hired a driver with a small, beat-up Toyota car. We headed out early the next day, going through numerous checkpoints in and just outside of Freetown. My mind kept flashing back to being a Peace Corps Volunteer, traveling along the same roads with the tall elephant grass on the sides and the many small villages with mud-walled houses.

This time, however, some villages were destroyed and most houses were shot up. People looked much thinner than I remembered, and their clothes seemed more tattered, too. There also was a roughness to the police and military personnel at the checkpoints, much different from the playfulness I remembered from years earlier.

Driving on, we crossed a bridge over the Rokel River. I thought about how Masongbo was upstream and flashed back to the twelve-day canoe trip with the Contehs.

On the other side of the bridge were several burnt vehicles along the road. John tensed up and said, "This is a perfect place for an ambush."

It was all so unreal. I just sat there, relaxed, thinking about the Contehs and then the people who had been in the destroyed vehicles, wondering what it must have been like to have gunfire suddenly appear.

When we passed the wrecked vehicles, John said, "We are not going back to your Peace Corps village. Don't even think about it. It's not safe to go into the bush."

The closer we got to Makeni, the more I thought about the Contehs and wanted to see them. To come so close after nine years and not to see them would be a shame.

Once to Makeni, we drove through the same streets I frequented as a volunteer. I looked at the various shops, to see if any of the owners I remembered were still there. One friend's store was completely burned and gutted.

We headed to the Catholic mission, where we were welcomed by Italian Bishop George Biguzzi, a tall, thin, soft-spoken man in his 60s. He and a few other Italian priests were there, having stayed through much of the fighting. The bishop said the fighting had been difficult for some of the priests, as they showed signs of post-traumatic stress disorder. The rebels had allowed the priests to live, but not without harassment. The hardest part for the priests was to see some of the young children they had taught in school turned into killing machines. The priests could not understand how it could happen.

Bishop Biguzzi seemed above the trauma, possibly in part because he was in charge of the mission and he needed to hold it together. He was happy we were there and was intrigued by the idea of radio being used for peacebuilding. He talked about the Catholic Church's plans of putting up a small FM radio station and asked for John's advice. The bishop liked that we wanted to create a studio that would support local community radio stations across the country by producing programs on national issues that the local stations could broadcast to their listeners. The studio also would support community stations by training their staff on how to produce programs that promoted peace and reconciliation.

When the bishop learned I had been a Peace Corps Volunteer in Masongbo, he offered to take us there the next day for Catholic mass. I smiled and held my tongue, not wanting to appear overly eager to risk my colleague's life.

When John asked if it was safe, the bishop insisted everything would be fine. He said having an old Peace Corps friend come back would be good for the people of Masongbo.

Back to Masongbo

The next morning my dream was coming true — we were headed to Masongbo!

Our rickety Toyota sped along the paved road, following the bishop who was with another priest in a small pickup truck. We reached the town of Bincolo, where a small mountain in the shape of a camel's back jutted out of the nearby rice fields.

I flashed back to a night when I climbed the mountain with a friend under a full moon.

We turned right and headed down a gravel road for the seven miles to Masongbo. The elephant grass gave way to rice paddies, and we drove slowly through a village as the taxi driver navigated between the chickens. I waved to a mother feeding her baby by one of the huts. She waved back with an enthusiastic smile that helped to assuage my apprehension about what we might find in Masongbo.

We were getting close; the houses had gone from rectangular mud houses with tin roofs to round mud-walled huts with steep cone-shaped, grass-thatched roofs. These were Limba huts, the Conteh's tribe!

We continued along, only to slow for a small bridge that linked two rice fields. As we climbed a small hill to enter Masongbo, I had my hand on the door handle. As soon as the car stopped, I jumped out. We were there! I could hear drumming coming from the other end of the village and saw a small Catholic church that had been built since I had left in 1989. I immediately headed toward the church, as if called by the drums, remembering the night I danced under a full moon with the entire village, celebrating Pa Conteh's funeral.

As I neared the front doors of the church, I stepped to the side and waited, allowing the bishop to enter first. As the bishop walked down the middle isle, a wave of excitement followed him, with people pointing and smiling. It was clearly a special treat for the bishop to be there. They did not notice John and me in the back.

After so many years away, my heart pounded. I began to sweat in the heat of the crowded church. Then I spotted Sanpha, clapping and singing. I came up behind him and tapped him on the shoulder. We looked at each other in amazement. His face turned into an ecstatic smile as he threw an arm around me. He pinched my arm to see if I was real. Then someone tapped me from behind. It was Moses!

And Bokarie! All the Conteh brothers were there! We sang and sang together, the same hymns we had sung when I lived there, the same ones I had sung in St. Mary's Church as a kid in Indiana, but now in an African dialect.

The mural on the wall showed a rebel boy shooting a nun, but our expressions were euphoric while the bishop gave a sermon on the importance of community during war. When the bishop asked me to say a few words, I walked to the front with immense emotions. I talked about how much I had learned from the people of Masongbo, how living with them had taught me the importance of community and of living simply, in harmony with nature. As I talked, I realized what I was saying was more for me and must have seemed strange, as it was all commonplace for them. I then told them how many people throughout the world were thinking about them, and that they were not forgotten, and that we all wanted to help end the war. This message seemed to register, as people clapped.

A wall mural in Masongbo's Catholic Church

After the service, men, women, and children crowded around to greet us: "Mr. Bob, Mr. Bob, you done come back." Children in tattered clothes handed me mangos, coconuts, or whatever they could offer. The village chief, who had lost weight from lack of food, handed me kola nuts, the symbolic offering of respect: "He who gives kola, gives life."

The Contehs then took me to the water well, to proudly show that it was still in use a decade after we had built it. They also showed us their oil-palm plantation, which they had doubled, from 250 to over 500 trees! I was thrilled to see that the work we had done together continued and had expanded!

The tone shifted, though, as the Conteh brothers showed us around, talking about the RUF rebels' occupation of the village. The rebels had beaten the elderly men in public, including the chief, took some of the children as combatants and "used" some of the women for sex, meaning they had been raped. The rebels also took whatever food they wanted and left little for anyone else to eat. Sanpha said the family nearly starved, surviving only by hiding in the bush for months on end. The Contehs were greatly relieved to have the RUF out of their village and were ready to get back to their lives as subsistence farmers, a life that was hard enough in itself.

Sanpha then pulled me to the side to show me something. With a big smile, he pulled out a stick painted red and white and that had shiny hooks hanging from it. Looking closer, I saw it was a fishing lure. "I made it last week," he said.

I was stunned. Looking into Sanpha's eyes, I listened as he said, "The RUF made me fish for them, but I always went to where there were no fish." My mind went to spots along the river where we knew not to fish.

"They got bored and quit," Sanpha continued. "When they were not looking, I went fishing on my own. With the fish I caught, I fed my family hiding in the bush."

Sanpha then held the lure out toward me, "Na for you," he said. Tears formed in my eyes as I smiled and gladly accepted the gift. We just looked at each other for several seconds, smiling. All of those evenings fishing, long hours of carving sticks and many nights eating together. There were we were, connected by fishing, a friendship, and a love that spanned a decade, an ocean, and a war.

Jennifer Wood

Children in Masongbo Village during a return visit.

The Contehs pulled out a container of palm wine and we sat together drinking. Even though I had given up drinking alcohol, I gladly accepted the warm, sweet, bubbly beverage. "From God to man," I said.

"Yeah Bobby," Sanpha said, "from God to man."

We all smiled and took turns drinking from the same plastic cup, enjoying the gift from nature and God.

The one person missing in the celebration was Adama Conteh. Moses said she had gone across the river and the brothers shook their heads, saying she would be so mad that she had missed me. I told them not to worry, that I would be coming back soon and frequently. Little did we know what was going to transpire over the next two years, and that Adama and I would never see each other again.

John reminded me we needed to get back to Makeni and then Freetown. I asked to speak with the Conteh brothers alone. We went into the house where I had lived, the one offered by Pa Conteh. I pulled out three U.S. $100 bills, one for each of them. I told them the money was from my family in America and that we hoped that it would help. I encouraged them to use the money slowly, and that I should be back in a few weeks in Freetown and told them how to find me. They said they could exchange the money in Makeni for leones, the local currency, when needed.

Moses said they had a live chicken for us and asked if we could take it. I thanked him and said we would be traveling and would not be able too. A live chicken was a considerable gift on their part. Their generosity — fruit, wine, and chicken — was still intact, even after surviving a terrible war.

Saying goodbye to the Contehs was a joyous experience, as I was relieved they were alive. I told them I would be back soon, at which point we all replied, "by God in power," meaning it was all in God's hands.

BBQ Smoke

Back in Makeni, John and I ate lunch with the bishop and a few priests. We were interrupted when a Sierra Leonean policeman came to the door. I could hear one of the Italian priests saying in Krio, "I only get one pair glove, I no believe am."

The priest was very animated when he came back to the table.

"I am sorry, I must go. I am the only one who will bury them and I only get one pair glove left," he said.

Seeing our confusion, the bishop said, "Necklacing. There have been many retribution killings against the RUF and junta members by mobs." The junta was the military that ousted President Kabbah and invited the RUF to join them. "If someone yells rebel, a mob will form and kill the person, even if he is not a rebel."

"And I am the only one who will bury them," said the priest as he walked toward the door. "And this na me my last pair glove."

John and I looked at each other and then he said, "Well, thank South Africa for teaching Sierra Leone how to do necklacing." John's demented sense of humor was ever-present, a result of years of being exposed to the impact of deadly violence.

The bishop asked if we wanted any more pasta. I declined, trying to understand what had just transpired and imagining the horror of a necklacing. The idea of placing a tire over someone's head and lighting it on fire just did not mix with eating more pasta. It was strange how lunch and necklacing had become a part of the priests' daily lives.

John thanked the bishop and said we should head back to Freetown while there was plenty of light.

We said goodbye and I thanked the bishop for taking us to Masongbo. He smiled and said, "I am glad. These friendships are important, especially right now."

Back in the taxi, we drove out the gate of the Catholic mission compound and past Pa Kargbo's, a bar I had frequented as a Volunteer. Another fifty yards and we were at an intersection where there was a large crowd. The taxi driver stopped and said, "Necklacing, na new one."

I looked past the crowd and could see a fire and black smoke.

"What do we do?" I asked John.

"I don't know," he said.

"Well, we are on an assessment mission, should I get pictures?" I asked, in a calm state of disbelief and not knowing what to do.

"I don't know," John replied.

Operating on autopilot, I jumped out of the car feeling completely safe, as if I were back in the Peace Corps, having just come from the bar. People started yelling for me to get closer, and I did as they said. Moving through the crowd, I came to an opening where I could see a wooden chair tipped over with a flaming tire under it. Tied to the chair was a body of a young man and his head was gone. A trail of blood went

A retribution killing of a rebel on the streets of Makeni, April 1998

from the neck into the crowd. Along the stream of blood was what appeared to be an organ, possibly the heart.

There were several hundred people standing, watching, most of them children. They were yelling for me to get closer and to take photos. I figured they wanted the world to know what was happening. I moved into the middle of the circle and toward the body. I was relaxed, probably in shock, as I took several photos.

Walking back toward the car, I did not realize that I had walked through the smoke. When I got into the car, John started yelling to the driver, "Go, get out of here now!"

John was nervous, and then started laughing hysterically, "Wait until I tell Sheldon (our supervisor) that you, the vegetarian, walked through the BBQ smoke."

I sat there, not sure what had just happened. On the drive back to Freetown, I recounted a barrage of images — driving into Masongbo, singing with Sanpha, Moses, and Bokarie in the church, the village chief handing me kola nuts, the decapitated body burning, hundreds of people watching ... images from the Peace Corps, dancing under a full moon ... all spinning through my mind. I eventually closed my eyes and tried to meditate, only to observe the thoughts in a motion picture–like fashion. I was in shock.

New York Times

A few weeks after the trip, I was back in Washington, DC working on the assessment report when news came from Sierra Leone that the RUF rebels were once again on the offensive.

Rex Features

Mariatu Kamara, at left, with her baby who died not long after, and her sister Adamsay. Both young women's arms were brutally cut off by the RUF. [5]

I walked into the office early one morning and on my computer keyboard was a *New York Times* left by a co-worker. On the front page was a photo of a Sierra Leonean woman with both arms cut off. I began to read in horror as the story told how the RUF had overrun

Makeni. My eyes hungrily read for information as fast as I could. Sure enough, Bishop Biguzzi had been captured and the Catholic Church was negotiating his release.

The woman in the photo was from near Makeni. The rebels were using a terror tactic of cutting off limbs, a scheme it had developed during the 1996 national elections. The then-candidate Kabbah had said, "The future is in your hands," so the RUF cut off hands so people could not vote.

My body began to shake. I looked at a photograph sitting next to my computer; it was a picture of the Conteh brothers and me under a full grown palm tree, one they had planted while I was living with them as a Volunteer. The photo was taken only weeks earlier during the assessment mission.

I looked back at the *New York Times* and the image of the woman without arms and then threw the paper against the wall. This was not another damn news story about Africa; this was about real people and my friends.

I wanted to scream but held it in and walked out of the room and into the fire exit. Alone, in a stairwell, I pounded my hand against the cement wall and began to sob.

Spirit of the Spring

Many are the names of God and infinite the forms through which He may be approached.
— Sri Ramakrishna

A friend told me, "Someone once asked Gandhi how many religions there were. Gandhi replied, 'in reality, there are as many religions as there are individuals.'"

This concept stayed with me.

After the assessment trip, I struggled with memories of seeing the deadly violence in Makeni and the fact that a wave of horrible atrocities was sweeping through Sierra Leone again. It was tormenting to think of the Contehs, A.K., and others having to face such horror.

I tried desperately to deal with the inner turmoil through meditation. Going inward to the place of the witness could bring temporary glimpses of peace, but for the most part, there was a torrent of disturbance from what was happening in Sierra Leone and what I had seen. I could not understand why such suffering existed in the world. I was looking for something beyond the witness, I was looking for God, both for comfort and to understand how in the hell He or She or It could allow such wars to happen.

The Kriya Yoga tradition challenged my concept of God and offered a new one to explore. While God was beyond and part of all creation, He/She/It could be worshipped in many different forms, both personal and impersonal, depending on culture and individual orientation. Impersonal aspects could be states of being such as emptiness, peace, bliss, light, or ecstasy. For many people in India, the personal aspect of God as the Divine Mother was especially appealing because of Her unconditional love. It was believed She, the Divine Mother, must respond to Her children if appealed to with strong determination and devotion. She was the one that comforted people. This was a new idea, as I had grown up thinking God was the old white man in the sky, keeping count of everybody's good and bad actions.

Sure, there was Mother Mary, whose statues adorned the St. Mary's Catholic Church I attended in Greensburg. I found Mother Mary to be a calming figure, but never thought of Her as an aspect of God.

Given all the inner unrest, I started to dive deeper into meditation and to experiment with praying to Divine Mother.

I clung to Kriya Yoga methods like a life raft. They were systematic in using breath and mantras to relax the body, focus and calm the mind, and bring energy and consciousness inward. From there, I would imagine energy being brought up the spine and focused at the spiritual eye, a point between the eyebrows, which was known as a doorway into subtle realms of consciousness.

The spiritual eye, with its yellow outer ring, was an old friend from my childhood, as I would go to sleep looking into it. I was learning in yoga that the golden ring corresponded with a frequency of vibration of energy and consciousness — that of Divine Mother, or the Holy Ghost, or great comforter, *Om*. This was the energy that created everything in the universe. Inside the golden ring was a field of blue, or Christ Consciousness — the intelligence that existed in and guided the energy manifesting creation. It was the consciousness that Christ, Krishna, and other holy people embodied. In the field of blue was a white star or Cosmic Consciousness or God the father that existed beyond creation.

Another way to think of it was that God, or Cosmic Consciousness, was beyond creation. The sound of Om, or Divine Mother, or Holy Ghost was the active vibratory force that created everything. Inside of the Mother was the son, or Christ Consciousness, which comes from the father, Cosmic Consciousness.

Sure, on an intellectual level, this all made sense, and I knew the golden ring was real through direct experience. Still, I was far from embodying and realizing any of it. I just wanted out of the distressing reactions and to understand "why?" So, I started to experiment with yogic techniques.

After sitting in silence for a long period I would start to pray deeply, with as much love and devotion as I could. The spiritual eye served as a sort of broadcasting mechanism, sending thoughts and prayers out, whether to a person, a saint, or an aspect of God. The heart was the receiving station, a place to feel a response.

I added a technique that intuitively felt right — while looking at the spiritual eye, I visualized the space around me and then on outward, to span all of the Washington, DC area, then United States, the western hemisphere, Africa and the eastern hemisphere, the Earth, solar system, Milky Way galaxy with billions of stars, etc.... until I could imagine billions of galaxies spinning. The idea was that imagination would help consciousness to expand and eventually embrace all of creation. Another effect was that the ego was completely humbled by the overwhelming awareness of the vastness of the universe.

At that point of expansion, while I imagined billions of galaxies, I prayed deeply, with all my attention focused on the spiritual eye, "Divine Mother, reveal yourself, reveal yourself!" I was pleading for Her to come, pouring extra energy up from my heart.

A few weeks after starting to pray to Divine Mother, I went on a trip to a friend's farm in Ohio. Given my monk-like habits, I got to stay in a small wooden hut next to a spring house and stream that fed a pond. The sound of the water was soothing, and I found myself at sunset, sitting next to the spring in silence. A friend from North Africa who was visiting the farm cautioned me, as he said spirits liked to hang out around water. His warning reminded me of the stories from Sierra Leone, yet I felt drawn to the water.

There was a peacefulness being so close to the water and to the woods. The hut had very

Whispers in the trees:
  Come play, come play with me
  Here I am, can you see me?
  Can you sense me? Can you feel me?
  Close your eyes
  I am here: in the silence, I am here

Be still
  I am with you
Be still
  I am your longing

Touch me, touch me with your breath
  Take me in, hold me deep in your lungs
Exhale me, slowly through your lips
  I will stay near

Drink in my waters
  Bathe in my delight
  Let me wash away your fears
Sit in my embrace
  Wade in my love
  I am the Spring of your youth

Open your heart
  And let me flow
Open your heart
  And I will carry you home

Shhh. Listen:
The frogs call your name
Wake up from your dream
I lie between worlds
Hiding behind a veil, I am waiting for you
Touch me if you can
Morning is for lovers, so roll over,
Be with me now.
Think me, I am near.
Think me, I am yours.

thin walls with large open slits between the pieces of wood, reminding me of the houses in Sierra Leone and how nature was a part of the homes.

The first night I meditated deeply and then prayed again for Divine Mother to reveal Herself. Afterward, I went to sleep and had a series of dreams of beautiful women dancing over the water. I felt almost drunk when I woke up. That entire day, I stayed near the water, listening. The second night, the same thing: more dreams and a feeling of deep peace.

On the drive home, I began to write poetry for the first time ever. The poems just flowed out, quite easily.

I continued the prayers, and a couple weeks later I went with two friends on a camping trip in the Shenandoah Valley near Front Royal, Virginia. We took a hike up a mountain trail, and I intuitively felt a need to be alone. One friend had been at the farm in Ohio and knew my inclination for solitude in nature. She went along ahead with her friend, talking about the real estate market in Northern Virginia.

Walking slowly, I started to bring all of my attention to the present moment, to my feet touching the Earth, to the feel of a slight breeze against my skin, to the sunlight shimmering through the leaves. Something was happening, as I felt energized and aware of a presence, almost like a life force in the forest. I began to giggle, imagining a two-way communication with a tree.

I was tuning in with something, some door had opened, a veil pulled back and I was allowed to walk through. Each step was slow and intentional, taking in the panorama of vibrations. And then, I became aware of the presence getting stronger, as if moving toward me, yet arising from inside at the same time.

I started to stumble, feeling like I was going to fall. I was becoming more and more light-headed, as if intoxicated. I paused and embraced a tree, and could feel the life force flowing down into the roots and up the trunk and out the limbs and into the leaves. I could feel the sun feeding the tree.

I was drunk on some invisible elixir that was springing from within and was permeating everything around me.

My friends came back down the trail, talking away. They looked at me, laughed, and said, "We'll meet you in the parking lot."

I slowly stumbled behind them, finding it more difficult to walk. I felt the presence getting stronger inside, so I hurried down the trail to the car.

We drove through the mountains to a campground in the national forest. The site we picked was in the woods, away from other people and close to a flowing spring. After getting the tents set up and a fire started, my friends offered to cook and agreed that I could take a walk.

Feeling a need to go somewhere but not sure where, I just headed into the woods. I thought about where to go and ended up in a thick briar patch. Stopping, I listened, heard water babbling, and moved in that direction. I came to a spring-fed stream and a small waterfall. I carefully stepped on stones to cross the water and then sat on a boulder along the bank.

There was the presence again, getting stronger. I was not sure what to do, whether to get up and walk away, or to stay.

Holding my legs close to my chest, I placed my head on my knees and looked to the left. Right there, a few feet away hanging on a tree limb was a rosary with brown and yellow beads and a white crucifix. Shocked to see the holy image of the cross, energy rushed through me. I surrendered and opened.

Energy exploded from inside and washed through me, flooding me with an overwhelming feeling of love. I began to moan as the energy went in wave after wave, pulsating through every cell. My mind tried to understand what was happening, and then all thoughts were rinsed away. I just opened, received, and experienced an indescribable flood of love.

Moans spontaneously poured forth, as my body pulsated in what felt like orgasms, one after the other, in a symphony of ecstasy. I grasped my legs tighter and squeezed. The love came from deep inside. On and on, the waves of energy came up the spine, blowing the heart open, clearing the mind, bursting through me. Several times I gasped for air, barely able to contain the ecstasy. I held back screams, muffling the sounds in my arms.

There was a period of timelessness, as the experience went on and on. At one point, my moans turned into passionate words of deep longing, as I found myself saying, "I've missed you, I've missed you."

As tears began to flow, I heard a voice in my head say, "Silly you, I am always with you."

As I felt the presence start to fade, to go back behind a veil, I mentally said, "No, stay, please."

I was engulfed by another wave of love and dissolved in the embrace yet again.

Exhausted, spent and energized, all at the same time, I eventually opened my eyes to see it was night. The sound of the babbling water came back into my awareness. There was a fire glowing only forty or fifty yards away. I thought, "Oh no, did they hear me?"

Blown wide open, feeling like a newborn babe, I slowly moved toward the fire. I sat near my friends, who were talking away. They asked if I was hungry and I replied, "Yes."

As I ate, I finally asked, "Did you hear anything?"

"Yes! We sure did," one friend said. "We did not know if you were okay, so we went to look and sat across from you for a few minutes until we realized you were more than okay. Whatever you had, can we have some?" she asked. They both laughed, changed the subject, and never said another word about the experience.

That night I slept feeling the Earth, the trees, the rocks, the sky, everything pulsating through me as I listened to the water babbling nearby.

Dancing Between Worlds

I cannot dance, lord, unless you lead me.
— Mechtild of Magdeburg

Needless to say, the experience with what I called the "Spirit of the Spring" confused the living daylights out of me. Being raised Catholic, there was no way I could have a spiritual experience that felt like lovemaking with God. Only later would I learn about mystics and their love affairs with the Beloved, such as the Christian mystic Mechtild of Magdeburg, Hindu mystic Mirabai, and, of course, the great Sufi mystic Jelaluddin Rumi. They all were lovers of God and wrote beautiful poetry about this all-consuming love.

My own small initiation with the Spirit of the Spring was so much more than meditating and witnessing thoughts and emotions rise and pass away. It was like the witness and the spiritual eye were a doorway and after knocking there was a response from the other side, from inside, that flooded my being ... a response that was both personal and loving. What was It or Her? How could She or It be coming from within? Was I going crazy?

At first, the experiences came frequently, whenever I would get alone, meditate, and imagine Her. I would feel the presence awaken within and be flooded with love. Saturday mornings and nights of a full moon were especially wonderful times to be with Her. I often prepared my bedroom, which was also my meditation room, for these special occasions with candles.

Cry Freetown

As I explored this new and familiar "relationship," I found the love to be a comforting and stark contrast to the news that was coming from Sierra Leone.

In January 1999, the RUF rebels made an assault on Freetown and over 3,000 people were killed. The RUF nearly took over the capital but for the heroic stand of the West African peacekeeping mission. There also had been a shipload of Ukrainian mercenaries, hired by President Charles Taylor of Liberia, that were bombed by a Nigerian jet off the coast of Sierra Leone. The mercenaries were preparing a rear attack on the peacekeeping mission, which could have been disastrous for Sierra Leone.

The assault on Freetown was recorded by a young filmmaker named Sorious Samura. CNN International played the documentary film, announcing ahead of time they had debated whether to show it. CNN said the level of violence was shocking and yet the world needed to know what was happening in Sierra Leone.

I watched *Cry Freetown* and was horrified. There were scenes of child soldiers, some younger than ten years old, as part of the RUF troops. The violence and killing was atrocious, as the streets of Freetown, places I knew all too well, were littered with bodies. The film included an interview of a Catholic priest who was trying to rehabilitate some of the children accused of being child soldiers. I was moved and impressed by the priest's resilience and relentless service in the face of ghastly events.

Cry Freetown did get the world's attention, and the United Nations sent a peace-keeping mission to reinforce and take over from the West African troops. The first wave of UN peacekeepers met with RUF resistance and over three hundred troops were captured by the RUF.

The British government responded by sending paratroopers. It was odd — during my Peace Corps service, many Sierra Leoneans had expressed a desire to have the British come back. It was happening, but not in the way people had hoped. The British troops provided a much needed hammer and punch to the UN troops and dealt decisive blows to the RUF, forcing them to participate more willingly in peace negotiations.

In the spring of 2000, Search for Common Ground received funding to start a program in Sierra Leone and a week later several colleagues left the organization for a new dot.com. Their departure led to my taking responsibility for overseeing the project in Liberia and hiring staff to head our program in Sierra Leone.

As I started traveling to Sierra Leone and Liberia to help set up the new radio project, I drew extensively upon my meditation practice to deal with the harsh realities of deadly conflict. Each trip began on a Sunday morning near Washington, DC, when I would go to the meditation center where forty to sixty people would gather for a group meditation and reading service. The center had a profoundly peaceful atmosphere and it was easy to go deep into meditation.

After the service, I would go home to Arlington, Virginia and finish packing, then take a taxi to Dulles Airport for a twenty-four-hour trip to Freetown or Monrovia. The contrast between a modern U.S. city, let alone a meditation hall, and war-torn African cities was remarkable and jolting.

The daily meditation practice became a traveling refuge, and I was so relieved when She, the Spirit of the Spring, was present on a few occasions, including the intoxicating time during meditation when I barely missed getting caught in the middle of a coup d'état in Freetown.

Internally Displaced

In the first few trips to Freetown after the failed coup d'état, I was quick to network with people to find out about my friends in Kagbere and Masongbo. I found A.K., his family, the chief, and many people from Kagbere living with their relatives and other people in Freetown. They were fortunate that they knew people who could take them in. This system of friends and family taking in others could not absorb all the people who ran from the violence, as hundreds of thousands of Sierra Leoneans lived in displacement camps set up by the United Nations around the country or refugee camps in neighboring Guinea and Liberia.

When I saw A.K., we just looked into each others' eyes and smiled. He kept saying, "*Kusheh* Mr. Bob, *Kusheh*." ("Hello Mr. Bob, hello"). A.K. asked if my family was okay, something that was so culturally appropriate and yet so strange when he had just survived a war! I wanted to know about him and his family.

A.K. looked thin and worn, yet his smile was huge. He told me about rebel attacks on Kagbere and how he and his family hid in the bush for weeks on end. I thought about Tendy, her gentle and shy nature, how she had cooked for me with great love and care. I thought about Josephine, carrying buckets of water on her head in exchange for school fees.

A.K. told me the house I had lived in was destroyed by an "RPG." When I looked perplexed, A.K. said, "A rocket-propelled grenade." I just could not understand how or why an elementary school headmaster would know anything about RPGs. I became furious and confused.

A.K. continued, telling me his house had been destroyed too, and that his uncle was killed. Then he said, "I tell God tanki they no capture and rape Tendy and di girls and make em sex slaves."

"What the hell," I thought? "Thank God that his wife and daughters were not captured, raped, and turned into sex slaves?"

There was a disconnect between hearing A.K's words and looking into his eyes and seeing his smile. There was a tremendous love between us, a sense of relief to have found each other. That love seemed to create an opening, and his words of atrocities found ample room to slide inside and then explode in my heart and consciousness.

A.K. then asked a favor, which was unusual for him. He said Josephine was a young woman, had finished secondary school, and was looking for work. I said I would pass along her information to our country director, Frances Fortune, who also happened to be a mother of two children herself. While I did not feel okay trying to influence the hiring of staff, I was relieved when Josephine was offered an internship where she could develop her office skills. Frances was adamant that the future of Sierra Leone and many African countries relied on women taking on greater roles and responsibilities, and positions of leadership. She made sure at least half of the staff members were women. Josephine and other young women were offered internships and mentored by Frances. Josephine also would later take classes and advance to a paid position in the finance department.

As for the Contehs, I sent a note to Masongbo via a public vehicle that was able to pass through RUF lines. With the tenuous peace process, there was some movement allowed. I was relieved when Bokarie appeared at the office days later. He and all of the Contehs had survived, with the exception of Adama, who had died while trying to give birth. I listened in dismay as Bokarie described how the rebels treated them again.

Bokarie Conteh

RUF combatants that occupied Masongbo under the command of teenage Colonel Rambo

I sent an inexpensive camera with Bokarie to get photos of the family. I was surprised when he came back with photos of the RUF combatants that were still holding Masongbo. All of them were child soldiers under the command of a teenage boy named Colonel Rambo. In one photo the child soldiers were posing like film characters.

A Jewish Yogi

My image of the U.S. changed yet again because of West Africa. While I was still uncomfortable with the vast waste and lack of awareness of the impact of our lifestyles on the environment and other countries, I also was grateful. To be able to live in a country without the fear of homes being raided and destroyed at night, without worrying about children being turned into soldiers, and with access to safe drinking water — all of this was not to be taken for granted.

I also found myself looking at police and military personnel with a new sense of respect and appreciation. Their age-old roles were ones that valued and protected families, communities, and countries. Seeing what happens to an entire country when police and military are corrupted or not available, and when the negative potential of humanity was allowed to run wild, was downright horrifying. While I believed in the positive spiritual potential of humanity, the fact was humanity's harmful side needed to be kept in check. The challenge always would be how to use police or military force wisely. Of course, the ideal situation would be to address the root causes of societal degradation — whether corruption, greed, poverty, political manipulation, or lack of education— long before they manifested into violence.

Being exposed to the atrocities in West Africa was wreaking havoc in me. Kriya Yoga meditation was helping, and at the same time the practices seemed to make me more wide open, allowing the stories of pain and suffering to enter more deeply. Even with Her occasional soothing love, I was not coping well with the dramatic contrast between the glimpses of divine love and the impact of deadly conflict.

One thing that drove me crazy was that I could leave Sierra Leone and Liberia and come back to the United States. Meanwhile, my friends had to stay and try to rebuild their lives in an uncertain world. "Why, why was I born in the U.S. and they were born in a country going through hell? Why?" I often asked myself.

Besides meditation, I tried to deal with the tormenting questions by connecting with my family more regularly. If my African family was going through hell, I could at least appreciate a sense of security through a strong connection with my family. I called my parents and a few siblings several times a week. I also threw myself more intensely into gardening, a hobby that I shared with my father and several siblings. Growing food was something that bridged my family in America and my friends in Sierra Leone. Gardening was a way to consciously follow the rhythms of nature and to connect with the Earth, something I enjoyed while living in Masongbo and Kagbere. Also, I found that I valued food much more when I grew it myself and was less likely to waste any. I often wondered if everyone grew some of their own food if there would be a greater sense of peace in the world.

I also created an intention of finding a healer rooted in the same Kriya Yoga tradition to help me deal with these inner quandaries. Shortly after setting this intention, a friend took me to meet Dr. Rick Levy during a free clinic at his office in suburban Maryland.

Arriving at the center, I signed the list for a free consultation and waited in line. When the time came for my session, I was escorted into a room by Rick and his partner, Lisa. Rick was a short, balding, and unassuming-looking man, Jewish by upbringing. Lisa was a tall blond woman with striking features. While greeting me, Rick looked above my head. Lisa did the same thing. They were looking at something; I was not exactly sure what.

After the brief introductions Rick explained that he was a psychologist and that his father had been a researcher at the National Institutes of Health. With his science background, Rick started practicing Kriya Yoga over thirty years earlier and had maintained a daily meditation practice of three or more hours a day, including frequent all-night meditations. He said he blended the science and yoga, allowing him to develop intuitive abilities, including the ability to see and interpret energies.

Lisa had also worked for the National Institutes of Health overseeing a billion-dollar health program, but had left that job to become a Methodist minister. She left the ministry just before the September 11 tragedies to join Rick's practice, as they saw a rising need in the world for applied spirituality and scientific healing.

Rick asked that I stand in front of a wall so he could see my energy field better. Again, he was looking above my head. He started talking about different colors and what they meant — green for healing, grey for negativity, orange for humility.

"So, tell me about this love of yours?" Rick asked.

His question surprised me. As I started to think about my experiences with the Spirit of the Spring, the love was right there, present.

"Ah, I see, you're a devotee of Master and Mother, very good," Rick said.

"It seems to be coming from inside; I don't understand," I said.

"You see, everything exists in a quantum field of energy and consciousness. The yogis knew about this field and could navigate it. When you start to meditate and are able to focus your energies, you can get a response from the quantum field. Being you, too, are made of that field, it can feel like the response is arising from inside of you," Rick explained.

"God responds to whatever form is dearest to the devotee," he said. "If you pray to Mother, it will be Mother, if you pray to Christ, it will be Christ. Some of the great saints, like Saint Francis, could bring such focus, love, and devotion to his prayers and meditations that he could actually get Christ to physically appear. It takes tremendous power and concentration to reach that place. Yogananda, Sri Rama Krishna, and other yogis were very big into Divine Mother, and they could concentrate enough so She would take physical form."

The idea of Divine Mother or Christ taking physical form as a result of a person's love and devotion sounded wonderfully comforting. I absolutely loved the idea of the Spirit of the Spring taking physical form!

"You know: 'Love the Lord your God with all your heart and with all your soul and with all your strength and with all your mind.' That is simply a reference to the laws of consciousness and energy. It's all about working with consciousness and energy," Rick said. "God being a jealous God simply means if your energy goes elsewhere, you cannot tune in as well. It is all scientific; it's just that the science has not caught up with what the yogis and saints of all religions have known for ages. Scientists are getting there, slowly, with quantum physics. Theory is one thing; being able to apply it is another."

Rick was silent, concentrating for a moment.

"There is also a deep sadness in you that is painful to be in front of. It has pretty old roots. You may want to come in and we can work on it sometime," Rick said.

"Well, I have been traveling a lot to Liberia and Sierra Leone. I used to live in Sierra Leone," I replied.

"Yes, that place is going through a really horrible time. I'm sorry to see it. It must be tough knowing people there. Still, the sadness in you is even older," Rick replied.

Levels of Awareness or Consciousness

I began to see Rick as a client on a regular basis. His ability to read energies, and his openness in talking about going in and out of different states of consciousness, was both surprising and helpful.

Rick could see the shifts in my consciousness with ease. Standing in front of him was like being completely naked — he could see the colors of my aura field, feel the energies in my body, and interpret their meaning. Basically, he could see the nuances of my inner self. There was no hiding anything. He saw the fear of loss of love that came from my family, the loss of my uncles, heartbreaks from relationships, the pain over the war in Sierra Leone, and even older events I was unaware of. He also saw a deep desire for God, hidden behind my confusion about the dualities of the world.

I took seeing Rick as an opportunity to face whatever was obstructing my spiritual path and to work through my quandaries about war and God. Over time, Rick became a trusted friend and mentor.

Rick encouraged me to keep loving God in the form of the Divine Mother and to remember that was only one form. He also told me not to get overly attached to any experiences happening in meditation. This was a key part of the Kriya Yoga teachings: not to look for experiences. If they happened, fine, just experience them, but do not go looking for them. Meditation, with or without experiences, would transform the consciousness over time, and the goal was merging with Cosmic Consciousness, not entertainment.

Rick also introduced me to psychological, mind-body awareness techniques that complimented the massage school training and Kriya Yoga practice. In one of the first sessions, Rick went over the basics of levels of awareness, or different states of consciousness.

"Your conscious mind consists of your thoughts, attitudes, and feelings — the parts of yourself that you are aware of," Rick explained. "Your conscious mind expresses itself as thought or reason. You are aware of your conscious mind, as it is with you while you are awake.

"The subconscious is the part of the mind that is hidden. It is full of memories, feelings, desires, motives, knowledge, and other parts of you that you may not be fully aware of. The subconscious mind is very big and powerful. Sigmund Freud said the mind is like an iceberg, with the conscious mind as the tip above the water and the subconscious as the big part under water."

"Yogananda talks a lot about the conscious and subconscious minds," I said.

"Yes," Rick replied. "The yogis and other masters have been aware of the subtle workings of the mind for thousands of years. Western psychologists and other scientists are just now learning about these workings.

"The subconscious mind guides your bodily functions," Rick continued, "such as your heartbeat, circulation, immune functioning, and so forth. It also has a collection of your life experiences and the thoughts and feelings associated with important events in your life."

As Rick described the subconscious mind, I thought about the Conteh brothers, A.K. and his family, and all the people across Sierra Leone. Their subconscious minds must be filled with incredibly horrible images and memories. I also thought about seeing the young man necklaced in Makeni and how that must be stored in my own subconscious mind and those of the people who were watching.

"The subconscious mind has even more to it. Carl Jung created the phrase *the collective unconscious* to describe the part of subconscious mind that includes underlying memories from man's ancestral past — the history of our evolution. We can tap into this universal part of the human mind. Included in the collective unconscious are *archetypes*, or basic human personality patterns such as warrior, caregiver, seeker, sage, fool, king, and so on. Many people subconsciously live out these archetypal roles."

I wondered about the collective unconscious mind of Sierra Leone, what archetypal energies and roles were being played out yet again by humanity; how children were absurdly turned into warriors.

"The subconscious mind communicates through deep feelings, stories, myths, and metaphors. Getting in touch with your subconscious mind can help you discover and release old trauma, emotional pain, or distorted beliefs that might be keeping illness in your body. You also can access your archetypal understanding of who you are and what your role in life is.

"The third level of human awareness is the superconscious mind. It has infinite power and no limits. Once you access superconscious awareness and learn to direct it, you can heal yourself and others and accomplish just about anything you want in life. The superconscious mind exists at the individual superconscious mind and the universal conscious mind."

"Is the individual superconscious mind the soul?" I asked.

"Some would say so, yes," Rick replied.

"And the universal conscious mind is Christ or Krishna consciousness?" I asked, referring to yoga terms.

"Yes, exactly," Rick said. "Universal conscious mind is Christ Consciousness. Cosmic Consciousness is God beyond creation and beyond duality.

"The individual superconscious mind is a level of awareness capable of sensing and guiding electromagnetic energy. Using the individual supercounscious mind, we can direct our own electromagnetic energy fields and influence the energy fields around us. You also can use it to improve your health, environment, and future more than you can imagine. The individual superconscious mind is accessed through intuitive thought — a deep, immediate, and accurate sense of knowing something that we could not necessarily know through logic.

"A vast majority of people have had an intuitive experience," Rick said.

"Is this what you are using to read people and to project healing energies?" I asked.

"Exactly," Rick said.

Rick was reinforcing the idea that energy followed focus and that wherever we placed our attention influenced a person's consciousness. If I focused on sports, I had sports consciousness, and it had a certain vibration. If I focused on the horrors of war, I had destruction consciousness and its vibration was sticky and burning, like hot pinpricks.

While in meditation, I could focus on the experience of calmness and peace, then that was my consciousness. However, I was clearly having trouble carrying that inner peaceful consciousness while interacting in the world, especially in going back and forth to West Africa.

What was interesting was that Rick and monks in the yoga tradition pointed out that thoughts and consciousness were universal. That when a person had a certain type of consciousness, he or she tapped into that same frequency in the universe, whether collective unconscious or universal superconsciousness. It was like tuning in to a radio station. A person then expressed that particular frequency through his or her individual nuances.

Through free will, people chose where they placed their focus. However, free will was often usurped by environment, habits, old wounds, and an array of social and cultural influences. The subconscious minds of most people, mine included, were filled with tons of memories, and as Rick would say, karmic seeds from this life and many lifetimes. Most people were and are puppets of these old habits.

Releasing Old Trauma

The purpose of these early discussions about levels of awareness or consciousness was to prepare me to clean out some of the old trauma that was giving me so much trouble. As Rick would say, I needed to become aware of the story behind the story, or the deep-seated patterns that were influencing my way of perceiving and interacting with the world.

Rick worked through several media: talk therapy, energetic healing, guided meditations, and deep meditation together. While he considered meditation focused on superconsciousness to be the most efficient way of healing, he also saw there were times to use the other methods. In my case, he saw there was a lot of old pain to be cleaned out of my subconscious.

Through a process of a guided meditation focused on the conscious and then subconscious minds, Rick helped me go into the sadness and grief buried in my subconscious mind. During the first guided meditation, I was surprised how alert I was, ever aware of what was happening. Rick's lulling tone of voice guided me into a relaxed state of being. He also was projecting energy into me even though he was sitting across the room.

Once completely relaxed, Rick asked me to focus on the sadness. I began to see images of Sierra Leone, back to the necklacing and then images of women and young children with their arms cut off.

Rick guided me to stay in those scenes for a short while and then to come out and refocus. He then guided me deeper yet again.

In the next scene, I was standing in a field, next to a village, burning. It seemed like a Native American village; I was not sure. I was there, standing, grieving, as smoke rose from the village.

I could see people dead, many people. They felt like family, like community. I could sense a sadness tearing through me, as I pounded the Earth. I was aware of everything, everyone that I loved, being gone. There was a vague memory from before this attack, of living with the community, close to the Earth.

Rick guided me through several scenes in the village, of bodies cut open, blood everywhere.

We stayed there, in this village, for some time, as I openly cried. I was aware that I had been spared because I had been away at the time of the attack. The overwhelming grief was mixed with a despair that I could not stop the killing, that I could not save my loved ones.

It seemed real, familiar, yet I also was aware of being in Rick's office. The tears kept flowing for several minutes.

When Rick guided me out of the experience, I opened my eyes and was relieved to be in the present. I felt exhausted and spent.

"Was that a real memory?" I asked.

"It does not matter if it was real or not. The subconscious mind is filled with many memories, from this life and many lives, along with images mixed together. This lifetime, the one you are in now, is the most important one, so do not get caught up in trying to figure out past life stories. Focus on the here and now.

"The main thing is to start releasing the big chunks from the subconscious. You can never clean it all out, nor do you want to try, as the world of duality will always keep adding things to it. That is one reason talk therapy can only get you so far; it is playing on superficial levels in a constantly changing world.

"We use the guided meditation into the subconscious just a little, the rest we will do with energetic healing and deep meditation focused on superconsciousness. Meditation actually rewires the brain, helping dissolve negativity through contact with superconscious states of being.

"The ultimate healing comes when you attune your consciousness with Christ or, even better, Cosmic Consciousness. That you will do through Kriya Yoga. We're just working to remove some of the tough barriers so you can go more deeply into meditation on your own and eventually anchor your consciousness in your soul and Cosmic Consciousness."

Mother, Child Soldiers, and Rambo

A Gift from the River

Even with the sessions with Rick Levy and meditation practice, I still found going back to West Africa to be a bizarre mix of experiences, from joyous reunions with friends, to being disturbed by violence, to fascination with peacebuilding. And then there were the rare occasions where I felt Her presence in surprising ways, including one time involving fishing.

On one trip to West Africa, I traveled with colleagues overland from Monrovia, Liberia to Bo, Sierra Leone, a town upcountry. We were having a regional meeting, and I knew there was a chance to go fishing, so I had brought fishing gear from the United States. The night before the meeting, I had a dream where a beautiful woman rose out of the river, and then I was flooded with an intoxicating love.

The next day I felt drunk the entire day, trying to stay focused on the meetings. I also was watching the time when I could get away to go fishing.

As the sun started to set, a colleague, a driver, and I headed out in a four-wheel drive vehicle for a nearby river. We were stopped at a United Nations checkpoint, and the vehicle was thoroughly searched. We traveled a little farther and then came to a river near the main road.

We went and asked the village elder for permission to fish, and then headed to the river. Several young men watched as I took water from the river and then poured a libation to the spirits, thanking them and asking for their blessing. I was ever-aware of the stories of "Mami Water" in Sierra Leone and how the same stories existed deep in the Amazon regions of Brazil. I figured they were all adaptations of the Divine Mother manifesting through those particular cultures.

My colleague, an inquisitive Jewish man from New York, did not pour a libation and he never got a single bite that night. As for me, I caught a five-pound Nile perch within a few minutes. The young men watching, many of whom I later learned were former combatants, were laughing, saying in Mende, their local language, "Look at this white man, he comes here and catches that fish when we fish here all the time and are lucky to get a few small ones."

A few minutes later I hooked a much larger fish. I was right back in fishing mode, as when I was with the Contehs. One of the young men got excited and tried to grab the fishing line to pull in the fish. I motioned for him to get back and let me battle the fish using the methods I had honed some twelve years earlier on the Rokel River.

The fish was big, and it took nearly twenty minutes to land. I was flabbergasted to see it was forty-four inches long and weighed over forty pounds, much bigger than any fish that I had caught during my entire four years in the Peace Corps. Between the dream the night before and catching that fish, I was ever-aware of some invisible hand having fun through me.

As for the people at the United Nations checkpoint, they too were astonished when they saw the back of the four-wheel drive vehicle completely filled with one huge fish. My colleagues at the regional meeting also were amazed. I gave the fish to one of our staff members so she could feed her family.

Back to Kagbere and Masongbo

Other trips to West Africa were a bit more challenging, especially the next time going back to Kagbere and Masongbo.

It was toward the end of a several-week trip in Liberia and Sierra Leone that there was an opportunity to go back to the villages. The situation in Sierra Leone had stabilized, and our staff members were able to travel throughout the country without harassment, largely because Talking Drum Studio, our radio programs, had an 89 percent listenership rate, determined by using methods

Hellmich and Josephine at the Search for Common Ground office, Freetown

developed by Ed Palmer (the person who dedicated the last two years of his life to figuring out how to measure the impact of media in conflict situations). People loved the programs, as they were produced by Sierra Leoneans in a variety of formats that were both entertaining and informative, all aimed at supporting the peace and rebuilding process.

With Josephine in the Freetown office, it was easy to get messages to Kagbere and Masongbo via a network of people traveling to and from Freetown. She sent word to both her father, A.K., and to the Contehs in Masongbo, that I was on my way.

The drive from Makeni to Kagbere was five miles on paved roads and then thirty-two miles on a dirt road fitting for a four-wheel drive vehicle. A driver, staff radio reporter, and I got a late start, so it was dark by the time we hit the dirt section. The road was clearly not traveled much in recent years, as the elephant grass on the sides was close to the road and well over ten feet tall. Early in the trip, we came across a human body in the road. I could feel everyone in the vehicle tense up. The driver swerved to the side, missing the body, and then sped up. My instincts were to stop and help. The driver looked at me and said, "There have been a lot of ambushes using bodies in the road as a trap."

From that point on, I was reminded that life was much different from when I lived there as a Peace Corps Volunteer. We were all relieved when we entered the village around midnight.

The village was fast asleep, but the sound of the four-wheel drive vehicle stirred people awake. Slowly, lanterns came out to see who was visiting, and then the sound let out: "Mr. Bob, e done come back." There was a joyous reunion for over an hour as familiar faces emerged from the darkness in a dreamlike fashion.

Over the next day, I visited with many friends, listening to their stories of how they survived the war. Everyone spoke about September 9, 1998, the day Kagbere was attacked by the RUF rebels. It was the day that changed their lives forever, just as September 11, 2001 changed the lives of Americans. Most villages across Sierra Leone had their own September 9 or September 11, and they spoke about those dates with the same eerie expression as people in America did about the Twin Towers and Pentagon being attacked.

It was a bizarre experience to see this picturesque village that was a second home, nestled on the edge of tropical hills, and to think of it being the scene of chaotic military attacks. In many ways, the village seemed the same as when I had been a Volunteer, with the rhythms of farming life underway and children going to elementary school. Yet, there were the reminders of the violence, such as destroyed houses and bullet holes in walls.

At one point during the visit, A.K. and I stood in front of the piles of mud and cement blocks that were once the houses where we had lived. I thought back to the many nights watching the moon with people walking up and down the village. I remembered those nights as tranquil and peaceful. It was hard to imagine rocket-propelled grenades being launched into those houses and the AK-47s being fired at my friends and the rest of the village as they ran into the bush to hide.

I thought back to A.K.'s words he had told me when we first met again in Freetown, "I am glad they did not capture and rape Tendy and the girls." It all seemed so absurd and surreal.

My experience in Masongbo a couple days later was very similar. There was another joyous reunion with the Conteh brothers and others in the village. Like A.K., the Contehs also were anxious to tell the stories of how the village had been sacked again and held hostage by a rebel group headed by a teenage boy named "Colonel Rambo."

Walking through Masongbo, I thought about the diabolical methods of creating child soldiers. Most children and youths were taken during raids on villages. Some children as young as eight years old would be placed on hard-core drugs, from crack cocaine to downers, for a few weeks. They would then be forced to commit atrocities, often against their own family or other community members. The children and youths were psychologically and emotionally shattered, and systematically cut off from their families and communities, and their own humanity. With no hope of returning home because of their actions, they turned to their abductors as new family and followed them into battle.

Martin Lueders

Some child soldiers were as young as eight years of age

The process of creating a child soldier was almost the exact opposite of a yoga practice, while both were working with consciousness. In yoga, a person weeds out negative behaviors and develops those that help him to focus his consciousness on his soul and/or aspects of God. The first step is *yama*, or rules that are prohibitive, such as avoiding injury to others, untruthfulness, stealing, incontinence, etc. Yama is similar to the Ten Commandments, and rules or guidelines from other spiritual traditions. The second step is *niyama*, or that which a person should do, such as purity of body and mind, contentment, self-discipline, self-study (contemplation), and devotion to God.

After yama and niyama, there are six more steps, all increasing in subtle sophistication and ability to control and direct prana. It was scientifically impossible for a person to reach the higher levels of consciousness without the foundation of yama and niyama. The cause-and-effect karmic seeds of negative behaviors would keep a person entangled in endless battles as their actions come back to roost in this life or another one.

Also, hallucinogenic drugs were strictly forbidden in yoga, and many spiritual traditions, including Umbanda, because they opened a person's consciousness to outside influences, including negative vibrations of consciousness and disembodied souls from the astral realms. The few spiritual traditions that do use hallucinogenic drugs do it under the strict guidance of a very advanced teacher, who then leads them into the other realms of consciousness.

Drugs were an essential part of turning a child into a killing machine. And given Sierra Leoneans had a rich spiritual tradition involving ancestors and spirits, both good and evil, they were all the more likely to become open to the negative spiritual influences. Some rebel units, especially those in Liberia, were known to appeal to evil spirits through human sacrifices and cannibalism. These practices were taking the technologies of shamanism and using them for horrific causes.

Violent movies like *Rambo* and those starring Chuck Norris became training materials to saturate the minds of children with role models, thus further filling their minds and consciousness with images and thoughts of destruction.

From a yogic perspective, this focus on destruction and use of drugs was tuning the consciousness of the children into the universal consciousness of the same frequency so the child soldiers would express the most destructive aspects of human potential. It was no wonder they were able to commit atrocities such as hacking off the limbs of women, children, and the elderly, and cutting open the bellies of pregnant women. The children were puppets of these destructive energies and consciousness. They were expressing the horrific universal human potential that had plagued humanity throughout time. Just as yoga was teaching me to tune in with my soul and aspects of God as the Divine Mother, child soldiers were systematically trained to tune in with demonic forces of death and destruction.

What perplexed me was the same age-old question: *given everything came from and was part of God, how could She/He/It allow such destructive energies and consciousness to exist, let alone possess children?*

On one level, it was intriguing to think about the sophisticated influences of human consciousness and the lessons that could be learned from yoga, shamanism, and other traditions, along with mind-body medicine and quantum physics. On the other hand, it was so demented and downright wrong to think of the systematic manipulation of children's consciousness to turn them into murderers. Seeing the impact on the lives of my friends in Kagbere and Masongbo grounded it all in a nightmarish reality.

While I was in Masongbo, Bokarie took me to Adama's grave. He talked about how much he missed her, and how he often put flowers on her grave. We recounted a few stories about the canoe trip we took together and how Adama loved smoking and selling fish. We laughed thinking about her ambitions of being a market woman, someone who sold goods.

I held back tears, thinking about Adama trying to give birth, only to die in the process. Even though that was not an uncommon experience in Sierra Leone, the fact that child soldiers denied her access to medical care angered me.

Jennifer Wood

On a later visit to Masongbo, Sanpha offers a thirty-pound fish and home-made fishing lures. The Contehs' love and generosity was overwhelming, especially when they had so little.

In both Kagbere and Masongbo, I slept in the mud huts of friends. A.K. and the Contehs were apologetic for the bedding. In Kagbere, A.K, and Tendy gave me their bed, which was a sheet and blanket thrown over thin straw mats covering sticks. In Masongbo, Moses, Sanpha, and Bokarie found the nicest straw mat in the village and put it on a dirt floor. Even though I slept little, I was simply happy to be with my friends and gratefully appreciated their hospitality.

I gladly ate with my friends the food that they prepared and accepted their generosity with an open heart. At the same time, I was aware of the level of poverty, much worse than anything I had ever seen before. My friends' faces were thin and hair tinted red from malnutrition. Their clothes were more torn than I remembered from my Peace Corps days. They were living on far less than a dollar a day.

Over dinner and throughout the day and night, A.K. and the Contehs frequently told stories about the rebel abuses, how they took whatever they pleased, including the women for their sexual pleasure, basically raping them. Hearing Bokarie say, "Colonel Rambo," the name of the teenage rebel commander, just grated on me. I thought about Sylvester Stallone and wondered what he and Chuck Norris would do if they knew they were role models for child soldiers? I was pissed at what I perceived to be Hollywood's mindless money-making machine, spewing out endless violent films with no clue of their impact in the far reaches of the world and on the minds of young people with little media literacy or the ability to distinguish fiction from reality.

Jane Shaw

Members of the Conteh Family and Hellmich during a later return visit.

The impact of Hollywood, Bollywood, and other film industries in creating a culture of violence had increased after the war. Thousands of video parlors popped up across Sierra Leone and much of sub-Saharan Africa. For a small fee, children and youths in towns and villages could watch movies on a TV/DVD setup in a tin shack. The most popular films were the most violent ones, thus reinforcing role models that were all too real and believable.

When telling the stories of the rebel abuses, A.K.'s eyes, the Contehs' eyes, would glaze over and become distant as if remembering a bad dream. The storytelling seemed to be a way of relieving a large burden, a small piece at a time. I reflected on what I had learned about mind-body awareness in massage school, and how Rick Levy was helping me release trauma from my own subconscious. It was mind- and heart-boggling to think about the scarring that occurred and how it was imprinted in the cells of my friends' bodies and deep in their subconscious minds. It was even more overwhelming to think of how healing would ever occur.

A.K., the Contehs, and others in Kagbere and Masongbo were delighted to be interviewed by our staff radio reporter. Interviews were a big part of the work we were doing, giving voice to people throughout the country so they could talk about the impact of the war and their efforts to rebuild their lives. This work was an attempt to facilitate healing on a societal level.

Bokarie, Moses, Sanpha, and I went back to the river to fish one evening. There was a lulling and soothing effect of being at the river with them, each of us rhythmically casting and retrieving lures. We were pleased to catch a fish, one that another Conteh sister then prepared for dinner. Still, the fishing was overshadowed by the realities of life in the village and the memories of the war. I kept imagining what it must have been like to go to the river, not knowing if there would be a band of armed rebels.

While we were smiling much of the time and simply happy to see one another, life was different, much different, than when I had lived there. The social fabric of the villages had been torn apart and it was trying to heal. There was an air of uncertainty and a grinding angst that must have been perpetuated by the poverty.

Bokarie, Moses, and Sanpha on the Rokel River during a later visit

The combination of poverty and trauma was downright disturbing. A deep sense of grief and despair started to stir inside, a sense of loss for a way of life, one that I may have romanticized yet it felt gone. I felt a strong desire to help my friends, and at the same time there was a sadness for what they had experienced and the poverty they had to endure.

To deal with these brewing feelings, I focused on what could be done in the moment. I was relieved that the water wells were still being used, and that the Contehs' oil palm trees and fishing lures were producing food. My family had sent money for me to give to A.K.'s family and the Contehs. With A.K., we discussed his options as an aging teacher and what would help him in the long run. We agreed that a fruit tree farm and an expansion of his vegetable farm would be a wise investment.

The Contehs were most concerned about shelter. They wanted to build two mud-block houses with tin roofs that would last for several years, to keep from having to replace grass-thatched roofs on a regular basis. Moses, Bokarie, and Sanpha still had a tenderness and caring for the elders and children in the family that was endearing. They simply wanted to provide shelter for them.

The money for helping A.K. and the Contehs was such a drop in the bucket, especially when thinking of all the people in need across the country. I also gave the Conteh brothers laminated photos of Christ and my guru, and encouraged them to pray to them any time they needed help. It was touching to watch Sanpha, Moses, and Bokarie take the photos, kiss them, and then place them over their hearts.

Josephine agreed to be the point person for keeping in touch with her parents and also the Contehs. She had an email account, and I gave her a digital camera so she could send photos occasionally. Josephine wanted to continue her education, but, as a single mother living away from her parents, she was financially stretched. Frances, our country director, was helping Josephine and other young women interns as much as she could. Josephine was in a good place to learn and grow for several years and had strong role models to inspire her.

When leaving Sierra Leone I felt a range of emotions — joy for having seen friends in Kagbere and Masongbo, along with the grief, sadness, and despair for their lives. At the same time, there was a poignant sense of guilt that I could leave and that I wanted to be home, in a safe place, out of reach of trauma and poverty.

Landing back in the United States, I cringed as the news featured the latest exploits of Britney Spears and Lindsay Lohan, and how many people talked about the most recent episodes of *Survivor*. Did America not have anything better to do than to idolize these ridiculous people?

Life is a Bitch and Then You Reincarnate

I form the light, and create darkness:
I make peace, and create evil: I the LORD do all these things.
— Isaiah 45:7

After the trip to Kagbere and Masongbo, I came back to Rick Levy pissed off. I asked Rick, "What the hell is going on? Why does God allow such horrible suffering to take place? I don't get it! Meanwhile, I can have blissful experiences in meditation and even intoxicating experiences of divine love. I just don't understand!"

In my mind, I could hear Mickey saying, "Who asked you how it should be anyway?" Would I ever understand what Mickey meant?

Rick sat back in his chair and said, "Look, if you view this Earth as a place where everyone can get what they want and live happily ever after, you are in for serious disappointment. If you view this planet as a place for souls to evolve over many lifetimes, it is perfectly designed to facilitate that process.

"Remember, God created everything, including the light and the shadows, the positive and the negative, the good and the evil.

"Everything is from God, and it is all an illusion.

"You know the metaphors — picture God as the ocean and all of creation as waves, or view this world as a motion picture of light and shadows coming from the projector of God's consciousness? This world is one big drama of God's production, and we are the actors, our souls, lifetime after lifetime.

"Souls go through hundreds, if not thousands of lifetimes, back and forth, from the astral planes back to the physical world, reincarnating. This does not include the thousands of lifetimes as plants and animals prior to becoming human. There is a general progression where new souls often do not even survive birth. Later they will get to the place where they live for a few years and then die. People who are victims many lifetimes then become perpetrators. Over many lifetimes, souls learn to survive on Earth and then to thrive. After many lifetimes of thriving, souls learn to be generous toward their families and eventually expand that generosity and love to their communities and others.

"After many, many lifetimes, souls tire of coming back over and over again. They tire of the fluctuating dualities of pleasure and pain, life and death, sickness and health, and they have a vague memory of their true essence of peace and bliss. Souls then start to look for freedom, thus they start their spiritual journeys in earnest. By that point though, they have acquired so much karma from the previous lives that they have to work it out before they can merge back into God.

"You have no idea how fortunate you are to be asking these questions and to have an opportunity to grow spiritually. It could have taken you hundreds of lifetimes to get to this place, and now the only lifetime that really matters is this one," Rick said.

As I listened to Rick, I was still pissed and remained silent.

"Look, all of God's creation is ruled by natural laws, you know this," he said.

"Yes, I know, cause and effect, the law of karma," I replied.

"Yes, the physical world is designed around duality and polarity, light and shadow; the contrast is needed to create motion. There are many natural laws on how the system works, with karma being the big one, and scientists are constantly discovering these subtle workings.

"When the soul identifies with thoughts, emotions, and physical bodies, it allows the traction for karma to form around the soul. Desires and fears are the main reasons karma forms — wanting something or trying to avoid something in a world of duality.

"However, the entire system is designed so that we will not find lasting happiness on Earth and that we experience the impact of our individual and collective actions. All the suffering that takes place, even the natural disasters, are the result of individual and collective karma, man's misuse of free will. The pain is simply a whip to drive us to seek God."

"How does Divine Mother fit into it all?" I asked.

"She is Shakti, the active part of Creation. She is the creator, the sustainer, and the destroyer. While She loves all her children unconditionally, Her natural laws apply to all of us. If you stick your hand in the fire, you get burnt."

After listening to Rick, I had one question: "Why did God create this damn drama?"

"Master (our guru) used to argue with God, saying it was not right to create a world where people have to suffer, even if it is all delusion. Master would say God was bored being all by Himself and wanted to experience Himself, so He manifested as all of creation. All the saints who have merged back with God say there is a beautiful plan behind it all that is based on love. For those of us stuck in the delusion, it can be a nightmare until we merge our consciousness back with God.

"You have to remember," Rick said, "It is all *Maya* ("delusion"), and our souls are never really affected by it. You know, be in the world and not of it."

"So life is a bitch and then you reincarnate," I said with sarcasm.

"Yes, like it or not, that is the game," Rick said. "My, oh, Maya," he added, not resisting the chance to throw in a pun.

"Look, the early Christian church accepted the doctrine of reincarnation, including the Gnostics and numerous church founders, such as Clement of Alexandria. Reincarnation was first declared a heresy by the Second Council of Constantinople in 553 AD. They thought it gave men too much time and space to seek immediate salvation. By getting rid of reincarnation, they also gave the church more power and control as they were the only way to salvation.

"Reincarnation was voted out of the Bible by bishops by a vote of three to two; go figure."

"That sure was some swing vote," I added, picking up on Rick's humor. "Do you think if Congress voted climate change or gravity out of existence it would work?"

"Well, they do seem to be trying on the climate change," Rick responded, smiling. "Look," he continued, "you have to find God in order to get out of the delusion."

"You mean find the one that created the whole damn thing?" I said.

"Yes, love Him, or Her in your case, with all your heart, mind and soul!" Rick said.

"How in the hell am I supposed to love Her for creating this show? My friends in Sierra Leone went through hell and now they live in utter poverty. I don't get it," I replied.

"Look, the human mind cannot comprehend God, so do not even try. God as Cosmic Consciousness is beyond duality. The human mind and all of creation is subject to duality and polarity. You are stuck in duality and delusion. Yes, I know it's pretty horrible out there. Like it or not, that is the way it is!"

Seeing I was still angry, Rick added, "Look, I am sorry what your friends experienced in Sierra Leone, I really am. You are facing an existential question that has haunted men and women for centuries. It is a big one that drives us back to God.

"Meditate; go deep into meditation, and then you can go into higher states of consciousness, far beyond your own mind. You have to get out of your mind and thoughts. Cosmic Consciousness is scientifically beyond the mind. You will still have to play your role in the world; we all have to play our roles. It is easier to play when you anchor your consciousness in God.

"Your karma over many lifetimes has placed you where you are. Your *dharma,* or duty, this lifetime, is peacebuilding, mine is healing, and other people's are different. Your dharma is your path to liberation specific to you; you have to play that role; you cannot play someone else's role. You are an actor in God's production.

"Read the *Bhagavad Gita,* the conversations between Arjuna and Krishna. Arjuna did not want to go into battle against his family, but that was his duty. Granted, the *Gita* is a series of metaphors for the internal battles we all face.

"The key is to play your role, the one given to you by God, to the best of your ability while completely absorbed in the blissful state of being merged with God. Whatever comes, good or bad, you can stay even-minded, anchored in full awareness that it is a dream. You know what Master writes, 'stand unshaken amidst the crash of breaking worlds.'"

That was my guru's and Rick's mantra: meditate, more, longer, and deeper; then, perform duties diligently without attachment, giving the fruits of all actions to God. Be in the world and not of it. Rick had reached the point where he was by meditating three to four hours a day for over thirty years. It was all much easier said than done.

Section Three

Transforming Self and Societies: Moving Toward Oneness

Mass media, particularly in democratic societies,
can make a considerable contribution to world peace
by giving greater coverage to human interest items
that reflect the ultimate oneness of humanity.[6]
— His Holiness the 14th Dalai Lama

Voice of the Present ~ Children and Youth in Conflict

As I reflected on the conversations with Rick, I was still overwhelmed by the realities of deadly violence, especially the impact on children and youths. In the early 1900s, 10 percent of the causalities of war were civilians. A hundred years later, 90 percent were civilians, with a large part being children and youths. If humanity was becoming more evolved, at least through technology, we had not fully caught up with the impact of our advancements. The deadliest of new technologies were the light automatic weapons, such as AK-47s, which could be carried by small children.

Sure, on one hand, I understood, "we are all one," we all come from one source, God/Universe/Spirit, and I could appreciate that we were all moving back toward oneness, at least in some larger scheme of things. But, to be honest, there was a huge cavern between the theoretical idea of souls evolving and all being one, and, how to deal with the here-and-now realities people faced in Sierra Leone and beyond. While I strongly believed if more people meditated the world would be a better place, I also knew it was not the immediate solution to the problems in Sierra Leone.

I became very curious about the inner process of moving toward awareness of the soul and oneness with God, and the parallels with outer peacebuilding efforts in the world. My hunch was there were core principles and approaches to the inner disciplines of yoga and other traditions that were being applied across the continuum from inner to international peace. I wanted to understand the practical application of these principles and approaches across the continuum, especially on societal levels.

Search for Common Ground allowed a perfect vehicle to learn from a number of inspiring colleagues dealing with very harsh situations. I continued to make trips to Sierra Leone and Liberia on a regular basis, and later started to travel to other parts of Africa, including Guinea, Ghana, Ivory Coast, Nigeria, Democratic Republic of Congo (East and West), Rwanda, Burundi, and Angola.

Even though most co-workers seldom talked about quantum physics or spirituality, they seemed to be tapping into and leveraging universal aspects around consciousness.

What I came to see is that all of my colleagues held similar beliefs: violence was destructive, period. It destroys lives and infrastructures and starts a cycle of cause-and-effect events that spirals into more violence. This perspective I found similar to the law of karma in real time or, as some cultures would say, "What goes around comes around" or "Do unto others as you would have them do unto you."

More importantly, all of my colleagues believed in the positive potential of humanity, that there was a basic goodness that could be leveraged to help people deal with conflict constructively. This was consistent with the idea that each person has a soul that comes from one source that has qualities of peace, love, and compassion. And with that said, my colleagues were clear that there were people who were so far disconnected from their own humanity, such as Charles Taylor, that they had to be dealt with sternly and directly.

This was similar to what Rick described: souls are in many different states of delusion and enlightenment, such as His Holiness the Dalai Lama, who was on his fourteenth round as the Dalai Lama, and then Charles Taylor, who hopefully will not come back as the same villain. The assumption I had was the more advanced the soul, the greater likelihood that person would be to express wisdom and compassion; and, the more deluded a soul, the more likely that person was to commit horrific actions. Of course, there was probably a wide range of grey and exceptions to any rule.

The challenge was to appeal to and awaken humanity's positive potential, or soul qualities, on a large scale in difficult situations.

Engage and See the Possibilities: Golden Kids News

There was an expression in Kriya Yoga that a saint is a sinner who never gave up. A colleague at Search liked to say that no one would have believed in 1942 that France and Germany would peacefully share open borders and the same currency. The idea was to believe peace was possible in order to make it a possibility and to see opportunities to make it happen. This idea was similar to emerging theories in quantum physics — thoughts influence physical reality.

Another similarity between yoga (and other spiritual traditions) and Search's work of transforming conflict was to face harsh realities head-on, accepting that such situations exist. Tara Brach, a psychologist and Buddhist meditation instructor in the Washington, DC area, called this *radical acceptance*, a cornerstone, she believed, to applying spirituality in daily life.

There was nothing "Pollyannaish" about Search's work. You did not have to like the fact that child soldiers existed, you had to look at it for what it was and seek out opportunities to transform it. The word "transformation" was used instead of "resolution" because the idea was to transform how people deal with conflict, whereas resolution implied addressing a specific conflict. Conflicts would always exist, so the goal was to increase people's capacity to deal with them constructively and, in the process, transform the relationships of the people involved in conflict — to go from adversarial relationships to cooperative problem solving.

There were a couple other foundational beliefs to Search's work. The founder, John Marks, often quoted Woody Allen, "Ninety percent of life is showing up." I took this as "being present." Another quote John Marks liked was from Napoleon; when asked how he was successful in battle, Napoleon said, "I engage and see the possibilities."

With these basic beliefs in the positive potential of humanity, and in showing up and engaging in possibilities, there were often unexpected opportunities that arose in the moment that proved more powerful than anything that could have been planned. A classic example of engaging to see the possibilities was *Golden Kids News*.

Search's radio studio in Monrovia, Talking Drum Studio, was composed of staff from the different ethnic and political factions. The staffing was a key component to the operations of all programs — people from the various factions involved in a conflict, and people who believed common ground was possible. The goal was to move beyond the human tendencies of duality and polarity by having elements of the various opposition parts working together to identify ways to influence the greater society. The staff became the think tank for identifying ways to use media together with other activities to influence the greater society.

The team in Liberia produced radio programs, such as news, feature stories, music, and soap operas, to encourage dialogue and defuse violence. Unlike traditional journalism, Talking Drum Studio programs had an agenda: transform how people deal with conflict, away from adversarial approaches and toward collaborative solutions. They knew radio programs dramatically impacted people's thinking, and that in a postconflict situation they had a huge responsibility to make sure the programs reduced tensions while also helping look for and highlight solutions to problems that were emerging in society.

Our staff began working with children and youth when a sixteen-year-old boy named Kimmie Weeks walked into the studio saying he was from the Children's Bureau of Information and he wanted to give a voice to children in Liberia. The staff member who told the story smiled and laughed, clearly tickled by the boldness of Kimmie to make up a Children's Bureau. Kimmie had an idea, and he needed help in making it happen. Our staff engaged Kimmie and taught him how to become a radio producer.

Before long, the Children's Bureau of Information and Talking Drum Studio were producing a weekly show entitled *Golden Kids News*, which was aired by local radio stations. The impact was almost immediate: children's voices were being broadcast and people stopped to listen.

Golden Kids News was such a hit that, before long, there were more people walking through the doors of Talking Drum Studio, including representatives of the United Nations High Commission on Refugees, asking whether we would produce another program. The result, *Children's World*, was a program "by and for children affected by war." This weekly program shared the experiences of children who were displaced by war and were trying to rebuild their lives. With adult support, the children of *Children's World* broadcast poetry, songs, storytelling, news, and music to thousands of listeners every week. From the ashes of war came the creativity and dreams of children.

I later learned that Kimmie Weeks had almost died in a refugee camp as a child. When he was given up as dead, he prayed to God, promising to work for peace if allowed to live. Kimmie Weeks had a spark of light that persisted in the face of tremendous darkness. That light found full expression through *Golden Kids News* and *Children's World*, thereby allowing other children and youth to share their light. The key was to highlight and amplify the light so that it would spark the light in others and together drive reduce the power of the darkness. Talking Drum Studio was doing just that — it was showcasing and awakening the human potential for positive ways of being.

The first time I watched a *Children's World* program being produced in Liberia, I was immediately impressed by the image of a small child with large headphones speaking into an even larger microphone: "My name is Brandy Crawford, and this is *Children's World*, a program produced by children for children affected by war." I suddenly understood on a visceral level the power of the programming. I struggled to hold back tears as the innocence and purity of a child reaching out to other children in the face of horrible atrocities stirred my own heart to compassion, beauty, and hope, the very essence of the human soul, all of which would need to be cultivated to move beyond war.

Standing next to me at the time was Joe, the older and seasoned producer who had lived through the war. He was a very tough, burly kind of guy. When Joe saw me tear up he said, "It happens to me too."

There was something so powerful about the innocence of a child's voice and the juxtaposition of violence. If each person does have a soul, which I believed was true, then these child producers were reaching them. They had reached mine at least.

When we started Talking Drum Studio in Freetown, Sierra Leone, *Golden Kids News* was the first program our team produced. The impact in Sierra Leone was even more striking than it had been in Liberia. Soldiers in the UN peacekeeping mission, market people, and taxi drivers all stopped by the studio to comment on the children's programs.

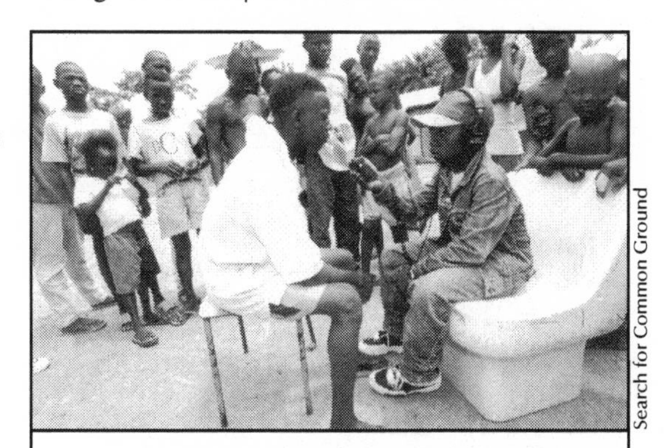

Search for Common Ground

A *Golden Kid News* reporter interviewing other children in Sierra Leone

Golden Kids News also became the way for me to face feelings about what child soldiers and the rebels had done to the Contehs, A.K.'s family, and other friends in Kagbere and Masongbo.

One of our producers in Sierra Leone was a young man named Stephen who had been abducted by rebels at the age of twelve and was forced to become a killing machine. After four years of fighting, he was able to put away his gun and go through a demobilizing and reintegration process.

When I first met Stephen, he stood off to the side and did not talk much. Frances, Search's country director, explained to me his situation and said she was giving him a chance to get to know the studio and the people working there. The next time I came through, months later, Stephen had joined *Golden Kids News* as a "cub reporter." Stephen was part of a broader team of *Golden Kids* cub reporters, many of whom had not been child soldiers or sex slaves, so Stephen could remember what it was like to be a youth.

Stephen helped me rehumanize the rebels and to put a face on a child soldier. Over time, he became a trainer of other youth producers. He seemed so soft-spoken and gentle; it was hard to imagine he was once carrying an AK-47.

Stephen was later featured in a United Nations film called *What's Going On*, and was interviewed by the actor Michael Douglas, who was visiting Sierra Leone. As Mr. Douglas pointed out in the film, Stephen had joined *Golden Kids News* as a way to put his horrific past behind him and to help the other estimated fifteen thousand child combatants. "I interviewed some of my colleagues to explain their stories," Stephen said to Mr. Douglas, "so the people in the community, they would be able to accept them back."

There were several things I loved about Stephen and *Golden Kids News*. First, it was a very practical example of awakening what I believed to be the soul of humanity by meeting people where they were — it was produced by Sierra Leonean kids in their own language. Second, it was a clear example of showing up, being present in a culturally appropriate way with an eye toward creating a possibility that had not existed before; in this sense, it was transformational. And, third, it acknowledged children and youths had played a role in the war, and it created an opportunity for them to play a positive role in the peace process. One friend called this a "five-degree shift" — take the same leadership skills a combatant has and then make a five-degree shift so they apply those skills in a new, constructive direction. In essence, *Golden Kids News* was creating a space for children and youths to experience themselves in a new way across an entire society.

An evaluation of *Golden Kids News*, using methods created by Ed Palmer, showed the program had reached approximately 89 percent of people in Sierra Leone within the first year of being broadcast. Over 70 percent of the people who listened said it had changed their perspective of youth to a more positive one. It was especially satisfying knowing the Contehs, A.K., and others in Kagbere and Masongbo were listening, and, that Josephine was part of the staff at Talking Drum Studio. These programs were reaching the people I loved.

Similar children and youth radio programs were later produced by Search in Angola, Democratic Republic of Congo, Burundi, Rwanda, Nepal, and beyond.

As for Kimmie Weeks, who had walked into Talking Drum Studio with the idea for *Golden Kids News*, he had to leave Liberia because he started to become outspoken against Charles Taylor's involvement in the training of child soldiers.

Kimmie received political asylum in the United States and went on to become a child ambassador for UNICEF. He received a full-ride scholarship to Amherst College and later received a master's degree from the University of Pennsylvania. Kimmie started his own nonprofit organization called Youth Action International with the mission of providing education, healthcare, and economic empowerment for children and young people living in postwar African countries.

In 2007, Liberian President Ellen Johnson Sirleaf, who later won the Nobel Peace Prize, awarded Kimmie with Liberia's highest honor by decorating him Knight Grand Commander in the Humane Order of Africa Redemption. But the most important of Kimmie's achievements must be that, while still only a child himself, he created a platform for children everywhere to voice their hopes and fears, and to teach us all something about the human spirit.

Namaste Street Kids

There were two other stories that helped me bridge the conversations with Rick Levy and the study of yoga with the children and youth work in Africa. I heard author and corporate consultant Robert Cooper give a presentation in Washington, DC about building trust. He told a story about going to Tibet and traveling to visit a sacred Buddhist monastery. When he got there, tired and hungry, he found the monastery closed and a Chinese guard at the gate holding an automatic weapon.

Robert was furious. He had traveled all the way to Tibet, hours by bus, and he was deprived of visiting the monastery. He also was angry at everything the guard represented.

Robert then saw a Tibetan family walk up to the guard, listen to the news of the monastery being closed, and then bow to the guard, saying, *namaste*. The family then walked to the side and sat down to eat lunch.

Robert approached the family, curious how they could be so calm and polite. They engaged in a conversation and Robert learned the family had traveled for days on foot. The young girl of the family offered to teach Robert Tibetan words in exchange for learning English. Namaste was one of the words, "I bow to the divinity in you that is also in me."

She then asked Robert how to say namaste in English. Robert was dumbfounded and thought for several minutes. There was no such word in English.

When Robert got back to America, he began an experiment. When he said hello to people, instead of automatically saying "hello" and walking on, he paused, said "hello," listened for a response and inwardly acknowledged the divinity in each person. Over time, he found that his relationships changed, that more trust was developed.

This story provided a lens to another of Search's youth activities in Sierra Leone. Elections had been brutal in 1996, with the RUF hacking off people's limbs. (The movie *Blood Diamond* would later have a horrific scene where this happens. It was just gruesome, and unfortunately, accurate.)

When the Sierra Leone elections were approaching in 2002, our staff knew there was potential for violence. They also knew that many youths living on the streets had been manipulated for political intimidation and violence. What our staff did was to go interview kids and to ask them about their lives on the streets and their experiences during elections.

Our staff approached the kids as if they mattered, similar to Robert's namaste experiment.

The young kids responded and talked openly about the harsh economic realities of being homeless. They also talked about how politicians came in with money and promises. After the elections, the elected officials would forget all about the kids until the next elections.

A few days later, our staff went back to the kids with radios and a bag of rice. They ate together and listened to the radio program with the kids' voices on the air. The kids were thrilled! They were important; they were being heard across the country.

Through several conversations, the kids were asked what they would like to do, if given the chance. They said they would like to register voters. Our team put them in touch with other local organizations that trained them to register voters. They reached many places where adults were afraid to go. The kids were next trained to become election monitors. The efforts of hundreds of kids monitoring election booths, combined with real-time radio results and other national and international efforts, contributed to the elections being largely violence-free. The youth monitors were visibly recognized and applauded by their communities for their efforts, which only reinforced their positive behavior.

Acknowledging the value of the kids and creating an opportunity for them to be heard created an opening for them to bring forth their positive potential. The techniques were so simple and were ones I found being applied by colleagues in several countries as an integral part of peacebuilding. When I later traveled to Nepal, I was thrilled to be in a culture where the greeting actually was "namaste."

The acknowledging concept and technique was so easy to apply on a daily basis, yet its power of awakening the soul was profound.

Based on these experiences, I started to apply the same technique back in the office in DC. One of my favorite experiments was to see how long it would take a new receptionist to go from being cool and formal to open and friendly. By slowly greeting and stopping to listen, I found that, within a week or two, even the shyest person would start to greet me with a big smile. What went around came around.

Societal Healing ~ Reweaving Social Tapestries

In many ways, Search and many partner organizations were working on societal healing. The social tapestry of Sierra Leone had been ripped apart by the years of violent conflict, as was true for Burundi, Liberia, Angola, Democratic Republic of Congo, and other countries. The violent conflict had destroyed infrastructures, denied youth education, etc.... and put into place a cycle of violence, poverty, etc. Many of these countries were considered "failed states" by the world community and would become more important, at least to the U.S. government, when they were seen as being connected to terrorist groups.

There also was a level of complexity on both the individual and macro level. It was hard to imagine the depth of trauma that individuals experienced by being exposed to violent conflict. I remember looking many times at the photo I had taken in Makeni when the young person was necklaced. In the crowd surrounding the burning body were dozens, if not hundreds of children and youths. It was so hard to imagine the impact such scenes had on an entire generation, and difficult to see how people could engage in a peace process with such trauma.

If we all do have conscious and subconscious minds, which Freud, Carl Jung, and my yoga traditions taught and I believed, then there must be layers upon layers of impact stored in the subconscious minds and in the cells of bodies. In terms of karma, the idea was that there were grooves formed in the minds and those groves would stay with us for lifetimes, shaping our very DNA and influencing every action we take.

The individual trauma contributed to what Carl Jung described as the collective unconscious. There also was a new scientific study about how the minds of people were entangled. Dean Radin, a scientist at the Institute of Noetic Sciences (IONS) and author of *Entangled Minds,* conducted research that proved thoughts could be perceived by people in other locations. With these emerging scientific studies, it was easy to imagine how Sierra Leone and other countries had an invisible collective environment of thought, emotions, and consciousness that was impacted by trauma.

Environment was recognized in yoga as having a tremendous effect on a person's consciousness. It was very difficult to rise above the conditions of environment, whether physical, emotional, or social, especially if there was tremendous stress and/or fear. Thus, outer conditions do greatly affect the ability to experience inner peace.

Healing of the individual and collective psyche were already complex and daunting challenges without adding the fact that Sierra Leone was becoming more entwined in a rapidly growing interdependent and interconnected world. There no longer was the possibility of reweaving an ancient African society that had been around for generations. No. The village life I had experienced as a Peace Corps Volunteer had already been influenced by the global economy. Fifteen years later, that village life had been dramatically impacted by the war and was again being radically altered by quickly changing technologies, global economy, and mass communication.

In 2000, when Talking Drum Studio started, there were only a few radio stations in the country. Within a few years, that number would grow to almost forty stations. Over the same time period, cell phones would spread across the country, and internet cafes would appear in Freetown and other towns. People in villages were able to talk with families in America and elsewhere. Josephine was able to send me emails with photos of A.K., Tendy, and other friends in Kagbere. This was unthinkable only fifteen years earlier when I was a Peace Corps Volunteer.

Meanwhile, the war also had changed the roles of women and youth, creating more opportunities for self-expression and power from a culture that had been largely led by male elders. Sierra Leone was a rapidly shifting context trying to recreate itself. When I later visited Congo, I saw the dynamics there were even more complex with all of the countries involved in its conflicts and the resources being collected by international corporations.

Trying to comprehend the complexity was overwhelming, and I always marveled at the nuanced analysis our staff had of local situations, far beyond my comprehension.

This was where I drank the Search Kool-Aid. Conflict was going to be an integral part of Sierra Leone's reconstruction for years to come; the goal was to transform how people dealt with conflict, not to resolve any one particular issue and then leave. Our approach was different from that of most other organizations, which focused on a sector, such as education or small business development, or a particular issue, such as refugees or reintegrating child soldiers.

When I was negotiating potential financial support from a British funding agency, I was asked by one program officer what Talking Drum would do after the soldiers were disarmed. I replied, "We will move on to the next issues: return of refugees, reintegration of combatants, pre-election education, election results, education and economic opportunities for youth, and eventually address root causes of conflict, such as corruption.... Each step of the way will have conflict. We can provide Sierra Leone with continuity on approaching conflict constructively." This was a novel concept for the donor and, in fact, most donor agencies were not designed to support such a long-term transformation of mindset.

If people in a society learned to deal with conflict constructively, then conflict could become an engine for growth and transformation each step of the way. It was really about a slow and gradual shift in mindsets and consciousness. The communications media was especially good for going broad in facilitating a change in consciousness. Outreach activities, such as working with the youth election monitors, could go deeper into communities. Together, it was a powerful combination, one that thrilled Ed Palmer before he died, as the approach was far beyond traditional journalism of just reporting the facts. No, this was sophisticated media with an agenda of promoting common ground.

Search's programs were very strategic in having studios that produced programs that were given to local radio stations. This strategy strengthened the capacity of the local stations and increased the number of people listening to the same programs broadcast by several stations. By being in a country for years, the studios gained trust with listeners and could address the issues as they changed. The radio programs also brought attention to other organizations that were doing positive work, thereby creating synergy between them.

Radio had become a part of the local environment and was facilitating societal healing and transformation of mindsets. Search's work, and that of other organizations, was dealing with societal consciousness, which required long-term commitments in order to bring about transformation. In essence, the peacebuilding work was allowing an entire society to experience itself in a new way.

The methods for bringing about this incremental societal transformation were highly creative and always couched within the local cultural context.

The Power of Storytelling

Based on the success of radio soap operas in Burundi and Liberia, the Sierra Leone program produced a soap opera called *Atunda Ayenda,* which translates into "lost and found." The fictional story line was based on real-life situations people had encountered during and immediately after the war. Listeners could easily identify with what was happening because of how close it was to reality. This allowed the producers to then guide people through how to deal with difficult situations constructively and to also heal through shared traumas.

For instance, Makunda was a fictional character who disappeared in the early episodes. She was the sister of one character, the lover of another, and the desire of an evil rebel officer named Dragon. For weeks, people in the radio series would ask, "Where is Makunda?"

It was so much fun arriving in Sierra Leone and encountering people at the airport and in taxicabs talking about Makunda and Dragon. Even the Conteh brothers and other people in remote villages were caught up in the story. The entire population seemed to be listening closely, following to find out what had happened to Makunda.

On the hundredth episode, Makunda arrived unexpectedly on a flight from Nigeria. Listeners learned she had escaped from Dragon, had traveled to Nigeria as a refugee, and found her way into the care of a wealthy Nigerian businessman. The fact that Makunda had been a refugee resonated with many people in Sierra Leone.

There was a huge celebration in the radio program about Makunda's return, and listeners celebrated, too. Makunda's mother was so happy to have her home that she asked Makunda to sleep in the same bed the first night. The next morning when Makunda awoke, her mother was dead.

Some of our staff reported women in several parts of Sierra Leone openly grieved over the death of Makunda's mother. It was clear they were grieving the loss of their own loved ones who had died during the war. *Atunda Ayenda* was taking all of Sierra Leone through a collective healing process through the power of storytelling.

Steady Bongo and the Cultural Heroes

One thing I loved about Sierra Leone as a Peace Corps Volunteer was the music and dancing. The memory of dancing after Pa Conteh's funeral had left such a strong impression on me. It was no surprise that this tradition of using music and dance had become an uplifting tool for societal healing across the continent. In Burundi, our program sponsored annual festivals where Hutu, Tutsi, and other musicians from around the country performed together. In Angola, our team coproduced an album of musicians from different political orientations.

Music had an ability to transcend the mental and emotional wounds and to open what I imagined to be the soul's innate capacity for joy even in the midst of dire situations. One of the most inspiring stories in Sierra Leone happened early in our work and involved a Sierra Leonean pop musician named Steady Bongo.

A year after our program started, there was a tenuous peace agreement between the government and RUF rebels. At that time, the RUF held most of the northern and eastern regions of the country while UN and British peacekeepers controlled the rest.

Search for Common Ground

Steady Bongo and the Cultural Heroes during a peace concert tour in an RUF area.

Word came to Frances, our country director in Sierra Leone, that the RUF were harassing UN workers who were trying to get humanitarian aid to the region. Steady Bongo was visiting Frances at the time, and she had a hunch that Steady should go with her to the front lines. Keep in mind, the RUF had committed terrible atrocities — people were terrified of them and rightly so.

Frances and Steady drove more than ten hours across the country. When they arrived at an RUF checkpoint, teenage boys wielding AK-47s and smoking pot started harassing Frances. She calmly asked if they liked Steady Bongo's music, to which they replied, "Yeah sure — he's our man." Then, she pointed to the back seat. When they saw Steady Bongo, the combatants went from being thugs to young boys. They danced and sang, "The war done, done, Steady Bongo done come!" Then, the gruff, hardened commanders met Steady; they went from being terrorizing combatants to starry-eyed fans in seconds. The RUF commanders asked Steady to play some music and Frances jumped in, sensing an opportunity.

Ultimately, the RUF commanders agreed to give safe passage to Steady Bongo and his band, provide security, pay for half the expenses, and allow Talking Drum Studio reporters to interview people for radio programs. In return, Steady Bongo and his band the Cultural Heroes did a peace concert tour across the RUF area, helping to open the lines to humanitarian aid. Steady and his band were greeted by enthusiastic combatants and civilians alike. The Talking Drum radio programs were broadcast across the country, carrying the voices of young RUF combatants who said they were tired of fighting and wanted to end the conflict. The Talking Drum interviews started to rehumanize the RUF rebels, allowing the slow process of reconciliation to begin.

Meanwhile, Steady went on to do many more peace concerts across Sierra Leone. Frances later told me that there was an interesting healing aspect to the music and dancing. She said that an international manual on trauma healing suggested exercise, a strange idea for a country of subsistence farmers. Frances did say that immediately after the war, people danced and danced and danced, often throughout the night. They danced with an intensity she had never seen in her twenty years of living in Sierra Leone. They danced and sang the trauma out of their bodies, minds, and souls.

Trow Away di Gun

Steady Bongo, *Atunda Ayenda,* and the other radio programs were changing the stories in Sierra Leone and, in this sense, working with the collective unconscious. *Golden Kids News* was telling the story that it was possible for children and youth to play a positive role in society instead of being destructive warriors. *Atunda Ayenda* had situations where people were able to forgive and reconcile with people who had committed atrocities against loved ones.

Another radio program that I loved was *Trow Away di Gun* which was produced by two former military officers from different sides of the conflict. Foday had been a high-ranking training officer with the *kamajors* civil defense forces. Rashid had been a military officer with the RUF.

Their radio program ran during the disarming and demobilizing phase of the peace process, shortly after Steady Bongo's first peace concert tour. Together, Foday and Rashid talked on the air about the services provided by the United Nations, the Sierra Leonean government, and nonprofit organizations to help combatants disarm and learn new skills. People across the country recognized the two personalities. The civil defense fighters trusted Foday, and the RUF trusted Rashid. Their being on the air together was a tangible example that it was possible to come back together peacefully.

Before meeting Foday and Rashid, I was somewhat hesitant and also curious. By getting to know Stephen, I had learned to see him as a tender-hearted young man, someone who had been forced to be a child soldier. Stephen helped me to see child soldiers as children and begin to heal from my own anger about what happened to my friends in Masongbo and Kagbere. Rashid, though, was a grown man who had been part of the RUF.

I was surprised to find Foday and Rashid behaved like brothers, almost connected at the hip. They moved together, and often stood close to one another. Foday was stout and muscular, Rashid thin with piercing eyes. They both had a very strong, solid, and unflinching presence. It was clear they both had seen and commanded troops in deadly conflict. It was interesting to see how they interacted with one another, almost affectionately.

When relaxing over Star Beer, the local brew, they would laugh and tell stories. Foday liked to say how he used to beat Rashid after he had been captured. Rashid laughed too, saying he was thankful Foday had not killed him. I just marveled at how they had moved beyond their differences, and found myself learning from them about how to let go of my own prejudices.

Traditional African Spirituality and Conflict

There was a part of Sierra Leone's violent conflict that added a bizarre mixture to the already complex global context of the war: the role of local traditional secret spiritual societies.

While I was a Peace Corps Volunteer, I was fascinated by the secret spiritual societies, yet did not have access to them beyond the public ceremonies when there was dancing and singing, often with a "devil," a person dressed in a colorful outfit. On many nights in the dry season, I would listen to women and young girls sing in the "sacred bush," as the new initiates went through weeks of training to learn how to become a woman in the community.

I came away from my Peace Corps experience with tremendous respect for the secret societies and the rights of passage that young boys and girls went through, which involved entire communities. The secret societies served as a bridge between the spirit world — ancestors, spirits, etc. — and community, farms, and nature. I often marveled at the sense of deep connection my friends had on so many levels.

These secret spiritual societies, one for men and another for women, existed side by side with Islam and Christianity, and were an essential part of the community tapestry.

During the wars in Liberia and Sierra Leone, African spirituality took on a very destructive aspect, as leaders such as Charles Taylor, Foday Sankoh, and others used human sacrifices and cannibalism to extract spiritual powers to help them and their troops in combat. These horrific stories were so far removed from what I remembered in Masongbo and Kagbere, where the worst I ever heard was people using witchcraft to protect their homes.

What was interesting about the Sierra Leone conflict was that traditional spirituality was used to protect communities, one of the first times in modern

African history to have it happen on such a large scale. Traditional warriors arose out of necessity.

At first, people in rural communities in Sierra Leone welcomed the RUF rebels because they were seen as a way to overcome decades of government corruption. But when the RUF turned against the civilians, then communities were left to the protection of the government troops. Because the government soldiers were not paid regularly, many became "So-bels" — soldiers by day and rebels by night, thereby stealing from the people they were supposed to guard. Eventually, a large part of the government army held a coup attempt and invited the RUF into the government.

The traditional hunter-warrior secret societies responded by training young boys and men to go into battle to defend their communities. People called "initiators" would initiate young combatants, giving them spiritual powers to shield them from bullets and knives. Thousands of traditional warriors were initiated across Sierra Leone, organized around communities. Foday, the radio producer of *Trow Away di Gun*, went through such an initiation.

Some initiators were known to be more powerful than others. There also were stories of how the rules of the "medicine" needed to be followed exactly, otherwise the powers could be weakened, such as by having sex.

These initiators and the local militias had tremendous power over entire communities during the war, and they played a huge role in helping stem the tide of the rebels and rogue government forces. After the war, it was not clear how the initiators and traditional spiritual ways could be brought into the peace process. They were largely sidelined by the government and international community.

Shortly after I started making trips to Sierra Leone, Rick Levy told me that he was available to help in Africa if needed. He said he had worked with shamans in South America and other parts of the world, that they recognized him as a fellow spiritual healer. I had no clue what this meant or how it could be relevant. Months went by.

Finally, I had a discussion with Frances about the initiators and the local militia in Sierra Leone. We agreed that they represented a powerful part of society and could probably be more integrated into the peace process. When she came to Washington, DC on a business trip, she met Rick Levy and agreed it would be worthwhile to have him come to see what would happen. No expectations, just curious.

We planned a trip for Rick to Sierra Leone in 2002. Rick and I met a few times to prepare for it. He said he was meditating on the situation in Sierra Leone and had made contact on the astral plane with one of the shaman-like traditional spiritual leaders. He did not know if we would meet this man in person.

This all stretched my sense of imagination, and I just had to go on good faith that Rick knew what he was talking about.

Just prior to the trip, Rick asked who would be taking us around to meet the traditional leaders. I informed him we had Foday, our staff person who had served as an officer and trainer for a local militia group. Rick said we would need someone else and asked about Frances's husband, someone he had never met. I checked with Frances, and her husband Cyril was available.

The week-long trip in Sierra Leone with Rick was a memorable adventure, as it brought a whole new dimension to the war and peacebuilding process. As soon as we got there, Rick began reading the energies of Freetown, pointing out where horrible things had happened, which was just about everywhere. He read the energies of staff and other people, often discreetly.

We traveled to Cyril's farm, a four-hour drive from Freetown, just outside a town called Bo in the Southern Region. Foday met us there, and we discussed our plans for the next few days. Instead of looking at everything from a logical perspective, Rick asked for a map, waved his hand above it and then pointed out where we needed to go. He was reading the energies. Foday looked intrigued to see a white man doing things that were in the realm of what a Sierra Leonean traditional healer might do.

The next day Cyril, Rick, and I went to Bo and found that Foday had had a motorcycle accident and broken his arm. He would not be available to help us, thus Cyril was needed, something Rick intuitively knew prior to the trip.

When we visited Foday a few days later in the home of his friend, we saw a wall calendar from 1996 featuring Indiana courthouses. I looked closer, and was startled to see a photo of the courthouse from my hometown, Greensburg, Indiana. I was beside myself with fascination. Rick just shrugged it off as another manifestation of Spirit at work. This was just one of many intriguing experiences that happened over the course of the week.

A calendar in Sierra Leone of Indiana courthouses featuring Hellmich's hometown

Rick, Cyril, and I then went on to meet with local initiators. The first person we met was Timday, a man who had been a famous warrior. He said he had been having dreams of two white people coming on a plane to visit him. Rick confirmed that Timday was the man he had met in meditation. Rick and Timday talked as if they knew each other.

Over the course of the next few days, we met a handful of other initiators, including one woman. Cyril was the perfect guide, as each person knew and respected him. Cyril opened the door for Rick to engage the initiators as a peer, a fellow spiritual healer who could work with energies and the invisible realms. Rick had three ways of looking at the initiators: 1) purity of heart, 2) spiritual wisdom, and 3) spiritual powers. Each person had different levels of each.

Another person we met was Alieu, a very well-known initiator who later stood trial for human rights violations. He had strong spiritual powers, yet abused them. Alieu welcomed and invited us into his sacred hut, a mud hut with white polka dots covering the walls and an altar of various artifacts, including a horse-tailed whip. Through a translator, he proceeded to tell us his story.

When the rebels came to the area, they wanted to capture Alieu because of his spiritual powers. When the village came under attack, Alieu ran into the bush to hide. He tripped and fell, hitting his head. For three days he was unconscious. During that time, spirits of people who were killed during the war came to him, saying he must do something to stop the fighting. They then showed him different leaves and roots in the bush that could be used to create a medicine that would protect warriors from bullets and knives.

When Alieu regained consciousness, he shared his experience with the village elders. They agreed it was important, and that they needed to test it out. Alieu made the medicine, placed it on a termite hill and then someone fired a gun. Nothing happened to the termite hill.

Next, they tried the same process on a dog. Again they fired the gun and nothing happened to the dog.

The moment of truth came — testing it on a man. Timday stepped forward. He was treated with the medicine and the gun was fired. Nothing happened; at least this was what we were told by both Alieu and Timday. These men went on to initiate hundreds of young men who fought to protect their communities.

The stories told by Alieu, Timday, and the other initiators were so far beyond my experience, yet, it was clear they had tremendous power over and respect from their communities. Meanwhile, Rick was having conversations with the initiators that were meeting them right where they were — exploring the invisible dimensions of the conflict.

The initiators confided in Rick that the conflict was happening on other realms of existence, that the initiators and other healers were battling forces and entities, such as disembodied spirits and demonic beings. They said they were tired and that they needed assistance, including help in training the next generation of healers, given that many young people no longer believed in the traditional ways. Rick told me that he was working with the healers in these other dimensions and did quite a bit of "combat" to help them drive out some of the nastier spirits.

After the assessment trip, Rick and his partner, Lisa, wrote a report that was sanitized of phenomena and could easily be given to mainstream organizations. They recommended a network of traditional healers in Sierra Leone and West Africa be established and supported in various ways, including helping them pass on their trade to the next generation. The network also was to have exchange programs with Western scientists and healers, looking at African means of curing diseases.

It was difficult to validate Rick's experiences, or the stories of the initiators. What I do know is that throughout Africa, including Uganda, Sudan, Congo, and elsewhere, there were many stories of African spirituality being used for a wide range of destructive and manipulative activities in conflict situations. The Lord's Resistance Army in Uganda was widely known to use spiritualism, and Joseph Kony, the head of it, openly claimed he was a medium for God. (Others said he was a pawn for a deranged spirit.)

In the yoga tradition, there were strict warnings to stay away from spiritualism — the channeling of disembodied souls — something I encountered in the Afro-Brazilian shamanistic tradition. The yoga tradition described the different levels of existence that souls go through from causal, astral, and physical planes. There were souls on the astral planes that wanted to come back to Earth for selfish and/or destructive reasons and would look for ways of entering the consciousness of people. The Kriya Yoga tradition strongly advised staying away from narcotic drugs, which were commonly used by rebel groups, as they opened a person psychically to disembodied souls from the astral planes. In yoga and Tibetan Buddhism there also were references to *asuras*, very powerful and evil entities that could play havoc in human affairs by using willing or unknowing people as puppets.

While it was hard to discern what was really happening on these different levels of consciousness, it was clear that the proud, beautiful, and powerful African spiritual traditions that were once the foundation of communities were being diluted and/or warped by the onslaught of Western ways and chaotic warfare, something that was later suggested by traditional African healers I would meet in India.

Common Humanity ~ Awakening Compassion

Love and compassion are not luxuries, they are necessities.
Without them, humankind cannot survive.
— His Holiness, the fourteenth Dalai Lama

Susan Collin Marks, the senior vice president at Search for Common Ground and a long-time peacebuilder from South Africa, once reminded me that most conflicts in the world were handled peacefully or at least nonviolently, a fact easily forgotten when traveling to war-torn countries or watching the evening news.

Another core principle Susan taught was that conflict was neither negative nor positive. If approached constructively, conflict could be an engine of growth and transformation. If approached destructively, conflict could cause tremendous suffering.

I reflected on these principles for years, trying to see how they fit with my meditation practice and exposure to other spiritual traditions. I also wondered how spiritual teachings related to the level of violence that took place in Sierra Leone and in other countries, such as Rwanda.

Separation: A Root Cause of Conflict

On one level, yes, conflict was a natural result of differences — differences of opinions, political parties, religions, etc. From a yoga perspective, it went much deeper: conflict was integral to the very fabric of the universe. A senior member of the Kriya Yoga community in Virginia, Gene, helped me understand this idea. An engineer and scientist by training, Gene enjoyed talking about yoga in terms of consciousness and energy, and often quoted yoga texts about the *gunas*, or qualities that make up the physical universe.

The three gunas are: *sattva, tamas,* and *rajas*. Sattva is the positive attribute that influences toward good — truth, purity, and spirituality. Tamas is the negative attribute that influences toward darkness or evil — untruth, inertia, and ignorance. Rajas is the neutral attribute, the activating quality working on sattva to suppress tamas or on tamas to suppress sattva, creating a constant activity and motion.

The concept of the three gunas was consistent with themes and stories told throughout the ages by different cultures about how good and evil were constantly in battle. Gene brought it to the scientific level, highlighting the composition of subatomic particles of energy and consciousness, that the positive and negative are required in order to have movement. He also talked about how the universe was expanding and contracting at the same time; how God had created everything (expansion) yet was drawing it back (contraction). He described this dynamic in terms of laws of gravity and love, the power drawing everything back,to Source, or God,and that ultimately love would prevail. Thus, love was the strongest force in the universe.

People were born with more sattva or tamas qualities depending on where they were in the cycles of death and rebirth, in their own evolution. In yoga, the idea was to use sattva, the positive, to pull out tamas, the negative, and then pull out rajas, the motion. Final liberation comes when throwing out sattva, too — God, or Cosmic Consciousness, was beyond the duality of positive and negative and was changeless, at least as told by the yogis and other saints who had fully merged with Cosmic Consciousness.

Bringing it all down to individuals, a person was born into this realm of duality and then subjected to the positive and negative, and the dynamic between the two. A resulting source of conflict for people was the ego — a soul's identification with the thoughts, emotions, body — and its emotional reactions to the inevitable changes of the phenomenal universe. In this sense, conflict was a natural result of the soul's deluded sense of separation from God, and conflict was an integral part of the spiritual journey.

Tara Brach, the psychologist and Buddhist meditation instructor in the Washington, DC area, explained this sense of separation by saying we identify with our thoughts and emotions, and then believe they are real. This belief starts a process whereby we separate from others and everything around us. With separation comes fear, which in turn gives rise to the "wanting self" (i.e., I want to be happy and avoid suffering). Everyone on the planet has this basic operating software package running — we are all trying to rearrange a constantly changing world to avoid suffering and get what we want.

Conflict is inevitable, as a result. It also is a natural part of the human experience, as we bump into other people trying to avoid suffering and create happiness. A child wants a toy to be happy and will fight with another child to get it, adolescents struggle over identity and romantic relationships, and adults continue the drama with even more involved conflicts. The mere process of surviving — food, water, and shelter — can create conflicts of its own, especially where there is rampant poverty and/or natural disasters. Also, in a warped way, the people who sold AK-47s and RPGs to the rebels in Sierra Leone were doing so to make money so they could be happy.

Meanwhile, humans are governed by spiritual laws, including free will; cause and effect, or karma; and a more subtle law, evolution. Often, free will is usurped by emotions, societal expectations, cultural norms, or subconscious patterns, whether from this life or another one. Still, we slowly learn by trial and error, and by reaping the fruits of our actions, how to choose behaviors that benefit us and those we love. In this way, we evolve.

I kept asking: *how did the horrible violence happen in Sierra Leone, or the genocide in Rwanda* (a country I visited too)? Sure, there could be individual and collective karmic reasons that go back lifetimes, or collective unconscious forces at play, but those realms were beyond my immediate comprehension. All that kept coming up was that, when conflicts are handled destructively, fear becomes the driving force.

In Sierra Leone, it was hard to see the patterns of conflict as there were no clear ethnic, religious, or political divisions. Rather, there was a complete breakdown of civil society after decades of corruption, all while the country was caught in a web of international politics and economics, with opportunistic power struggles by malefactors like Charles Taylor and Foday Sankoh.

It was when I started to travel to Burundi and other countries that I started to see a pattern to many destructive conflicts. It seemed people become polarized, and that extreme positions drove the agendas. The people with the loudest voices often used fear as a tactic to unify their group against "the others." As fear increased, people narrowed their multiple identities (such as father, mother, musician, artist, sports fan, farmer, teacher) down to just one — whether an ethnic group ("I'm a Hutu and you're a Tutsi"), a religious sect ("I'm a Muslim and you're a Jew"), or a political party ("I'm a Republican and you're a Democrat"). Instead of seeing what they had in common, or what connected them, they saw only how they were different and what separated them. (In this sense, it was not so much religion that drove conflict as the human tendency toward dualistic and polarizing patterns of thinking.)

In Rwanda, this dynamic played out to an extreme level. In the early 1990s, radio programs amplified the fear and mistrust by fueling ethnic tension. As fear increased, people became more polarized, thinking in terms of "us and them." Tutsis and Hutu moderates were identified as the problem. To get rid of the problem, the radical Hutus believed it was necessary to get rid of the Tutsis and even the moderate Hutus. As in all destructive conflicts, the aggressors created an atmosphere where it was possible to strike out and kill — first stereotype and then dehumanize "the others." Thus, Tutsis were called dogs, since it was easier to kick a dog than a human. Then, they were called cockroaches, as it was easy to kill a cockroach.

I once heard a Jesuit priest quoted as saying, "I knew evil existed when I saw a wave of killing come over the hill." Just imagining the collective fear that mobilized the killing reminded me of Dean Radin's research on entangled minds, where thoughts from one person were picked up by others, and how they leveraged the collective unconscious. In Rwanda's case, people's thoughts and consciousness formed a mass frenzy of fear, allowing the collective group consciousness to become a channel for universal tamas (negative consciousness) to manifest on the physical plane.

By exploring this dynamic, I was reminded of what Mickey had told me when I was searching for a spiritual path: "You have it set up in dualism already." There was a human tendency to think dualistically — us/them, good/bad, either/or, etc. John Marks, the president of Search for Common Ground, liked to say, "When it is either/or, it is usually both." Dualistic thinking was a part of human consciousness; it stemmed from feeling separate from God/Universe/Spirit. When experiencing intense fear, human consciousness contracts around the small self, the ego, and goes into a survival mode. Dualism was part of the operating software package of humanity and fear and love, and contraction and expansion were some of its chief functionalities.

In yoga, fear dissolves and duality disappears when a person expands his or her consciousness, taps into the soul's essence, and merges with Spirit, at least so I heard from yogis, though I had had only glimpses of such states of consciousness. Search for Common Ground was doing a similar process of helping people expand their identity to see their common humanity with "the other." The idea was to expand the middle — the number of people who did see their commonality — and reduce the power and influence of the extreme positions. While leveraging common humanity was a core part of the work in Sierra Leone, the clearest example of moving beyond polarization and dualistic thinking was in Burundi.

The Voice of Hope

The Search for Common Ground program in Burundi started in 1995, a year after the genocide in Rwanda, and later became the inspiration for the programs in Liberia and Sierra Leone. The first time I went to Burundi, in 2003, I was nervous because the Rwanda genocide was such a hallmark of horror. But I was amazed to walk into the Search office and see a large team of people busily producing radio programs, all committed to working together. One of them was Adrien, a tall, soft-spoken man with deep, compassionate eyes. He was a Hutu; in his youth, Adrien took time off from school only to have his entire class massacred by Tutsis. In the office next to Adrien was Agnes, a powerful, robust Tutsi woman who had lost seventy-nine members of her family to the ethnic violence. Indeed, everyone on the staff had a story of personal loss, yet each was willing to take a stand, together, for a new way of resolving conflict.

Coming from a large family and having seen the impact of war on A.K.'s family and the Contehs, it was both mind- and heart-boggling to imagine working side by side with people from an ethnic group that committed atrocities against loved ones. Adrien, Agnes, and others across Africa became my teachers on the practical ways to embody compassion and love, and how to promote those values across multicultured societies.

Agnes, Adrien, and the other staff members were helping Burundians face their harsh realities together. The idea was to shift the focus from what separates people from their perceived enemies to what they have in common — their common humanity. In one sense, similar to yoga, this good work was moving souls back toward union.

Again, the *common ground approach* was based on an implicit trust in the human spirit. When there is recognition of common humanity, innate spiritual qualities of tolerance, compassion, forgiveness, and love can be awakened. With these positive human qualities present, it is easier for people to shift their mindset. A new consciousness arises, one where they can start to discern that the "others" are not the problem, but rather that they may share similar problems, such as poverty, corruption, or political manipulation. From there, it is possible to face problems together instead of attacking each other. In essence, the approach was similar to a meditation practice: help a person move beyond fear, expand their identity or consciousness, and experience a sense of oneness or connection with other people and nature. This process opens people to their innate spiritual potential and allows them to tap into collective creativity and possibly higher states of consciousness to identify win-win solutions.

In a sense, Adrien, Agnes, and the others were introducing positive, or sattvic, thinking into a tense, negative, tamas, environment. Many motivational speakers and spiritual teachers talk about the power of positive thinking and positive affirmations. Some spiritual teachers say if you want to reduce the power of negative influences, do not battle the negative; rather, increase the positive. Paramahansa Yogananda often said, "Change your thoughts if you wish to change your circumstances."[7] This sounded idealistic when a society was facing potential genocide, but that was exactly what our staff in Burundi were doing — helping an entire society to begin thinking it was possible to peacefully coexist.

It was profoundly inspiring to see these universal principles around consciousness in action to inspire societal shifts.

One of the Search radio programs produced in Burundi was a radio soap opera called *Our Neighbors, Ourselves*. It told the story of a Hutu family living next to a Tutsi family. Like all good soap operas, it was filled with laughter, tragedies, drama, and love affairs. Through more than one thousand episodes, the program helped rehumanize Hutus and Tutsis to each other by highlighting what they had in common. Nearly 90 percent of the population listened to the show. Adrien told me it had become so popular that during a break in programming, a general in the army came to our office and demanded a copy of the next episode! He said his men were anxiously waiting to hear what happened next.

Our Neighbors, Ourselves was creating a story where Hutus and Tutsis were living peacefully side by side, much different from the story that came out of Rwanda in 1994. The core message of *Our Neighbors, Ourselves* was pretty close to: "Love thy neighbor as thyself." Without using any religious references or overtones, Adrien, Agnes, and other staff were modeling behaviors taught by the great spiritual traditions and they helped reweave the social tapestry of their society with compassion and love.

Heroes: What You Appreciate Appreciates

Another radio program in Burundi was called *Pillars of Humanity*, or *Heroes*, which featured the stories of people who had risked their own lives to save the lives of others. One of the radio producers told me people were initially hesitant to tell their own story out of fear of retribution from their own families and communities. But over time, the radio program began to catch on and develop a following.

In this sense, *Heroes* was an example of wherever you place your focus, that was where your energy and consciousness went; or, what you appreciate appreciates. On a deeper level, *Heroes* was tapping into the collective unconscious and awakening the idea of a hero as someone showing compassion. In this sense, it was changing the story behind the predominant story. This program was taking the same concepts of healing and transformation that could be applied by individuals and doing it on a societal level.

On the tenth anniversary of the Rwanda genocide, our team sponsored an historic three-day Heroes Summit, where people from across Burundi, Rwanda, Congo, and even Nigeria gathered to tell their stories of helping one another in times of crises and to discuss their visions for peace and reconciliation. The summit was broadcast live on national radio and was carried by a number of media sources.

There also were Playback Theater performances, where actors recounted the stories of individuals. One story told was about a Hutu woman who had hidden her Tutsi neighbor in a field, protecting her from the Hutu militia. Once the militia passed, her brother tried to escort the woman to safety but they were caught by a Tutsi mob that killed her brother because he was a Hutu. The woman was labeled a traitor by her own family. When she watched the actors tell her story, she sobbed, believing she had done the right thing.

Over the course of three days, many such stories where told, stories of people bringing incredible courage and compassion at great risk to themselves. Their bravery was acknowledged during the summit. A colleague who was the director of the studio was quoted in a report, "There is an inspiring face of Burundi that has been hidden from the world. The Summit has been a celebration of humanity."

Facing Problems Together

A key part of the common ground approach was not to advocate for any sides or positions; rather, it was all about process. In this sense, common ground was sacred space, as it created the opportunity for humanity — stuck in cycles of polarization and duality — to experience itself in new ways and to shift dynamics from spiraling downward into cycles of violence to spiraling upward into new levels of cooperation.

The purpose of *Our Neigbors, Ourselves, Heroes,* and the other radio programs, together with the music festivals and other activities, was to help people reconnect with their common humanity and to awaken qualities such as compassion, tolerance, forgiveness, and even love for once-perceived enemies. There was endless creativity that had been engaged to find culturally appropriate ways to help people rediscover their commonalities.

Once this base of common humanity was established, and innate spiritual, or soul, qualities awakened, then it was possible for people to stand side by side to address shared problems. It is amazing the amount of ingenuity and creativity the human spirit can muster when channeled and focused harmoniously together on problems instead of battling one another. Shared problems, together with the natural laws of free will and cause-and-effect, ultimately force us to come together and evolve as individuals, communities, nations, and a species.

One of the clearest examples of facing problems together came from the youth in Burundi. Like Sierra Leone, Burundi had a problem of young people being manipulated for political violence. When I met some of the Burundi youth, they had already moved beyond their differences and were working on a range of activities, including organizing the music festivals.

How they got together, though, was an amazing story.

A film company had been engaging youth from two ethnic rival groups in Burundi in an attempt to bridge their differences. These Hutu and Tutsi youth groups had been responsible for horrendous violence and even murders. Both sides were given video cameras to document their lives and share their films with the other side. The two groups slowly learned about the plight of the other.

Our staff got involved in facilitating the exchanges, and over time, the youth in the two groups slowly started to see the similarities of their experiences: the loss of loved ones, the pain and the suffering, the poverty, and also the manipulation by political figures to incite fear.

When the leaders of the two groups were finally brought together in person, everything almost fell apart after they discovered that one leader's brother had been killed by the other leader. It took incredible skill to navigate the tensions and to help both to remember their shared experiences of pain and loss.

The dialogues continued, and the two youth groups were brought together to play soccer and to have sleepovers in a camp environment. On the first night, many participants almost did not sleep, out of fear of being killed by the other. Over time, the groups gained trust in each other.

They separated out the problem from "the other." They both were experiencing poverty, lack of economic opportunities, and, more importantly, manipulation by political figures to incite violence. Together they created ideas on how to address shared problems. They all loved comic books, so they co-wrote a book about the realities they faced, expressed through fictional characters.

Through the help of our staff, the comic book was brought to the attention of the Minister of Education, who then worked with the youth to edit, publish, and distribute the book to schools across the country. This was the first of several joint activities by the youth groups.

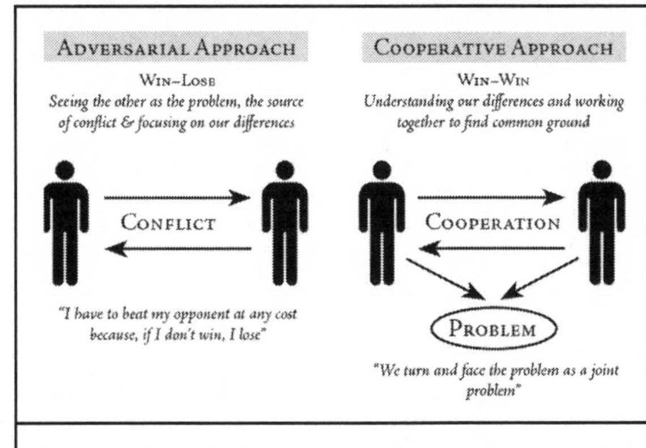

Diagram from the book *Watching the Wind: Conflict Resolution during South Africa's Transition to Democracy* by Susan Collin Marks

In looking at the experience of the Burundian youth and other examples I witnessed across Africa, it was clear that the process of helping people discover common ground began with creating a safe space for people to experience themselves in a new way. It required complete belief in the positive potential of humanity and dogged persistence and ingenuity. Once that space of common ground was created and trust gained, then it was possible to discern the shared problems. When facing those problems together, a collective consciousness would arise — again, thinking about Dean Radin's work on entangled minds and yoga's precept that all thoughts are universal — creating a container for creativity and innovation to arise.

It seemed so simple. Instead of battling each other, face the problems together and free up the energy and resources to tap into higher states of consciousness, far beyond the range of solutions that would come from a state of fear. Or, to paraphrase Einstein:, *you cannot solve problems with the same mindset that created them.*

Thohe complexity of problems facing Burundi, Sierra Leone, and many other countries was daunting, especially given the influences of the global economy. An ongoing challenge for these countries will be to reweave the social tapestries and integrate the best of traditional African cultures with the positive aspects of globalization. A driving force of evolution will be how people deal with conflict, whether they/we narrow our human potential because of fear or expand our possibilities by leveraging our capacity for love and compassion.

Leaky Pipes

Like a plumber with leaky pipes, I had a lot to learn about conflict. Africa once again provided a new lens for me to view myself and life in the United States. One thing was definite: "being spiritual" did not mean I knew how to deal with conflict, nor did people in the United States have it down pat.

Shortly after the 2004 presidential elections in the United States, one of my siblings called to tell me what happened to my mother. My then seven-year-old nephew, Jake, looked to my mother and said, "Grandma, I can't come visit you anymore." When my mother asked why, Jake replied, "Because you are a Democrat," and he walked out the door. My mom, who had raised eleven children and had always advocated for tolerance, cried for hours. Later that day, flowers arrived from her Republican son, apologizing for his son.

After the elections, several siblings and I exchanged heated phone calls. Our behavior was somewhat surprising because most of my family members, including me, were conflict avoiders, a trait we picked up because our parents seldom argued in front of us, plus we needed to work together so we could thrive on limited resources. My siblings and I had little experience with having heated arguments with someone we loved; we found it all emotionally disturbing. (One African colleague went so far as to say I was passive aggressive, which was humbling, given I was working in a conflict tranformation organization.)

I surprised myself, the "common ground" person of the family, in how I enjoyed being self-righteous and adversarial around the *red-blue* divide. However, when my mom mentioned that my *red* sister Sue and *blue* brother Jim, had had terrible arguments and were no longer talking, it struck me that the red-blue divide was similar to conflicts in Africa: polarization based on identification with one group, extreme positions were driving the agenda with anger and fear, and there was a sense of win-lose mentality. The most disturbing similarity was the dehumanizing of "the other" — my brother is blue, my sister is red, so they didn't speak for a few weeks (they eventually got over it).

While the impact of the red-blue divide in my family was upsetting, it was even more distressing to see the toll it was taking on the nation. The reds and blues spent considerable time, energy, and money — literally billions of dollars — battling each other over who was going to have power instead of working together on shared problems. There was political gridlock on major issues that affected millions of Americans and billions of people around the globe.

I often thought: the American bald eagle flies because the right and left wing work together. Democrats and Republicans have a lot to learn from the national symbol.

In an attempt to bring home the lessons from Africa and my yoga practice, I found myself applying the same tools I learned from my colleagues. I started practicing the namaste concept, listening to my siblings as if they mattered, making sure they felt heard. I found the listening relayed both respect, and, more importantly, love.

The impact was immediately noticeable. One sister began to cry when I said, "I disagree with you, and that's okay. We can agree to disagree, and I still love you." She confided that she had been feeling isolated and sad. She had found it easier to avoid political discussions, only to have an underlying tension. She said that our conversation had surprised her. "It was pretty neat, to agree to disagree," she said. "It really helped me feel less alone."

In talking further with my siblings, I began to see that underneath everyone's positions were similar interests: a deep concern about their children's future — would their kids have a safe world, would they have good educations and a prosperous economy? These interests were universal in Africa too.

Fear and anger were leading to the heated discussions in my family and across the country, all fueled by extreme positions on both sides, and exacerbated by radio programs that demonized the other. Some siblings listened to Rush Limbaugh, another brother to ultraliberal radio stations in Northern California, and others to NPR. Where we got our information shaped our political viewpoints, just as radio influenced mindsets across Africa. It is safe to say the radio programs by Search for Common Ground in Africa were more sophisticated in dealing with conflict in a constructive way than the radio and TV programs in the U.S.

From this experience with my family, and with my trips across Africa, I came to see the human tendency toward stereotyping, demonizing, and attacking the other as a very slippery slope. It was an ingrained part of the human software package, one that desperately needed to be upgraded. While the impact in Rwanda was genocide, the impact in America had become increasingly dramatic in political polarization and gridlock. In many ways, the U.S. had a political civil war underway, and the casualties were all Americans and people around the world affected by our policies.

Forgiveness at Home

The African colleagues also inspired me to address a deep-rooted part of my family's history.

My grandmother, my father's mother, had asked if I would say something at her funeral service. Prior to each trip to Africa, my mother would remind me to write a eulogy in case my grandmother died while I was traveling and I could not get back home. However, I never felt moved to write the piece.

The examples of forgiveness that our staff demonstrated did motivate me to write my father about the anger he felt toward his father. I reflected for a long while about how anger hurt the person feeling it and how it rippled to those near him. Trying to put myself in my father's shoes, I wrote a heartfelt letter, encouraging him to pray for help in forgiving his father, suggesting he did not have to condone what his father had done, rather simply let go of carrying the burden of anger and resentment.

A few days after I mailed the letter, a hurricane hit the East Coast of the United States. There was a strange sensation in the air from the approaching storm, coupled with a feeling that my grandmother would be visiting me. I cleaned the house from top to bottom, as she loved a clean house. I then went to my meditation area, lit a candle, and meditated. At that point, I sensed my grandmother was dying, so I started to write her eulogy, and it flowed easily as if she were speaking through me.

She did in fact die around that time in the hospital back in Greensburg, Indiana. My parents, two of my siblings (a brother and a sister), and other family members were with her. My brother Trevor had just arrived a few moments before she passed. One aunt said, "She must have been waiting for you, Trevor," at which point he responded, "Yes, she was waiting for her Republican, Baptist grandson."

Everyone laughed, as my grandmother was a die-hard, so to speak, Democrat and Catholic; and, as she was passing over to the other side, political and religious differences did not matter.

When my father went home following his mother's passing, my letter was waiting for him. He suspected something was up and asked my sister to read it to him. The timing was poignant, as both of his parents were dead. As my sister read the letter to my dad, he cried, nodding his head. It would be days before he and I could speak about it.

The whole family came home for my grandmother's funeral service which was held at St. Mary's Catholic Church. As I looked around the church at the paintings and statues, I thought about the Contehs and the Catholic Church in Masongbo with the mural of rebels shooting a nun. I thought about all the loss that the people of Sierra Leone, Burundi, and elsewhere had experienced at the hand of deadly violence; and, how fortunate we were to have my grandmother die of old age.

The eulogy was well-received, as I tried to say what I imagined my grandmother would want to say. Following the service, my father and I talked about the letter. He agreed it was time to let go of the hurt that his father had caused him.

I could see my father was doing his best, just as the people in Sierra Leone, Burundi, and elsewhere were doing their best with what life was bringing to them.

Section Four

Soul Searching

Ervin Laszlo ~ A Spiritual Crisis

A human being is a part of a whole, called by us "universe," a part limited in time and space. He experiences himself, his thoughts and feelings, as something separated from the rest — a kind of optical delusion of his consciousness. This delusion is a kind of prison for us, restricting us to our personal desires and to affection for a few persons nearest to us. Our task must be to free ourselves from this prison by widening our circles of compassion to embrace all living creatures and the whole of nature in its beauty.
— Albert Einstein

The more I reflected on the parallels between inner and international peace, the more it was clear that conflict was an integral part of life, starting deep within the soul and running through interpersonal, community, national, and international levels. I was intrigued by the insights Kriya Yoga, Rick Levy, Dean Radin, and others were providing into Search's work in transforming consciousness on societal levels and the parallels with quantum physics.

An idea emerged to explore the consciousness around transforming conflict at the various levels. The idea was to bring together the societal conflict transformation practitioners, such as colleagues from Search for Common Ground, with scientists researching consciousness, along with contemplatives, or mystics, of different spiritual traditions. I thought for sure the three broad perspectives could shed insight into a deeper understanding of consciousness and why certain conflict transformation techniques worked and others did not. Likewise, I thought the practitioners could expand the realm of possible applications of the science of yoga and the emerging scientific studies of consciousness.

I wrote a concept paper and pitched it to the president and vice president of Search for Common Ground. They loved the idea and encouraged me to pursue funding. Meanwhile, another senior manager asked me to move from the Africa programs to a new fundraising department so I could provide stories that were needed to inspire investors. One-fourth of my time could be used to seek funding for the new consciousness program.

I was thrilled! This was the closest to realizing the dream of inner and international peace that I had gotten. Plus, telling stories about the work was a natural for me.

There was one major foundation that was an ideal match for the consciousness project. I was thorough in developing relationships with the foundation's staff and board members through the help of friends. The process was moving slowly, so I started to explore different scientists for the dialogue.

One of my favorite scientists was Ervin Laszlo. I heard him speak at an IONS conference; in twenty minutes he summarized ideas I had grappled with for years.

Mr. Lazslo outlined the evolution of humanity over the past thirty thousand years. He showed how humanity advanced in a stair-step fashion. There would be a plateau until enough momentum and pressure would build and force humanity to leap to the next level of consciousness and social complexity, such as from hunter-gather to agriculture. Industrialization was another major step.

With the advent of modern technology — computers, global communications and travel, etc. — the world was rapidly becoming more interconnected and interdependent in a very short time. The global economy had grown in leaps and bounds, creating both economic and environmental problems more complex than our current mindset could handle.

Mr. Lazslo predicted, well before Hurricane Katrina or the 2008 economic recession, that the world could face catastrophic economic and/or environmental disasters. He talked about how the speeding economic system would only further impact the environment and/or cause violent conflicts over resources.

What surprised me was how this scientist said the problems were not technological, but rather a spiritual crisis. He said we had to expand our sense of identity and compassion from family, community, and nation, to identity with and have compassion for all of nature and all of humanity. Einstein had said something similar, which sounded very much like what the Dalai Lama promoted.

As Mr. Lazslo spoke, I kept thinking about going from mud huts in Kagbere and Masongbo, to meeting my first computer...how the fax machine was invented after my Peace Corps service......how diamonds were used to buy weapons from the Ukraine...how Rambo movies were used to train child soldiers...how vast rain forests were clear-cut by Charles Taylor in Liberia and bought on the international markets…how Sierra Leone had gone from a few radio stations to over forty in a decade…how cell phones had spread across Africa.

All of this and more had happened in less than twenty-five years, and that was only one small part of a larger global tapestry. I kept thinking how each of us wants to be happy and wants to avoid suffering…how our individual pursuit of happiness through consumerism, combined with new technologies, was fueling massive consumption and creating collective problems. Meanwhile, within each of us was a soul, a reservoir for deep peace and wisdom that was connected to everything else through a quantum field of consciousness and energy and how that universal field of consciousness could be tapped for innovation to address shared problems.

Lazslo brought it all back to awakening the human spiritual potential. He also said the first step to determining whether we had a breakthrough or breakdown was how we dealt with conflict, as there would need to be cooperation to find solutions to the complex problems.

Shortly after hearing Lazslo speak, I met people from *What Is Enlightenment* magazine. They were holding "salons" in DC where they would discuss the work of Ken Wilbur, Andrew Cohen, and Don Beck. Over time, they began to hold the salons in the Search for Common Ground conference room, after hours, as they liked the atmosphere and the applied nature of Search's work.

The salons would have twenty-five to fifty people sitting in a circle. They would start with an article by Ken Wilbur or Andrew Cohen on integral thinking or *evolutionary consciousness*, that humanity was the product of consciousness evolving and expressing through us. Most people in the dialogues where familiar with Don Beck's work of *Spiral Dynamics*, a sophisticated system of viewing how *memes* (systems of core values or collective intelligences, applicable to both individuals and entire cultures[8]) evolved through a spiraling process. Dealing with conflict constructively and in ways appropriate for each "meme" was a cornerstone of Beck's work.

Invariably the discussions would lead to awareness that the group itself was forming a collective consciousness. This was one of the intentions of the people organizing the salons — they were aware of Dean Radin's research on entangled minds and that groups of people formed a collective consciousness. They were using the methodologies to focus the collective on topics of global significance so the group *container* could inspire new ideas to emerge. This dynamic felt similar to what Search was doing on societal levels, yet here was a group anchored by a spiritual teacher, a philosopher, and a conflict specialist, consciously applying it at home in the United States.

I would meet yet another group exploring the idea of collective consciousness. A former Search colleague introduced me to his mother, Lori Warmington, a cofounder of The Aspen Grove Experiment. Lori and a group of people, including the Christian mystic Father Thomas Keating, had responded to the September 11 tragedies by getting together to have dialogues about how to approach global issues. Many of their discussions explored how to bridge the inner realm of being with the outer realm of doing. It was taking the idea of brainstorming to a whole new level.

The Aspen Grove was a metaphor, as aspen groves are the largest living organism in the world. Aspen trees are all connected by their root system.

When I attended my first Aspen Grove gathering, it was facilitated by Lori and other "stewards," including Michael Abdo who had been a monk for thirty-two years. The group would go into silence, and individuals would speak only when inspired, similar to a Quaker gathering. The stewards were intentional about forming a group consciousness container and encouraging each individual to use whatever method of meditation they knew to tap into higher states of consciousness.

I attended a number of the Aspen gatherings over the years and would come to be one of the stewards. I always was amazed to watch thoughts rise and pass during these gatherings, only to hear someone else express those same thoughts. It was clear that thoughts did pass from person to person, and that the quality of the collective consciousness would influence the type of discussions taking place.

I would later meet yet another person exploring the emerging science of collective consciousness being used to inspire innovation to address critical issues in the corporate and social entrepreneur arenas. Sandra de Castro Buffington was a brilliant public health professional who would later work with Hollywood script writers to insert public health messages into mainstream television programs such as *House M.D., ER, Scrubs,* and others. Sandra was very aware of the power of collective consciousness and had attended a week-long gathering in France where several economic theorists and social entrepreneurs applied similar group consciousness techniques to explore ideas around creating a potential global currency.

Meeting all of these people only further inspired the idea for the consciousness and conflict project. Over the course of a year and a half, I developed a solid list of potential participants. During an annual meditation retreat in California, I relaxed and went into a deeper calm state within, looking forward to the possibility of a new phase of work.

When I returned to Washington, DC, I learned that the foundation program officer had come to Washington to meet with our staff. The consciousness project was pulled off the table because another program needed funding. Just like that, the project was gone.

I sat there, listening to the news, thinking about Mickey, how he said, "It could all be gone tomorrow and it would not matter." I simply experienced what was happening, trying not to judge or be attached, curious what would unfold.

The following months I reflected on what was next. I was not sure. My job was to raise funds. I believed in doing whatever job was in front of me to the best of my abilities because it all came from Spirit. I also wanted Search's work to be better funded, as I knew the positive impact it was having. So, I did everything I could to raise money. Still, my natural tendencies were to see parallels between the process of transforming consciousness on inner and outer levels, across a continuum from inner to international.

India and the Divine Feminine

The Global Peace Initiative of Women

For the next year, I focused intensely on fundraising. The most rewarding part was taking donors to Sierra Leone so they could see our work. During those trips I was able to visit the Contehs and see Josephine and A.K. On one trip, Sanpha knew we were coming to Masongbo and he was waiting for us with a thirty-pound Nile perch he had caught the night before. He was thrilled to present it, fishing lures, a live chicken, and palm wine to me and the visitors.

The Contehs' generosity in the midst of poverty stunned the donors, who were having a hard time reconciling the horrors of war with the love of my friends, and the inspiration of Search's work, let alone being given gifts by people who lived on less than a dollar a day. The visits to Masongbo and Sierra Leone tended to rip people open, exposing them to the wide range of human potential. For me, it was one more sign that Africa had much it could teach the rest of the world.

Even with the trips to Sierra Leone, I grew restless. I wanted to explore the spiritual and consciousness aspects of conflict and peacebuilding. Needing a creative outlet, I started giving presentations on spirituality and conflict, including a talk at IONS in California. James O'Dea had become the president of IONS after leaving Amnesty International in Washington, DC a few years earlier and after a short stint as the head of the SEVA Foundation in Berkeley, California.

James provided an opportunity for me to speak at IONS, as well as share with me the latest research from Dean Radin and other scientists, which only convinced me further of the need to bridge the inner and international. A couple of the IONS staff members, Stephen Dinan and his wife Devaa Haley Mitchell, were especially excited about the presentation. Afterward, they talked about their ambitions of creating a large-scale initiative called Summer of Peace that would look at peacebuilding from the inner to the international levels. They were so turned on by the presentation that they became supporters of Search for Common Ground, and Devaa volunteered for our programs in Democratic Republic of Congo and Angola.

Giving presentations on spirituality and conflict appealed to many audiences, convincing me there was an opportunity to make a bridge between the inner and outer aspects of peacebuilding. Still, I was restless for a more full exploration of the subjects.

On New Year's, I went on an annual meditation retreat in Encinitas, California where I met with one of the monks and explained my situation. He was straight to the point: I needed to take practical steps and to start networking, both for the fundraising and for my dreams around spirituality, consciousness, and peacebuilding.

I so much appreciated the monks and nuns in Self-Realization Fellowship because they were very clear: focus on God and play your role to the best of your ability. They often referred to a quote from Yogananda: "When you realize that life is a joyous battle of duty and at the same time a passing dream, and when you become filled with the joy of making others happy by giving them kindness and peace, in God's eyes your life is a success."[9]

Describing life as a joyous battle was back to the idea of conflict being a natural and integral part of the human experience!

While the monks and nuns encouraged daily meditation, they also provided practical advice on how to apply will power and a positive attitude to overcome life challenges. They very much taught engaged detachment, or, be in the world and not of it.

When I returned to Washington, DC there was a message on the answering machine from the monk telling me to call Dena Merriam, another member of our yoga tradition who lived in New York City. I did as he said and, a few weeks later, met with Dena in person.

Dena had started a nonprofit organization called the Global Peace Initiative of Women. It came about because, in 2000, the United Nations had gathered spiritual leaders from around the world. There were hundreds of participants, yet only a few women, at the international event. Dena and a few of the women gathered over lunch and decided there was a need to have women better represented in global matters of spirituality; thus, they formed the Global Peace Initiative of Women.

Dena and I hit it off as we both had a deep Kriya Yoga meditation practice and were drawn to bringing spiritual wisdom into the peacebuilding arena. Dena wanted the contemplatives, or mystics, of each tradition, the people who had profound inner realization, to participate more fully in peacebuilding dialogues and activities. She was not interested in interfaith dialogues that compared dogmas. We agreed in this area as I had little to no interest in dogma, as it only pertained to the mental plane, which was subject to duality and interpretations. Both of us saw a need for the deeper wisdom of all the spiritual traditions to be more present in addressing global issues.

Dena invited me to a conference that was taking place in a few weeks from that time in Jaipur, India. As soon as I decided to go on the trip to India, I could feel a burning sensation in my spine. One friend, another yogi who had traveled to India several times, simply laughed. He said, "Ah, the India burn! I felt it every time before a trip to India. It was usually a sign that Mother was going to clean me out. I hope you are ready for it."

Little did I know that this was the first of two trips to India that year and that they would start a period of deep purification.

Making Way for the Divine Feminine

Going to India was like a homecoming, especially given the theme of the conference: *Making Way for the Divine Feminine: For the Benefit of the World Community.*

It was such a rich experience to be surrounded by a couple hundred people from all different faiths — Hindu, Buddhist, Christian, Islam, Jewish, and indigenous traditions — all gathered because of a concern about the global situation and wanting to bring in more qualities of the human spirit to address serious issues. People had traveled from across Africa, Asia, the Middle East, Europe, Australia, South America, and North America.

In a statement to the conference participants, H.H. the Dalai Lama wrote: "... In the twenty-first century, when the world is so much more interdependent, compassion and warmheartedness are required. Women are more of this nature, while men are more brutal — for example I believe all butchers are men. In order to create a genuine, peaceful society we need more warmheartedness so the role of women is important...." I thought Frances Fortune, Search's director in Sierra Leone, ßwould agree with His Holiness.

The conference aimed to bridge spiritual ideals with the practical process of peacebuilding, as there were speakers who were seasoned peacebuilders and social activists from areas like Iraq, Afghanistan, Israel and Palestine, Kenya, and many other countries affected by deadly conflict. There also was a strong emphasis on the role of youth in bringing forth such feminine qualities and in creating an intergenerational dialogue between youth and elders. At times there was a clear gap between some spiritual leaders and youth, as the youth claimed the spiritual language and traditions did not translate into their daily lives.

At the event there were some well-known spiritual figures, including H.H. Sri Mata Amritanandamayi Devi, the hugging saint. Amma, as she was affectionately called, traveled the world speaking to thousands of people at a time and then hugged each and every person that would line up. It was common for people to wait six to eight hours to receive a hug, and yet Amma never tired. She was connected to an inexhaustible source of love.

Global Peace Initiative of Women

Amma at the Global Peace Initiative of Women in Jaipur, India

Amma was believed to be an incarnation of the Divine Mother, and I naturally was drawn to her. She had dozens of devotees, all dressed in white or ocher, who were there with her at the conference, attending to her every need. The devotees and other people swarmed around Amma like bees to honey. Her magnetism was powerful as she was clearly "plugged in" to a source of loving conscious energy.

Amma's presentation was in Hindi and translated into English. Her words were similar to the Dalai Lama's, in that they were simple and profound. She talked about the growing global environmental crisis being a manifestation of greed, and that people needed to go inward, to reconnect with their own divine essence. She was eloquent about the need to bring more of the divine feminine qualities of love, compassion, nurturing, and community into action in the world. As she spoke, it was easy to feel that she was deeply attuned with a spiritual essence, that she embodied those divine qualities.

Amma's words were backed up by a tireless dedication to serving people around the world through numerous volunteering initiatives, including building and servicing health centers and feeding and sheltering the homeless. She channeled all of her energy and the money that came in from devotees toward spreading her messages of love, teaching yoga techniques, and doing volunteer service.

As Amma was leaving, people gathered around her to shake her hand or receive a hug. I later met a woman who received a hug from Amma that day. She said, "I have never experienced anything like it before. I was skeptical about Amma or other yogis being an embodiment of higher consciousness. As soon as I thought this, Amma looked at me, moved people to the side and then hugged me. I was filled with a surging energy of love that pulsated through me for days."

That potent magnetism was something I experienced every time I went on a meditation retreat in California where Yogananda had lived. Yogis and other people who are spiritually advanced carry a tremendous amount of powerful conscious energy that permeates around them and leaves an impression where they had lived or visited. That conscious energy has the same quality of vibration that exists in everyone's souls and serves to awaken an awareness in people that stirs them to seek it for themselves.

What was nice about the conference in Jaipur was that the *presence* of holy people saturated the gathering and the discussions. There was a heightened level of energy and consciousness. The challenge was to translate the ideas of the various traditions into meaningful actions to address global needs. There was a daunting gap between perceived global crisis — climate change, economic challenges, and geopolitical tensions, including wars in Iraq and Afghanistan — and the innate wisdom and power of the human soul that could be used to address the root causes of human suffering.

I participated on two panels, including one about media and peacebuilding. People were intrigued how Search for Common Ground's work with radio and TV encouraged people to rediscover their common humanity and to awaken qualities such as compassion and tolerance, qualities consistent with the feminine principles spoken about by Amma and other speakers. On the panel was Pooran Pandey from the Times of India Foundation, which published a column on mind-body health. Pooran was a thoughtful and wise person with a deep sense of spiritual devotion and call to service. Pooran's humility hid his lifetime of accomplishments in helping thousands of people in India who were living in poverty. I later introduced Pooran to Rick Levy via email, which would result in yet another trip to India a few months later.

The other panel on which I participated was on Africa. The night before this session, I had a clear dream that Africa's ancestors were angry, that the spiritual traditions were no longer respected or practiced. On the panel was a traditional healer from South Africa. She was adamant that the traditional African spiritual ways had been lost and, as a result, there was an identity crisis, one where the African roots were disconnected from their source. She claimed that many of the African spiritual ways were diluted and, in some cases, were being used for negative purposes.

As she spoke, I could see a young man from Sudan nodding his head in agreement. I later talked with him and learned that many combatants in Sudan used witchcraft and spiritual powers in combat. It seemed the use of traditional African spiritual ways in conflicts was common in many parts of Africa.

It was interesting to hear the perspectives from the African healer and to think about the important role of spiritual traditions in grounding individuals and entire societies in ways authentic for them. What was nice about the conference was that there was respect for each of the different traditions and a general consensus that each tradition needed to bring its wisdom forward. I did not know what that meant for Africa and its years of colonialism, missionaries, and adulterated spiritual traditions. Meanwhile, there we were in India, a country with spiritual traditions going back thousands of years, including a Kriya Yoga lineage that was scientific in nature and was taking me deeper into my Christian tradition and own self awareness.

Nepal and Kali ~ Increase Positive to Overcome Negative

On the flight home from India, I came down with a horrible case of dysentery and spent much of the time in the bathroom. I lost nearly ten pounds over a couple days.

A few days after getting home, my father had a heart attack, which shocked my family, as my parents had been healthy prior to that point. Six siblings and their children were with my parents within hours. There were so many people home that I was advised to wait and to spread out the love and support.

I was supposed to fly to Nepal a week later for a trip with donors to see our work there. I debated whether to go. My family discussed it and encouraged me to go, because canceling the trip would send a message to my father that his case was bad.

Before boarding a flight at JFK airport in New York, I called my mother and father. They were at a hospital in Indianapolis. I pictured my mother, next to my father. They had been married since the age of seventeen and had lived in Greensburg, Indiana all their lives but for a few months. My mother and father were both scared, and so were the rest of the family and me.

My father needed to have open-heart surgery for a quadruple bypass. The operation could be any day. When he got on the phone, his voice was weak. He kept saying, "I love you, have a good trip." I broke into tears. My heart was being ripped open.

The flight was tough, as I was thinking about my mother and father. I kept thinking about a story my brother had told me. When my father had the heart attack, he and my mother were out walking. He could not get back into the car, so my mom called my sister-in-law. She called 911.

The people on the fire department rescue team that responded knew my parents because the fire station was a few houses from my parent's home. My mother and father routinely brought cookies and other baked treats to the fire station every holiday. The emergency squad took incredible care of both my father and mother, telling my mother not to worry about anything, that they would even take care of their car. A few days later, while my father was in the hospital, my mother baked cookies and took them to the fire department.

There was something about the small-town human connection that touched me and reminded me of Amma's talk about love, compassion, nurturing, and community. It reminded me of the love and connection I felt in Kagbere and Masongbo. It was the human connection that opened my heart and seemed to be a pivotal part of awakening the soul in conflict situations I had seen across Africa.

During a layover in Dubai, a friend and donor, a fellow Indiana Hoosier, and I took a taxi around to see the incredible skyscrapers. It was amazing to see all the wealth, a result of the oil money flowing from around the world to the Middle East. I thought about my dad and his small pickup truck, buying gas in rural Indiana. I thought about Sierra Leone and the frequent fuel shortages that happened when the government did not have enough money to pay for a shipment of fuel. Our trip to Nepal almost had been cancelled because of a national fuel shortage too. The world really was so interconnected, and the expression of that interdependency was a massive transfer of wealth that was being spent on fabulous, artistic skyscrapers and man-made islands in exotic shapes. It seemed ridiculous to have monuments to wealth at the expense of millions if not billions of people, yet this was a human practice throughout the ages.

On to Nepal we went. We arrived in Kathmandu in the evening. I was exhausted and went to bed early.

The dreams were very vivid. I was being attacked by a dark, shadowing man. He was climbing over a rooftop to get to me. I prayed deeply for God and my guru to intervene and raised my hands to send energy toward the person. That did not stop him.

He threw a live chicken at me, which I immediately used to make a sacrifice. A beautiful woman then appeared. She looked at me and said, "The way you overcome the negative is by increasing the positive." She then raised her hands and blasted the man with an immense amount of light and love. He disappeared.

I awoke buzzed, completely in bliss. The sadness had dissipated and I knew my father would be okay, no matter what happened. A small group of us took a walk around Kathmandu with our local guide, Sanjaya, the husband of our country director, Serena. Sanjaya was by far the sweetest and most gentle man I had ever met, as he took great care of each person.

Sanjaya and I quickly developed a friendship and a sense of brotherhood rooted in an appreciation for the subtle and nurturing qualities of the human spirit.

As Sanjaya took us around Kathmandu, I felt drunk from the dream. I loved that the streets were filled with images of the Divine Mother and that people openly paid homage at different shrines.

We came to a temple to the Goddess Kali. The temple felt so familiar. I asked Sanjaya if there were ever chickens sacrificed to Kali. He smiled and said, "Yes, how did you know?" I felt a wave of love flow through me and just smiled.

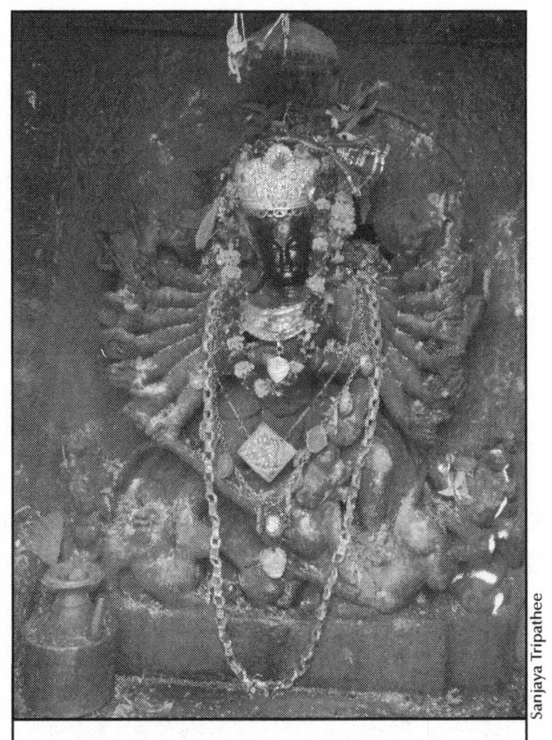

Sanjaya Tripathee

Goddess Kali/ Bhagawati in Nepal

The strong spiritual vibrations continued throughout the two-week trip. There were many times I felt I was in love and did not know who or what I was in love with. I so welcomed having the strong feminine spiritual presence again; it had been a couple years since I had experienced Her presence so directly.

I later learned that in a yoga/meditation practice, there often can be gifts early on, to inspire the yogi to go deeper into a practice. Once established in a daily practice, the gifts and experiences can disappear for long periods, leaving the yogi with the choice of continuing the hard work through difficult periods or to go back to his/her worldly habits and interests in human distractions.

Feeling Mother's presence in Nepal was like coming to an oasis during a long dry journey. It also provided a special lens for viewing the peacebuilding work in Nepal.

Manifesting the Divine Feminine

Our group of ten was composed of people from the United States, England, and Denmark. We were there to learn firsthand about how Nepal was emerging out of an eleven-year civil war and was on the brink of a new democracy. We were to meet with people who were partnering with our youth programs and to see how those programs were impacting their lives.

I loved that people in Nepal greeted each other with "namaste" and then bowed with folded hands! I felt so at home!

We flew from Kathmandu on Buddha Air to the eastern part of the country. I was so tickled that the pilot was a woman named Yasodhara, the same name as the Buddha's wife. We then traveled for two days by four-wheel drive vehicles to a small, remote part of Nepal in the foothills of the Himalayan Mountains. The views were stunning!

A highlight of the trip was when we met with representatives of a district youth peace network to learn about their efforts in promoting peace in Nepal. We hiked for hours into the hills to a small village. Under a tree, near a schoolhouse, over twenty young people were waiting for us, having walked for hours from nearby villages.

After brief introductions, I asked if any of the youth listened to the radio soap opera *Naaya Baato, Naaya Paila* (*New Path, New Footprints*). The radio program, written by Nepali youth and produced by Search for Common Ground and a partner organization Antenna Foundation Nepal (www.afn.org.np), was about youth in a fictional village in Nepal's hills who come together from across dividing lines to find positive ways of contributing to the peace process.

Immediately after I asked the question, several of the youth became animated, speaking out. One voice emerged from the rest, a fifteen-year-old girl named Pushpa, the vice president of the youth network. Pushpa said she listened to the program regularly, and that her favorite character was Kamala, a high-caste girl with a disability. Even though Kamala sometimes made mistakes, she always kept looking for ways to bridge divides in her community.

Leaning close to Pushpa was another girl, Sushila, treasurer of the network. There was clearly a deep friendship between the two, as they were affectionate with one another and talked quietly between themselves. Sushila jumped in by adding that the soap opera had shown how girls could play a positive role in their communities and that it was okay for her and her friends to do activities outside of the house.

Like other girls in the youth club, Sushila's parents did not want her to be away from the house unattended. However, over time, Sushila and the other youth demonstrated that participation in the youth club was a thing to be proud of and that they contributed to the community. One example Pushpa and Sushila gave was that their club took the initiative to repair a three-kilometer section of road leading to the village school. Like Kamala in the radio program, they did not wait for the government or other people to do what was needed. When the adults saw the youth take the lead, they joined in to help too. Thus, Pushpa said, "Youth and adults can work together, just like a tree: the youth are the branches and the adults the roots," the first of many tree metaphors she would use in the conversation.

When asked what it was like to have boys and girls working together, Pushpa, without pausing simply referred to the wheels of a cart. "If they do not move together, they will not achieve." She then smiled and giggled, reminding us she was a young girl.

Even though Pushpa was lighthearted with us, I later learned that she, like many youth in Nepal, had overcome tremendous adversity during the war. Her younger brother had found a pipe bomb which exploded, leaving him seriously wounded. When Pushpa participated in a Search workshop in 2007, she and other youth had an opportunity to talk openly about their hardships. One exercise they did was to give voice to Peace, Truth, Justice, and Mercy. When asked to speak on behalf of Mercy, Pushpa put aside her personal anger and pain by saying, "There must be Mercy for all sides; otherwise the peace will not last. We have to see the light in everyone, to give space for their light to shine."

In Nepal, *Naaya Baato, Naaya Paila* had a 27 percent national listenership rate after two years of broadcasts, according to a BBC survey, which was quite high given an abundance of media in Nepal. It was the most-listened-to radio program in the country, second only to a BBC program. Search reinforced the messages in the soap opera through public service announcements on radio and through an extensive youth leadership program that involved training events and opportunities for youth to network with one another and to design community peacebuilding projects.

One of the challenges facing Nepal was the reintegration of children back into their communities after they had participated in violent conflict. One activity Search specifically designed to address the issue of reintegration was the use of *dohiris*, traditional live drama performances where an improvised dialogue takes place through singing. Search conducted a dohiri workshop for youth and adults to explore the issues around reintegrating youth combatants. The participants created and performed dohiris in their communities that were intergenerational conversations between fictional parents and their children returning from service in armed forces. Performed in villages across Nepal, these dohiris attracted audiences anywhere from two to six thousand people and were broadcast live on the radio.

In one dohiri, which was completely improvised, three thousand villagers watched spellbound as a group of young women, some of them former child soldiers, sang the part of sisters who had gone to war, and the group of boys sang the verses of a brother, pleading with his sister to come back to her community, reminding her she was still loved. In the audience, contrary to Nepali culture, people openly wept.

Sushila (left) and Pushpa (right), making way for the feminine in Nepal.

Pushpa and Sushila said the dohiris used the conversational singing style to give voice to real concerns of people in the villages. When a dohiri they participated in resulted in the reunion of the family members, Pushpa said the village erupted into applause. Michael Shipler, the director of programs for Search in Nepal, said, "When people come together across dividing lines and find profound commonalities, they also find elation." There was something about the human spirit that responded to reconciliation from a place deep in the heart. It was an awakening of the soul. I had seen this time and time again across Africa.

Here was yet another example of it being possible to help people access their positive human qualities of love, compassion, tolerance, and forgiveness; and that a natural result of reconciliation was joy and warmheartedness. The methods for inspiring these qualities were free of any religious or spiritual traditions.

Two clear examples of this human potential were Pushpa and Sushila. One of the major issues confronting youth in Nepal was overcoming the effects of the caste system. When asked about this issue, Pushpa reached out and put her arm around Sushila. She said, "I am from the Brahmin (high) caste and my friend, Sushila, is a Dalit. We are not to associate with one another. This is a tradition that is no longer useful. Traditions, like all trees, must decompose and give space to new trees."

A boy spoke up, "The roots will rot eventually, naturally."

"No!" said Pushpa, "The roots of the caste system are made of plastic and they must be burned out!"

Sushila smiled, laughed and agreed.

As Pushpa and Sushila spoke, it was clear they were embodying and giving expression to profound feminine spiritual wisdom. I was awestruck, as many of Pushpa's words echoed those of the Dalai Lama, in his letter to the Jaipur conference, and of Amma and the other spiritual leaders at Jaipur. Yet Pushpa and Sushila delivered their messages with such joy and celebration, free of any religious overtone. Pushpa and Sushila, along with thousands of other youths, were making way for the Divine Feminine in Nepal.

The Divine Feminine was and is a part of all humanity, it is a part of our very soul essence, it is a part of the quantum field of energy and consciousness, and it was arising and giving expression. It was the Divine Feminine that was expressing itself through the resilience of people in Sierra Leone, Liberia, Burundi, and other countries coming out of war. I like to think that the work of Search for Common Ground, my colleagues, and other peacebuilders were simply instruments of Her, that She was manifesting through all of us.

Kali ~ Burning Off Dross

You cannot make steel until you have made the iron white-hot in fire.
It is not meant for harm. Trouble and disease have a lesson for us.
Our painful experiences are not meant to destroy us,
but to burn out our dross, to hurry us back Home.
No one is more anxious for our release than God.[10]
— Paramahansa Yogananda

The trip to Nepal was yet another inspiring affirmation that it was possible to facilitate helping people bring out the best of humanity, their sattvic positive qualities, even in difficult situations. It gave me a profound sense of hope for humanity that a new level of consciousness was in fact emerging and giving expression to positive aspects of humanity and the Divine Feminine in unique ways through individuals and organizations around the world.

The inner dimension of peacebuilding took an unexpected turn, however, for me. Through another trip to India, I would learn firsthand about the aspect of Kali as the destroyer. In my case, as in many spiritual aspirants' lives, She would burn away parts of my consciousness that were keeping me from merging more fully with my own soul and Her.

The lessons came via a tragic ending of a romantic relationship. In the past, romantic relationships had been challenging teachers for me, as my unconscious fear of loss of love influenced my dynamics in them. After years of work on the "story behind the story," I thought I had gotten to the place where I was ready for a loving relationship with a partner.

I had been dating Carrie, a brilliant and beautiful woman who also had been a Peace Corps Volunteer in Africa. Even though she did not practice yoga or meditation, we shared a love for the outdoors and international work. There was an ominous sign from day one, as she had created the intention of meeting her soulmate by the last day of September. We were introduced by a mutual friend and exchanged phone calls. Lo and behold, we finally met in person on September 30. I arrived at her door with a white rose, having come from a yoga ceremony, not knowing about her soulmate wish.

The relationship started as a friendship and slowly evolved over months. She was reluctant to open her heart, largely because of a recent engagement to be married that ended badly and because she had lost her parents in a tragic car accident several years earlier. Also, I was not exactly what she imagined her soulmate would be like. I persisted, as I was genuinely attracted to her, and I was optimistic that her heart would heal and open. Heck, any woman who wanted to build and live in a mud hut in the States after returning from the Peace Corps had my attention — not that she'd actually done it, yet!

Right when Carrie and I were starting to get closer, Rick Levy invited me to attend a trip to India to meet with people at *The Times of India*. Going on the trip were Dena Merriam and Rick's partner Lisa, all of us from the same Kriya Yoga tradition. It was going to be a combination of business trip and spiritual pilgrimage, thus it did not make sense for Carrie to join us.

As soon as I said yes to the trip, the India burn started again in my spine. This time, however, it was stronger. Something was happening.

The day before the trip, Carrie emotionally pulled back, which started an emotional reaction in me. She then chose to cut off communication for most of the trip, which I imagined was her way of protecting herself from yet another man possibly leaving her.

During the trip, Rick and *The Times of India* agreed to publish a series of his books. They were intrigued that a Western scientist and yogi was coming back to India with wisdom gained through yoga. The staff at *The Times of India* were concerned that the young people in India were caught up in consumerism and chasing material happiness at all costs, creating a range of individual, social, and environmental issues while leaving India's rich spiritual wisdom and heritage behind. Rick's credentials as a psychologist from a scientific family boded well for catching the attention of readers in India. It was interesting to see the *The Times of India* staff having similar concerns that had propelled me to look at peace from the inner to international levels and that were inspiring Dena to bring together contemplatives from different traditions.

After several days with *The Times of India* at various functions, Lisa, Dena, and I headed out for Rishikesh in the foothills of the Himalayas. The area was renowned for having been the home to many self-realized saints throughout the centuries. On the first night in Rishikesh, we were staying at the Parmarth Niketan Ashram next to the Ganges River. Swami Chidananda Saraswati was active in the Global Peace Initiative of Women's dialogues, including ones that brought together India's yogis with Pakistan's Sufi masters. Swami shared Dena's interest in bringing the inner science and wisdom of peace from various mystical traditions into more prominent roles in outer peacebuilding.

The room I stayed in at the ashram had a window overlooking the Ganges. The sound of the river was so loud, and the energy of the ashram so strong, it was hard to sleep. I listened to the rapids, thinking about all the people who had worshipped along the banks of the sacred river for thousands of years. I was surprised when my cell phone rang and to hear Carrie's voice. She was stunned to hear me answer, thinking she would leave a message. We had a brief and enjoyable conversation, not knowing that the next day would change both of our lives.

Hellmich and Rick Levy on the Ganges River near Rishikesh, India

The next morning, Rick, Lisa, Dena, and I visited the cave of Vasishta, the guru of Rama who had lived over three thousand years ago. I was amazed that there was a small ashram near the cave and that several swamis in ocher-colored garb were tending to the cave, conducting rituals, and chanting at the cave's entrance. It boggled my mind that a sacred site could be revered and tended to for over 3,000 years. I had never encountered anything like it in my travels across Africa or the U.S.

The power of a living tradition with roots so deep was energetically palatable. While in the cave, I could feel a potent and peaceful vibration. We meditated for about an hour together. When I came out, I walked to the Ganges River feeling intoxicated. I stripped to my underwear and then bathed in the Ganges for the first time this life. It was strange, as I felt an age-old desire fulfilled — one that I did not even know I had! It felt like I had been baptized in a Christian Yogi way.

Meanwhile, the peaceful experience was coupled with a growing pain in my heart. I did not know what was happening, and figured it was associated with Carrie.

After our visit to the cave of Vasishta, we attended an *aarti* — a traditional Hindu ceremony. This aarti was performed on the banks of the Ganges River under a large statue of Lord Shiva. Swami Chidananda Saraswati led the ceremony, which was attended by several hundred people. Each of us had a banana-leaf raft with candles that we lit as a form of devotion to God and then placed in the river. Just after setting his raft afloat, Rick proposed to Lisa with a ring he had purchased in the Rishikesh market. It was a romantic moment, and I was touched to be the first to congratulate them.

The next morning we had one more dip in the Ganges and then flew back to Delhi, where Rick, Lisa, and I said goodbye to Dena and then flew to Calcutta. We arrived late at night, and our taxi drove wildly on the wrong side of the highway as there was no traffic. We were relieved when we arrived at the Yogoda Satsanga Society (the Indian counterpart to Self-Realization Fellowship) ashram in neighboring Dakshineswar. Over the next couple days we stayed in the ashram while making day trips to visit holy sites where Yogananda and his guru, Sri Yukteswar, had visited or lived, places that were very special in our yoga tradition and that also had strong energetic vibrations. The entire time I felt a mix of both deep peace and a growing anguish in the heart.

In Dakshineswar we took rickshaw carriages to the Kali Temple, a place where several Indian saints, including Yogananda and Sri Ramakrishna, had seen the Divine Mother take physical form. The vibrations were once again strong. Rick and Lisa were beside themselves with joy, especially Rick, as he had been practicing Kriya Yoga and reading about these sites for over thirty years. Rick's deep devotion and excitement reminded me of my grandmother when she went to Medjugorje to visit the site where Mother Mary had appeared.

Hellmich at the Kali Temple in Dakshineswar, India

At the Kali Temple, Rick immediately asked to speak to the groundskeeper, to whom he explained we had traveled from America and were yoga devotees. It was like magic to watch the groundskeeper rise up and then take us behind the scenes to the most sacred statue of Kali. The priests attending to the image offered us a special blessing with holy water, this time pouring water over our heads and into our mouths while we bowed at the feet of the holy image. An overwhelming feeling of love flooded each of us as tears streamed down our faces.

The Beloved Mother's image as Kali was terrifying and beautiful: black with a necklace of skulls, her tongue protruded outward and she had multiple arms, with one holding a sword. She looked like a fierce warrior and was revered for Her ability to destroy delusion from a devotee's consciousness.

As we left the temple, Lisa found an opportunity to repay Rick and me for the endless puns we had told her while traveling together. Lisa dropped the mother of all puns. "Look, it's the ferry ghat Mother," she said, pointing to a ferry landing at the temple's ghat on the banks of the Ganges River. Rick and I agreed her pun had topped all our silly humor, including Rick's mentioning of taxi drivers in Delhi that were playing hide and "Sikh."

We then loaded into the ferry and traveled to a temple to Sri Ramakrishna, another favorite yogi for Rick. Once again I was touched by the hundreds of people who were lining up in the temple to offer prayers and flowers. The level of love and devotion was impressive and moving.

The next day we visited places where Yogananda had lived or visited, including the attic in his family's house where he had meditated as a child. This attic room was especially inspiring for me, as when Yogananda had lost his mother, he went into such a state of despair that he prayed endlessly, demanding the Divine Mother's comfort. With the aid of a teacher, and through long hours of meditation and prayer, the Divine Mother appeared to him, assuring him that She was in fact always with him and that it had been Her in the form of countless human mothers over many lifetimes, ever watching over him.

This story of humility and deep love and faith had often moved me as my guru, too, was human, that the pain of tragic loss had driven him to the feet of the Beloved. As we meditated in the room, I offered my own prayers to Divine Mother, asking that She help me rise above the pain and suffering I had encountered over the years, that I too be comforted once and for all with the deep assurance of Her love. I also prayed for all my loved ones across Africa and beyond.

I did not realize that my prayers would be answered in part by giving me the opportunity to burn away layers of fears that had plagued me for lifetimes.

In hindsight, I could see how the strong spiritual vibrations at the holy sites in India were opening me on new levels, taking me ever deeper into a tradition that was slowly transforming my consciousness. This was one aspect of the spiritual journey that constantly surprised me: going deeper and being exposed to more and more positive energies and consciousness would shake loose parts of my own consciousness that were at a negative and lower vibration. The powerful positive energies also served as a counterbalance to the more dense and painful fears that were starting to rise, keeping true to a world of duality.

When I returned to the U.S., I learned that Carrie's ex-boyfriend and former fiancé had committed suicide on the day we were at the cave of Vasishta in Rishikesh. As I was being baptized in the Ganges, Carrie was losing a former lover and being thrown into the fires of a terrible experience.

When I saw Carrie, she was in complete shock, depressed and numb. Over the next few months, she became more withdrawn, refusing to seek any professional help and choosing to deal with the loss by herself. The romantic relationship was over, yet I tried to be a supportive friend, as there was no way I would leave a loved one during a time of need. I tried to maintain some boundaries, but the psychic and energetic connection was strong. I was being triggered with the same frequency of fears and began acting out from a place of sadness and neediness.

One thing I had learned over the years was that when I was close to someone or a situation with a fear or desire that also existed in me, that the seeds in me would resonate and become activated. It was all about energy and frequency of vibration. It was probably similar to group dynamics in situations where the collective unconscious is activated.

I was connected with Carrie, and she was living through hell. Not only was she experiencing the grief and anguish of a former lover killing himself — guilt, anger, rage, sadness — she was also dealing with all the unresolved emotions of the previous relationship that had ended badly and of the tragic loss of her parents, etc. And, as the yoga tradition had taught me and in my direct experience working with Rick, there were often karmic seeds from past lives that also kick in.

To top off all of the grief associated with and triggered by Carrie, my loving cat, Bob Cat, died from accidental poisoning, having eaten something in the neighborhood. My housemate and friend Kristen and I cried as we laid Bob Cat to rest in the Earth, at the feet of a Kwan Yin statue in the backyard. I said a prayer to Divine Mother, thanking her for the love from Bob Cat and asked Her to guide his soul to his next incarnation. As I placed a candle on the grave, it lit by itself before I even struck a match. Kristen and I looked at each other, aware of a blessing in the midst of all the pain, a reminder that even in darkest times there is light.

Releasing Sanskaras

Besides the brief glimpse of Mother's love at the grave of Bob Cat, I was in excruciating pain. On an intellectual level, I understood why. Mickey often had talked about *sanskaras,* or karmic seeds, being energetic patterns in and around a person. A sanskara is formed when a person has an experience and then becomes attached to or tries to push away the experience instead of letting it pass through; that is, the energy gets stuck in the person's energy field. It stays there with a particular frequency and vibration swirling in and around the person. (For people like Rick, who can see the colors of auras, it was possible to read the karmic tendencies in others.) A sanskara magnetically draws to a person, through patterns of thinking and acting, situations of the same vibration over and over again, until the sanskara(s) are released.

When a sanskara gets hit, or activated, by a situation, a person will have internal sensations rise up, similar to those experienced when the sanskara initially occurred. If a person has stacked up many such sanskaras on top of each other, then they become stronger and stronger. When one is activated, they all come flying up, and suddenly a person is reacting out of proportion to the stimulus, though not really sure why. Some sanskaras are pretty universal, such as loss of loved ones, and can be triggered by a sad movie or, as in the case of the societal healing in Sierra Leone, through a soap opera.

As Mickey would say, "When stuff gets hit and starts to come up, it is a wonderful opportunity to release the old stored-up sanskaras. Celebrate!" Celebrate is not what I had in mind; I just wanted out of pain.

The first rule in letting go of the old energies was not to blame the person or situation that triggered it. Blaming keeps a person stuck in the pattern and from taking responsibility. The way releasing happens is that the old energies start to express themselves as thoughts, emotions, and physical reactions. I knew if I blamed Carrie or her ex-lover, the triggers, I would engage in reactive thoughts and emotions, giving them more energy; thereby strengthening the sanskaras and missing the opportunity to release them. If I could simply relax and witness the triggered reactions, then the energies would dissipate. Mickey would say, "Learn to do nothing." Buddhists might say: *watch all sensations and thoughts rise and pass away, staying even-minded.* It was so much easier said than done.

Mickey also warned not to listen to the mind, as it would drive a person insane, trying to figure out a way out of the pain when in fact the burning was a necessary part of a spiritual process. Instead of fighting the burning, Mickey would encourage people at the Temple of the Universe to "assume the position" — lie on the floor, chest lifted, arms to the side, head arched back and pray "Mother, do with me what you will." I frequently assumed the position, yet, to be honest, in an attempt to get out of pain quicker than to joyfully participate in a sacred process of purification.

Some of my close yoga friends and I called this process "BBQ," and often joked about being slow-roasted over an open fire. It was a passage by fire of a spiritual journey. Rick liked to call it "burning off the dross," dross being karmic seeds in the subconscious and conscious minds that keep a person from fully identifying with his/her individual superconsciousness, also known as the soul or true Self.

Eckhart Tolle described another way to think of it — Carrie's pain body activated my pain body. Plus, there was a good chance I was taking on some of her pain body, or karma, in an unconscious attempt to be helpful. She was connected to the guy who killed himself, which did not help matters. The whole situation was a double whammy. In hindsight, it was all perfect, and only later could I see and be grateful for how it was cleaning me out of age-old fears and trauma.

The level and type of pain coming up was out of proportion to the stimulus, so it had to be old. As one friend said, "If you are hysterical, it must be historical." It reminded me of what I experienced in the early 90s, when I got "blown out of there with dynamite" and physically and emotionally burned for over two years. At that time I was dabbling with three or four different spiritual traditions and did not have a place to stand to ride through it all. This time I was firmly rooted in Kriya Yoga, plus I had Rick Levy as a mentor and years of practice with other tools. It was time to face the inner demons.

My meetings with Rick took on a new aspect. When I would openly grieve with him, he would look at me and say, "I could sit here and tell you how sorry I am about the relationship, blah, blah, blah. But I am not going to do that."

Ever calm, he said, "I am sorry you are in pain. You are burning off dross; it is difficult, I know. But you have to remember, this is not real. It is all an illusion. You are not the pain, you are not the emotions. You have to tap into a deeper part of yourself, your true Self, the soul. Sure, the whole situation is sad, but what keeps you hooked in it?"

Rick was tough during this period; he was pushing me, and he could do it because we had worked together for years and he had come through similar challenges. He knew my edge of growth, knew I was on it. He kept reminding me of the bigger picture: hundreds of lifetimes of identifying with the dualities — pleasures and pains, stuck in the unending cycles of birth and death. Meanwhile, the soul was untouched by any of it.

I somewhat understood what Rick was saying because there was a part of me that was witnessing the thoughts and the emotions. It was such a bizarre reality — lots of sadness and grieving, and at the same time a detached awareness about my own experience.

During those months of BBQ, I continued to go deep into meditation. At times I would experience peace and occasionally profound levels of bliss. Yet, when not meditating, I was ever-aware of a tremendous pain in my heart.

I often prayed to Divine Mother, asking for Her help, not realizing that She was already helping in Her Kali way. I missed the feeling of intoxicating love and, having experienced it before, I felt the sadness and grief all the more. I knew there was a profound sense of love available, but where was it? Was there no easy way out?

While I realized the BBQ was a purification of my consciousness, a burning-off of dross, managing the pain was not fun. I used every tool I knew: power of positive thinking; lots of physical exercise; long hikes in nature; gardening; long, deep meditations; affirmations; and prayer. Part of me wanted to drive the pain away with the tools, and another part knew that pushing away the pain would not work, as the old saying goes: "What one resists, persists." I simply had to be present and witness everything. My inner world was a battlefield.

Rick said there were several therapeutic approaches to release the old energies, with talk therapy being the slowest. He said we could do more guided meditations into the subconscious, which we had done before, and go back to the experiences, whether this life or another one, where the initial traumas occurred. However, he believed long, deep meditations into superconsciousness were the best way for me to slowly dissolve the karmic seeds.

In the Kriya Yoga tradition, it was believed it would take a person a million years of healthy living to spiritually evolve over many lifetimes. Kriya Yoga sped up the process through a scientific process working with prana, or conscious energy, and would systematically purify a person's consciousness. The techniques generated so much energy that a person had to slowly build up their capacity to handle them. The ultimate state of merging in Cosmic Consciousness would require and result in so much power that it would literally burn a person if they had not acquired the capacity to handle it. The metaphor was trying to plug a fifty-watt bulb into fifty thousand volts of electricity.

Knowing about the possible power generated in Kriya Yoga and other meditation traditions gave new meaning to the Biblical quote, "Love the Lord your God with all your heart and with all your soul and with all your mind and with all your strength." But I was having a hard time loving God because I was in so much pain.

The years of meditation and learning how to work with prana had brought me to the place where I was prepared to burn off a layer of old fear and pain. It was bizarre to think of the burning as a sign of progress, and I wondered how many more milestones like this there would be on the path toward self-realization. I felt like I was in first grade and ready for summer break!

While Rick encouraged me to keep meditating on my own, we also spent much of our time together meditating. Rick would project healing energies into me, helping dissolve what was arising. After each session I would feel an amazing clarity and peace that would last for a few days, reminding me that the pain was only temporary.

After Carrie and I officially called off the relationship, I took a lot of space and entered into a period of anger and rage. The pain in my body shifted from my heart to my solar plexus, symbolizing a loss of power. One close friend encouraged me to practice what he called the "fuck-you meditation," where I would just rant and rave when alone. Even though I knew not to blame Carrie for my reactions, I needed to do something with the anger, as I had gotten a urinary tract infection and my prostrate had become enlarged — a physical sign of pent-up anger. Rick seconded the idea, encouraging me to express and release the anger instead of suppressing it — but not to get caught up in identifying with it. He said, "Release, let go, and then focus your attention on God."

To compound matters, the funding for our program in Sierra Leone was suddenly dramatically cut when international donors changed their priorities. Donors just did not understand the need to make a long-term commitment to transforming how people dealt with conflict. Meanwhile, the root causes of the conflict in Sierra Leone were still there, waiting to resurface.

A large number of our staff in Sierra Leone had to be laid off, including Josephine, which resulted in Josephine and I not being able to stay in touch. Since Josephine was my connection with the Contehs in Masongbo, I also lost contact with them. Losing this connection with my friends in Sierra Leone added one more layer of loss and grief.

Meanwhile, the diamond mining in the eastern part of Sierra Leone was not yielding the same amount of stones, so people were getting desperate. There was an increase of rape with many of the victims being young girls. There also were reports of ritualistic human sacrifices to bring good luck for the miners.

The news from Sierra Leone was simply disturbing and I felt powerless to help. It pissed me off all the more, and I hoped and prayed that the work that had occurred in the past few years would take root.

The amount of rage was tremendous, and shocked me. How could I, who had been meditating for nearly twenty years, experience so much anger that just kept coming in waves? Again, there was a part of me, the witness, just watching the emotional outbursts as if they were a movie or a pressure cooker letting off steam. I was utterly fascinated by the whole process of learning about the subtle realms of peacebuilding and the inner root causes of conflict.

During this period of anger, I often thought about my friends and the staff in Sierra Leone, as well as our staff in Liberia, Burundi, and all across Africa, and people in other deadly conflicts, such as Israelis and Palestinians, who had suffered real losses in this life. I wondered how Agnes in Burundi could forgive the people who had killed seventy-nine members of her family. Was forgiveness out of necessity, in order to have a chance for peace to take root? If I had so much anger, how could I expect my friends in Sierra Leone, Burundi, or others in war-torn countries to let go of their pain and find peace with one another? Were they, too, carrying tremendous anger and rage stored in their subconscious minds, cells of their bodies, or in their energy fields as sanskaras? If so, healing could take lifetimes.

Then again, I truly felt that the anger coming up was far beyond the relationship with Carrie or the funding situation in Sierra Leone; it was old, very old, almost archetypal. I was all the more interested in understanding this old rage.

At times, I would see images of women with arms cut off or of villages leveled. Other times I would see child soldiers carrying weapons, or I would flash back to my grandfather and his inability to deal with the loss of his sons and how it impacted my family. There also was the awareness of how the global consumerism lifestyle was wreaking havoc on people in other countries and on the environment and how out of control it all seemed. Were we destined to trigger massive climate-change effects? There was such a range of different images and dreamlike memories, all flowing through. I often found myself at the end of a meditation, lying on the floor, holding the meditation pillow and just crying, asking, "Why? Why God, why? I don't understand."

The anger was giving way to a deep despair. I also realized, down deep, there was anger toward God for creating a world of duality, and yet I knew being angry with God did not make sense. I pictured Lieutenant Dan in the movie *Forrest Gump*, riding through a hurricane sitting at the top of a mast of the shrimp boat, yelling at God!

When I took these questions to Rick, he said, "Of course you are angry with God; many of us feel that way at times. It can be pretty horrible in this world and you've seen terrible things in Africa.

"Eventually you will come to see that most of the suffering in this world is a result of our own misguided use of free will. The quantum field of energy and consciousness is so interconnected that the cause and effect patterns manifest in ways we cannot even imagine. You've heard that when a butterfly flaps its wings, it can cause a tidal wave on a different part of the world? Well, what do you think happens when millions of people break moral laws in this life or another, let alone the impact of horrendous wars and massive environmental destruction? The cause-and-effect energies go somewhere. The natural laws balance it all out over time. It can seem pretty overwhelming, and that there is no hope. Trust me, it is all beyond human comprehension, so don't even try to figure it out.

"You also have to remember that it is all an illusion, and that there is a deeper reality," he said.

Rick paused and then continued, "I am sorry you are feeling despair. I am not surprised. Despair is a part of a spiritual path, especially the closer you get to the goal."

This comment totally intrigued me — despair as an important part of a path, especially the closer you get to the goal.

"Look, you are getting to the place where you realize, on a profound level, that lasting peace and happiness cannot come in this world. Even if the relationship with Carrie or someone else would have worked out, even if Sierra Leone had peace and prosperity, even if you had the dream job on consciousness and peace-building, even if you had loads of money, the nice house, two kids and everything, eventually there would come a time where you would feel emptiness, that something was not complete. You could go after a new relationship, buy new things to try to appease that emptiness. That void cannot be filled by anything in this world. It only can be satisfied by merging fully in Cosmic Consciousness or God and the gateway lies inside, in your own soul.

"That does not mean do not go for those things in this world. Absolutely, work to improve your life situation and to help others, but just do not be attached to it looking a specific way and keep your eye on the ball, the real source of lasting happiness. You know the sayings, 'be in the world and not of it' and 'seek ye first the kingdom of God, and His righteousness, and all these things will be added onto you.'" Rick loved quoting the Bible when bringing home a yogic principle.

As Rick spoke, I reflected on how he and Lisa often worked more than eighty hours a week helping people through healing sessions, writing books, producing films, and updating a website. Their entire lives were about service, and at the same time they often said it was not them doing the work. Like Mickey, Rick followed "the energy" or "spirit" and gave all the credit to Master, the one pulling his strings. He and Lisa were being called to bring spiritual wisdom into society through scientific healing methods. So when Rick said it was all an illusion, he was still engaged in this world.

"What you're experiencing is a part of the spiritual journey home. Many spiritual aspirants experience anger and despair before going into higher states of consciousness. You're okay, you're on track, trust me, I am not worried about you at all. I went through terrible despair and I have seen many people go through it before going into a place of deeper peace," Rick added.

As Rick said this, I thought about the thin line between hope and despair, how much of the peacebuilding work I had seen was about awakening and leveraging hope for a better future and bringing forth the soul's qualities. There also were conflicts where the situations had to get so bad before people were willing to participate in peacebuilding activities. I had realized despair and hope were an important part of outer peacebuilding. I had not thought that despair would be a natural part of an inner peace process, that it would be a driving force to seeking deeper peace.

If hope was to come from within, from fully anchoring my consciousness with the soul and eventually merging back with God, then I was going to need help. Then again, Kali was helping, as She had answered my prayers of helping me move beyond delusion. Such a good reminder: be careful what one asks for. I just had to ride it out.

No wonder there was so much conflict in the world if the path to fully merging with one's own soul and then Cosmic Consciousness, or God, was so damn challenging.

Contemplatives ~ Rooted in Peace

Let not your heart be troubled. Ye believe in God; believe also in me.
— John 14:1

The relativities of existence (birth and death, pleasure and pain) are overcome
by those who view this world with equal-mindedness.
Verily they are enthroned in the taintless, the perfectly balanced Spirit.
— Bhagavad-Gita V:19

During the BBQ months, I continued to explore with Dena at the Global Peace Initiative of Women how contemplatives from around the world could contribute to addressing global problems like climate change, environmental destruction, and geopolitical conflicts.

Talking with Dena and participating in dialogues with contemplatives was perfectly timed, as I was in the midst of my own inner battle. I wanted to be around people who had successfully faced their own inner demons and came through victorious. Yogananda had once said: *if you want to be a businessman, spend time with businessmen. If you want to be a saint, spend time with saints.* I wanted a deep sense of peace so I wanted to be around people who were rooted in peace, even in the midst of times of crisis.

The next contemplative gathering was in Aspen, Colorado the weekend after the 2008 U.S. presidential elections. "Change" was in the air, as Obama had been elected.

Rick, Lisa, and I flew out to join the gathering which was a continuation of the Jaipur, India conference. The theme was Gathering the Spiritual Voice of America, and an intention was to look at how to bridge the divides in America and to address climate change and other global issues by drawing upon the spiritual wisdom of different traditions.

In Aspen, there were eighty people for the first day and then an additional seventy people the second day. In the inner circle were a handful of senior established contemplatives from Hindu, Buddhist, Christian, Jewish, Muslim, and indigenous traditions. Some of the contemplatives were very well-known in their traditions, such as Father Thomas Keating, founder of Centering Prayer, a Christian form of meditation. There also were a few international guests, including Sufi masters from Pakistan and Iran, and delightful youth social entrepreneurs from China.

Hellmich with Father Thomas Keating and Emma Far Rawlings at the contemplative gathering in Aspen, CO

Over the course of the gathering, I noticed a profound difference between the inner circle of contemplatives and the rest of us. While the contemplatives shared a concern about global issues, they seemed to have a deep sense of peace, humility, and humor. I was so intrigued. There was no urgency, as was expressed by other people: *what can we do and we must act soon*! Many of us talked about what was emerging, that there was some quantum leap in consciousness that was unfolding, and we needed to facilitate its happening or otherwise there could be global disaster. One of the monks later explained, "Look, the way you respond influences the outcome. You cannot encourage peace by working from a place of distress. That is what Gandhi did, he knew he could not act from a place of anger and violence, as that would affect the process and outcome."

One of the other participants who shared my curiosity about the contemplatives' deep sense of peace was Greg Reitman. Greg had been exposed to deadly violence, and it had shaken him to his core. Thus, he started a search on the roots of peace through his own profession, filmmaking. Greg was at the gathering to interview contemplatives as part of a documentary film entitled *Rooted in Peace*. He also had interviewed a number of scientists, peace activists, and politicians for the film, along with pop figures such as Deepak Chopra and Ted Turner.

Greg and I would later develop a friendship and fuel each other's searching. The idea of conflict being natural and an integral part of the human experience was a new idea to Greg. Likewise, I appreciated his boldness to ask the difficult questions and desire to share insights with a broader audience. I became an advisor to the *Rooted in Peace* project and, after the Aspen gathering, Greg and I frequently had long conversations about the intersection of science, spirituality, and consciousness.

Another person at the gathering who left a lasting impression on me was Brother A, a senior monk from the Kriya Yoga tradition. Dena had asked me to accompany Brother A, so I had a lot of time with him, which was an incredible opportunity.

Brother A, an American yogi born in Montana, was over eighty years in age and still incredibly youthful in smile, fitness, and attitude. There was one story Brother told that really caught my attention. He said that he had been a successful engineer before becoming a monk. He had lots of money and yet he was unfulfilled and would frequently get very depressed. The bouts of depression persisted even after he had become a monk, and would last several days at a time. During one gloomy period, Brother asked himself and God why he got these terrible moods. The response he heard in his mind surprised him: "Because you like them. You must, otherwise why would you keep getting them?"

Brother reflected on this insight and saw that it was true. He was addicted to this deep gloomy feeling. He then used strong determination and will power to demand that the moods leave him once and for all, and, they did.

Brother amazed me. He was not going to allow the inner conflicts to come between him and his goal of merging with God or Cosmic Consciousness.

Brother later shared with us that the periods of deep depression came from an unconscious realization that nothing in this world could satisfy his inner longing, exactly what Rick had been telling me.

Brother also was open about his going into samadhi, a nondualistic state in which a person merges his consciousness with Cosmic Consciousness. A Buddhist might describe samadhi as a state when there is no longer a subject and object, simply oneness. A Christian or Sufi mystic might say a state of intoxication when the Lover fully merges with the Beloved.

Brother said our guru discouraged talking about spiritual experiences, lest they feed a person's ego. But Brother had gone into samadhi several times in public, so he figured he was being used as an example and it was okay to share the stories.

At Aspen, Brother told Rick, Lisa, and me about the first time he went into samadhi. He had been asked to speak at an event in India. Prior to going onstage, the feeling of samadhi came close and he drove it away, thinking, no, he could not go into that state when he had an obligation to speak.

When he did get onstage, he went into samadhi. He stayed motionless, unable to speak, completely entranced in the overwhelming feeling of being merged with Cosmic Consciousness. The people leading the event pointed to Brother as an example of what the people of India could strive toward — using their ancient science of yoga to merge with God.

As brother told this story, I could feel a tremendous presence coming from him. Even though he was quiet and humble, the amount of strong and peaceful energy emitting from him was noticeable. I was reminded that going into samadhi was like connecting with fifty thousand volts of electricity. To be able to handle "the juice" took great conditioning and burning-away of anything standing in the way of merging. He was practicing the presence of God, or Cosmic Consciousness, by simply being.

This was one aspect discussed at the Aspen gathering: the effect of presence in influencing situations in the world. There had been a documented experiment conducted by Transcendental Meditation practitioners who successfully lowered the crime rate in Washington, DC in 1993 by 25 percent through their joint meditation practice. People who meditate deeply often carry a presence that affects the consciousness of people around them. Many of the contemplatives at the gathering had a strong, peaceful presence, and it could be felt.

The Aspen gathering ended with a lot of enthusiasm and a very clear message: there was an "inner dimension" to climate change, environmental destruction, and global conflicts. It was clear that the rampant consumerism was the result of an inner hunger that could never be satisfied through material objects, and that consumerism was leading us, humanity, down a path of crisis. There was an agreement that the inner dimensions needed to be addressed. It was time for the wisdom of all spiritual traditions to come forward with a unified voice to encourage people of whatever faith to embrace the inner practices of those traditions.

I left the gathering uplifted by the growing consensus across traditions to bring the inner disciplines forward. I also kept Brother A in mind as an example of overcoming deep-seated despair and was happy to see him a couple more times over the next few months, once in Los Angeles and again in Washington, DC.

During conversations, Brother pointed out why he did not have a sense of urgency about the global situation. He said, "Yes, we are going to have difficult times. There always have been hard times throughout history. There is too much greed in the world today; it's going to have consequences. The crisis will get people looking for peace and meaning. Pain and suffering are whips that drive us to seek God."

When I asked Brother about being angry with God, he laughed, "That is stupid; God is what you want."

Somewhat embarrassed, I added, "But I have lived in villages sacked by child soldiers."

"I am sorry," he said. "I know it can be pretty horrible in this world. Master used to argue with God, telling Him it was not right to create a world where so much suffering existed. Many of the great saints have said there is some divine plan behind it all based on love. Still, it can be pretty horrible while in it.

"It is good to do what you can to help alleviate suffering. Master was very close to Gandhi and supported what he was doing in India," Brother said.

"You have to remember, God does not want us to suffer. But if we use free will to transgress the laws of health, prosperity, and wisdom, we must inevitably suffer from sickness, poverty, and ignorance. This is what is playing out in the world and it is being sped up through technology," he added.

As Brother mentioned this idea, I thought about all of my reflections over the years on how the individual pursuit of happiness created so much suffering. The collective pursuit of happiness through massive consumerism certainly was affecting the environment, and the global economy reached people even in remote parts of Sierra Leone. It seemed so strange that the "pursuit of happiness" was a cornerstone of the American Declaration of Independence, yet we really did not understand the science of happiness. We were creating bigger problems than we could manage because of how we "pursued" what sages would say already existed in our own souls.

This is where I found the mystical traditions of all religions offered insight to the global crisis — all people want to avoid pain and want happiness. Yet, it is in merging with higher states of consciousness, the one Beloved, or God (whatever word works for you) that we experience bliss. In this sense, the global crisis is a spiritual crisis, because we are seeking outside of ourselves what exists in our own souls.

Our guru often talked about the need for the West and East to come together, to bring the best of both ways. The West's industrial know-how could help alleviate physical causes of suffering and the East's ancient wisdom of the inner science of peace could help people in the West with the inner causes of suffering and the elusive pursuit of happiness.

"You also have to have a long-term perspective," brother continued. "You have to think in terms of hundreds if not thousands of years and lifetimes. Do what you can today to the best of your ability and be aware the results may not be seen in your lifetime."

He later added, "You see, the Earth goes through twenty-four-thousand-year cycles, with twelve thousand years of ascending consciousness and twelve thousand years of descending consciousness."

Brother was talking about *yugas*, cycles of rising and descending consciousness, a cornerstone of many Eastern spiritual traditions.

"We are just coming out of *Kali Yuga*, the most dense and lowest level of consciousness, that was focused only on the material plane. We are now in an ascending age of energy, where consciousness is rising and the old structures will give way to new ones. In this phase, *Dwapara Yuga*, there will be rapid advancements in technology and understanding of energy. It started about two hundred fifty years ago with the discovery of electricity and will go for another two thousand years. It is also a time of great challenges as humanity does not have the moral consciousness to handle all of the new technologies. There could be terrible wars and great disparities in wealth."

As brother described this phase, I thought about the previous twenty-five years and how Sierra Leone had gone from mud huts to cell phones and how the global economy had contributed to the conflict there.

Brother A was clear: "The Earth is not going to end until it has served its purpose in helping people evolve spiritually.

"Sure, there can be terrible things happening, but it is all karma being worked out." He also went on to say that the best thing people can do to overcome karma and to speed up evolution was to meditate.

I simply looked at Brother A and realized he had merged with Cosmic Consciousness. He had experienced nondual states and a depth of profound oneness with the universe, and he spoke with utter conviction, peace, and strength. He also had fought his inner battles and had won. He was quietly playing his role as a monk, serving at a temple, leading services, and counseling people. He was not seeking any worldly fame or fortune, and he deferred all credit to the lineage of gurus and God, none of it was him. He knew this was all a dream from direct experience, and that there was a more profound reality. He was at peace and had experienced heaven on Earth through samadhi.

I wanted what he had, and I was going to have to work to get there.

Inner Peace

Shortly after that conversation with Brother A, a CD arrived in the mail from the Kriya Yoga tradition of a talk entitled: "Inner Peace: Divine Antidote for Stress, Worry, and Fear." It happened to be by Brother S, the monk who years earlier had advised me not to become a monk. It was about the battle between the soul and the ego.

In this talk, Brother S too pointed out that we go around hundreds if not thousands of lifetimes and eventually the soul gets tired of it. The present life was the most important, as it was an opportunity to reach the hidden treasure inside.

He told a story of a great king in India who had everything but was still unhappy, until he met the Buddha. The Buddha taught him how to dive inward through meditation and to tap into peace and bliss inside. That peace was the buried treasure that existed inside.

Brother S was clear that peace does exist inside, and that it opens to bliss and then to fully merging with God. He also said it was the soul that drives a person to seek that inner happiness, to move beyond the drama of daily life. Yet, the ego — the soul's deluded identification with thoughts, emotions, and body — is that part of us that has been helping us through thousands of lifetimes to fulfill sensual and material desires and take care of us in the daily battles.

As the soul starts to awaken, the ego does its best to keep control. The ego always felt mysterious to me, and I later learned why: I was so identified with it.

"The ego's constant emotional reactions to the events of daily life keep us entangled with it," Brother S said. "Over many incarnations each of us have become an emotional specialist — some like to explode with anger, some like to become impatient and grit our teeth. Others fall into tears of despair and unworthiness, and others suffer from silent criticism and sullen moods, and so withdraw. These are emotional reactions. Often times we are reacting in the same way to different situations.

"We have become an emotional specialist in our reactions, this is the ego that needs to be tamed and transmuted."

As I listened, it dawned on me that, when in these states of anger or despair, all my energy and consciousness was focused on those reactions instead of identifying with the soul, the witness. In order to fully merge my consciousness with the soul and then eventually Cosmic Consciousness, I would need to free it from identifying with those states that seemed all-consuming and second nature.

The idea was not to destroy the ego but rather turn it into friend and servant of the soul. Brother S was clear: it was a battle and we had to be spiritual warriors. There had to be unconditional surrender of the ego to the soul.

He then quoted our guru as to the goal: "The spiritual aspirant is advised to conquer his emotional reactions to the inevitable dualities of the phenomenal universe and to remain like his creator in an even ecstatic state."

He went on to say, "Regardless of conditions, we have inner work to do. We do not blame others, situations, relationships. There will always be a new test and the ego will seek compromise and negotiation."

I listened to the CD numerous times, reflecting on the subtleties of the inner battles. When I started on the whole inner-peace–international-peace journey, I had no idea how deeply rooted conflict was to the human experience or how demanding it would be to find lasting inner peace, even though it was a treasure buried within my own soul.

Soul Mate ~ Take Two

Out beyond ideas of wrong-doing and right-doing
there is a field. I'll meet you there.
— Jelaluddin Rumi

Attitude of Gratitude

The great yogi-saint Lahiri Mahasaya often told his disciples, "*Banat, banat, ban jai!*" which translated into, "Doing, doing, at last done!" The idea was that a person just keeps on keeping on and eventually reaches the goal of merging his/her consciousness back into God. It was to offer hope that the goal was not out of reach. While I felt like I was in first grade and taking baby steps, there was no choice but to keep going.

Along with meditating, I became ever mindful throughout the day when I would get pulled into periods of anger or despair. I would remind myself: "This is my ego's habitual reaction to the phenomenal universe. This is not who I am. There is a more profound state, a place of peace that exists inside. That is my true identity." I would then close my eyes and remember the peaceful feelings from meditation and try to carry them throughout the day.

Another practice that I started to use to compliment the meditation and mindfulness about my ego's reactions was the "attitude of gratitude." I had learned it from Gene, one of the meditation instructors who lived in rural Virginia. Gene had been an engineer, scientist, and pilot who explained yoga in terms of energy and consciousness. Two of his favorite expressions were "the attitude of gratitude" and "altitude is determined by attitude."

Gene told our meditation group a story about when his late wife, Annette, was being operated on for cancer. During the operation, the anesthesia began to wear off where she could feel the pain from the surgeon's scalpel, yet she could not speak or move to tell them she was conscious. Having been a long-time Kriya Yoga practitioner, Annette began to pray to the guru in the midst of the terrible pain, asking what to do. The response she heard surprised her: "be grateful."

Annette had tremendous faith in her spiritual teacher and God. She understood that everything came into her life for her spiritual advancement. She knew the laws of karma were very subtle and complex and that she was being helped to remove a big chunk of it.

Annette began to pray with gratitude for what was happening. She became flooded with an overwhelming amount of love that saturated the operating room. The next day, the surgeon and each assistant came by to visit Annette and Gene. One by one, each person said they did not know what had happened, but they had been deeply changed by the operation. Each of them went on to explore their own spiritual paths.

There were many levels to this story and the application of the attitude of gratitude. Gene said on a very simple level, being grateful for everything in life brings one closer to God in that we are focused on the giver instead of the gifts. Praying before eating was a nice time to practice gratitude, at least being grateful for the people who brought the food to the table and for all the animals, fish, and/or plants that gave their lives.

The deeper level: when totally surrendering to God in a deeply personal relationship, a devotee begins to trust that everything comes into his or her life for spiritual advancement. The burning-off of karma can be terribly unpleasant and to do so, hand in hand with a spiritual lineage, with the clear intention of merging fully in God makes it not only more bearable but can also provide a deep sense of peace.

With this in mind, I kept on keeping on, doing my part. For some reason, my path had been one of exploring peacebuilding, both inner and outer. Why? Who knows? At times, I had wished I had pursued a totally different vocation in life. The edge of growth was to surrender, to see that this world was a place of constantly moving energies — positive, negative, and the dynamic between the two.

When lying in bed in the morning and night, I mentally thanked God for of all the positive things in my life, including the burning-off of the old karma. I became grateful for Carrie and saw how she had helped trigger the old anger and despair so I could release them. I also reminded myself how fortunate I was compared to the billions of people who were living in poverty or war-torn countries. My life was wonderful.

Another time I liked to practice the attitude of gratitude was when biking to and from the office, a sixteen-mile round trip. One aspect of the practice was that gratitude inspires positive feelings and can magnetically attract more abundance.

Gene also reminded us frequently about the gunas. He loved talking about them — sattva, the positive influence toward good; tamas, the negative attribute toward evil and ignorance; and, rajas, the dynamic between the two.

Gene, as a scientist, loved the idea of the entire universe being composed of positive and negative qualities and the dynamic between them. He reminded us all the time that the way out of delusion was to use sattva, the positive, to pull out tamas, the negative and then pull out rajas...and eventually to throw out sattva to go beyond duality.

Gene talking about the gunas reminded me of the dream about Kali in Nepal and then experiencing the flood of positive, loving energy. Awakening humanity's potential toward positive or sattva qualities, and the ongoing struggle with the negative tendencies, was such a core part of peacebuilding too.

On a practical and personal level, the daily battle was to focus on the positive, be grateful for the painful releasing of old anger and despair, and to keep bringing my attention back to the positive. I had to remember I was not the painful emotions, that they were my ego's emotional reactions to the constant changes of the phenomenal universe.

The other aspect I heard from Gene, Brother A, Rick, and others in the yoga tradition was that I could not do it alone. I needed God's help to get beyond the delusion. With that in mind, I prayed constantly, at the end of meditations and periodically throughout the day.

I also wrote a letter to Sri Daya Mata, the head of Self-Realization Fellowship, asking for her help. "Ma," as she was affectionately called by devotees, had been handpicked by Paramahansa Yogananda to lead the international organization and she had been guiding its growth for over fifty years. *Daya Mata* meant "true mother of compassion" in Sanskrit. Ma was known for her powerful spiritual presence, deep wisdom, and love, along with her humility. She never promoted herself, but always referred people to focus on their own relationship with God and guru.

Just writing the letter to "Ma" was comforting, as I felt I was writing to Divine Mother Herself. I explained all of my efforts to overcome my reactions to the horrible atrocities in Africa and the heartbreak in the relationship. Most importantly, I confided that I was concerned about my ability to love God in the face of such worldly suffering.

I sent the letter and then forgot about it, assuming Ma would be too busy to respond.

Comic Relief & Déjà Vu

To complement the letter to Ma, the attitude of gratitude, meditation, and everything else, I also called upon the time-proven method of comic relief. This was one thing I had learned from my African friends and colleagues: no matter how dire, humor could be invoked to lighten things up, and joy could be awakened through music and dancing.

Rick Levy was constantly encouraging me to read *The Onion*, his favorite source of humor. Another yogi friend was addicted to the comedian Eddie Izzard and frequently recited his lines by heart. I loved silly movies, including a short-film on Israel-Palestine called *West Bank Story*, a musical comedy about competing falafel stands in the West Bank. Adam Sandler's film, *You Don't Mess with the Zohan*, also had a hysterical take on the Israeli-Palestinian conflict. My favorite film, though, was Mike Myers's *The Love Guru*, a ridiculous spoof about self-help gurus in the United States. It received terrible reviews, with one person saying, "Just drive by the theatre, roll down the window, and throw your money out. Don't waste your time!" My yogi friends and I loved it! I especially loved how the greeting between the Love Guru and his devotees was "Mariska Hargitay," as the actress was (fictionally, of course) his largest financial supporter.

The most bizarre humor though came in real life in the form of déjà vu.

Several months after the break-up with Carrie, I went on another meditation retreat in Encinitas, California. I was feeling lighter and had absolutely no intention of seeking out a relationship with a woman. The retreat coincided with a public India Night celebration with over one thousand people from the surrounding area in attendance. It was a lighthearted and delightful evening of music, food, and presentations.

After the event I volunteered to help put away chairs and happened to meet a woman named Haleh, which was a Persian name for halo. She was on vacation from Canada and had been spiritually drawn to that area. Being I was dressed in traditional Indian clothes, she initially thought I was a monk but threw out that idea after we exchanged phone numbers. We met a couple times that week, including on her birthday.

We took a long walk on Swami's Beach just below the ashram, a place very sacred to me as I will have my ashes scattered in the ocean there when this lifetime is all over. As we walked, she was straight to the point: she was looking for a spiritual partner to marry. She wanted someone who loved to meditate and would want to go on retreats; seeking God together was the highest priority, and kids were optional. She was just starting to explore spirituality and was leaning toward Kriya Yoga. Even though she lived in Canada, she wanted to move in the next year and was open to possibilities.

Haleh basically said everything I had ever dreamed of in a relationship, plus she was drop-dead gorgeous. Yet, I was somewhat hesitant, wondering if it was a divine gift or a divine joke. As it turned out, just like Carrie, Haleh had set the intention of meeting her soulmate by a certain date, and that was when I met her. This should have been a clue — keep clear of a woman trying to manifest her soulmate by a specific date. When the music stops she'll grab anyone in sight, and the dream bubble is sure to pop later!

Haleh and I dated long-distance, and she came to visit twice in DC. It was simply delightful. Given she had come to see me, she canceled a retreat with James Arthur Ray scheduled to take place in Arizona. That was the retreat where three people died in a sweat lodge. Haleh would have been in the sweat lodge, and she was friends with the people who died. Knowing her strong will and determination, Haleh could easily have been seriously hurt or killed.

After the tragedy, Haleh became more withdrawn. When I went to see her in Canada, she was cold and distant. Two days after I returned to DC from visiting her, Haleh called to say old traumatic memories were coming up and she needed to deal with them. She was seeking professional help but could not be in a relationship.

At that point, I simply threw up my hands. I was glad Haleh was seeking help and even more relieved she had not been in the sweat lodge. I felt sadness for a couple days, and then was over it. There were only warm feelings for Haleh, no anger, and a bizarre sense of humor about it all.

I wondered if that was what releasing karma was all about: keep reexperiencing similar situations over and over again until all the old energy is released, until a person learns not to get caught in the emotional reactions or learns to laugh at the absurdity. In one sense, I was reminded of the movie *Groundhog Day*, where Bill Murray kept waking up on the same day until he learned how to selflessly love another person. Then again, I wondered if this was what Mickey meant when he realized someone else was pulling his strings?

Humor aside, Haleh provided several gifts: she helped me to let go of Carrie (evoking the Guatemalan expression *It takes a nail to drive another nail out of a board*), and she reminded me that each person really is doing the best that he or she can in this world of duality and karma.

I later met a young male yogi who also had traveled to India and visited the sacred cave in Rishikesh while going through a relationship breakup. We laughed so hard about what he called, "The disappearing carrot routine," when women would suddenly disappear, inspiring the yogi to seek a divine love. He thought for sure it was part of many yogis' paths.

Forgive and Surrender

After the experiences with Haleh, there was a breakthrough. It was early morning, and I had a clear dream with a phrase repeating itself: "It is time to forgive."

The dream was associated with a peaceful, almost blissful, feeling. I intuitively understood that it was time to forgive on many levels: Carrie and her ex-lover for the heartbreak; all the people and factors contributing to the war in Sierra Leone; and, most of all, myself for any suffering I had caused others and myself during this lifetime or any other.

I also experienced a surprising desire to forgive God for creating a world of duality and delusion. Yes, forgiving God, as crazy as it seemed. I kept thinking, "If You created us for your entertainment, I hope you are enjoying the show, because it is crazy down here!" Then again, I realized forgiving God meant I was still stuck in identifying with being separate from Him or Her, which was yet one more form of delusion. Oh well, one step at a time.

Several weeks later, I received a call from a senior monk in the Kriya Yoga tradition. He was calling on behalf of Sri Daya Mata. He explained that Ma had received my letter, and she wanted me to know she was deeply praying for me. Just hearing those words, I was flooded with an overwhelming feeling of love. I was once again grateful to be rooted in a spiritual tradition that offered so much support in navigating the inner realms of consciousness.

Even with her endless responsibilities of overseeing a large international organization, Ma still found time to reach out to me. I later learned that Ma did the same for thousands of people around the world who wrote to her for assistance. One monastic later referred to Ma's ability to personally care for thousands of people while fulfilling her daunting duties as a perfect example of the Divine Mother of compassion.

I later read in one of Ma's writings that the Divine Mother has many different sides, and that it is our consciousness that determines which aspect we experience. When we attune our consciousness with Her, we can experience deep love and bliss. It is when we feel separate from Her, from God, that suffering arises. The sense of separation can be caused by overidentifying with worries, worldly pursuits, and/or old habits. When suffering, Divine Mother can seem like a disciplinarian, especially when reaping the consequences of breaking natural laws.

While the monk on the phone was willing to talk about my struggles with duality and loving God, the shifts in my own consciousness were already taking place.

The next two nights, I had vivid dreams of Sri Daya Mata appearing in the traditional ocher-colored robes of a yoga nun, offering comfort and reassurance that, yes, in fact, God was love and that I needed to learn how to rise above duality and to deeply love Her. The sadness was giving way to an almost joyous feeling and I found myself wanting to offer the same love and compassion to others.

The way I acted on this opening of my heart was to send an email to Carrie, the first time I reached out to her in over a year. She responded almost immediately, happy to hear from me. We wrote back and forth about when to get together and realized we would both be traveling. It would be a month before we could see each other.

When we finally met, I was calm and peaceful. We took a walk along the Potomac River, something we both enjoyed doing. She told me about her work and sports, the two areas where she had channeled all of her energies — her way of overcoming the suicide. We came to a secluded spot along the bank and sat on some rocks. We went into a natural silence for a long period of time.

Sitting there, side by side, we watched the river flow by. There was a hazy mist over the water and large boulders protruding, similar to the Rokel River in Sierra Leone in the dry season. A fish jumped, and I was taken back to Masongbo, thinking about Moses, Sanpha, and Bokarie. I wondered where Adama's soul was, and wished her a deep sense of peace. I also was aware that Carrie, too, shared that love for West Africa and wondered if she would ever build the mud hut in the back of her yard. If she did, I wanted to see it!

The silence kept flowing with the river, no need to say anything. A deep peace and calmness entered my heart and seemed to be with her too. I felt a natural sense of compassion for Carrie and her soul's path this lifetime, realizing how challenging it had been for her to lose her parents and a lover. I could sense she was doing the best that she could do, and I wanted her to be happy.

I could sense that all people and their souls, everywhere, were doing the best that they could. The Contehs, A.K., and the Search for Common Ground staff across Africa were all living to the best of their abilities, as were my parents and other family members. I could sense how all of humanity was connected by a web of nature and also an invisible quantum field of conscious energy. We were all in this grand divine production together, learning to remember we are all from the same source and learning to behave.

We were all a manifestation of consciousness, or God, giving expression through each of us in our unique ways and, meanwhile, we all splashed around creating waves of cause and effect, creating joy and also suffering for ourselves and others around the world. Meanwhile, the Divine Mother was slowly calling each of us home through Her love and compassion, as well as Her discipline through natural laws.

Sitting there next to Carrie, I could feel my desire to know why it all existed just melt away.

I had no clue what was next in life — whether the world was going to hell in a hand basket or if the human spirit could in fact bring heaven on Earth. I was simply grateful for all the assistance along the way, from many people and Her invisible loving presence. I just hoped that I could learn to "follow Her energy" a little more gracefully and to be at peace with whatever came.

I could hear Mickey saying, "Who asked you how it should be?"

This time, there was no mental response. Instead, I was experiencing the flowing river in silence.

Women in Afghanistan

A friend asked me if a college student from Afghanistan could stay with me for a week while she looked for a place to live during her summer internship in Washington, DC. When I picked up the young woman from the bus station, I was immediately struck by her huge smile.

This young person, Simi, was bubbly, energetic, sweet, intelligent, and wise beyond her years. My housemate and friend, Kristen, and I had a room prepared for her in the basement. Within a day, Simi was teasing me about the spiders in her room and my lack of ability to see cobwebs. She was much tidier than I was.

Simi enjoyed being with Kristen and me, and decided to stay the summer with us, even though Kristen and I were not married and I was a single man, something that would be frowned upon in Simi's traditional Afghan culture.

Simi taught us to drink three cups of tea a day and found endless things to tease me about, including the small gut I had developed which she called *bibi gul,* Persian for "lady flower," insinuating I looked pregnant.

Every morning Simi and I would help one another in cooking breakfast and then would eat in the backyard next to a sanctuary to Kwan Yin with a small fish pond. We would talk about the fish and the two frogs, which we named Lilly and Pad. Over breakfast Simi would ask broad-stroke questions like, "Why are men bad" and then start to laugh. Another one of her favorite topics was, "Tell me about your God."

My reply was always the same, "Well, I think what is more important is what concept of God appeals to you. You know there is only one source and it can have many names."

Simi reflected on this question frequently and often said, "There is only one God, but we do have ninety-nine names for God in Islam."

We would finish breakfast and then do a ritual where Simi would accompany me. The first stop was bowing to a statue of Kwan Yin, ringing the wind chimes next to Her and paying our respects to Bob Cat, who was buried by Kwan Yin. We would then walk to a sanctuary of Mother Mary and bow to Her, a statue that had been my grandmother's. We would then continue to the garden and thank the land, vegetables, and flowers. Simi often added, "Thank you tomatoes and basil for growing, so we can eat you!" and then she would laugh.

Even though Simi did not relate to God as the Divine Mother, she was respectful and curious, especially since her major in college was women's studies and peace-building. I was intrigued how the divine feminine was expressing itself through Simi and other women she talked about in Afghanistan.

The morning ritual was then rounded out with a mile walk to the Metro (the Washington, DC area subway) station. During these walks there were endless conversations about frogs, men, and God. Simi also helped me start to understand the complexity of Afghanistan and how the U.S. had helped create the messy conflict. I was surprised how Simi said life was better for women under the Soviet rule and that the U.S. training and arming of Mujahideen, Taliban, and other groups fueled an old tension between people in the rural areas, who were more conservative, and people in and around Kabul, who tended to be more progressive, at least toward women's rights.

The U.S. support of the Taliban and other groups resulted in horrific atrocities against women after the fall of the Soviet-backed regime. Simi and her family fled to Pakistan, where they lived for several years. Simi was quick to say, "The U.S. was the only government to recognize the Taliban when they came to power."

The U.S. and NATO arrival in Afghanistan was welcomed, even though we were fighting people that we had once trained and supported. We were reaping what we had sown. It was all so complex, and there appeared no quick and easy answers.

Slowly over the weeks, I caught glimpses of Simi's life as a woman growing up in Afghanistan, and her struggle over identity. She was very traditional, and at the same time drawn to Western ways. She loved to comment about Western clothes, while at the same time staying modest. She was deeply loyal to her family and talked with them daily on Skype. She wanted to go back to Afghanistan to help, and at the same time she was carrying a deep grief and sadness inside.

The decades of fighting had profoundly impacted Simi and her family. Simi's grandfathers were killed in the war, and she had lost many uncles and cousins. Her mother had become so distraught from losing her father and brothers that she shut down emotionally. Simi said, "I never knew my mother's love, as she would never hug us or say she loved us. She was too much in shock."

One Saturday I served Simi a piece of watermelon on a plate. She got up and said, "I'll be right back." She returned with a piece of bread and put it next to the watermelon.

"This is what we ate during the two weeks of intense fighting in Kabul. We stayed in the basement, hearing the bombs, gunfire, and people screaming."

Simi went on to say, "Once, when I was nine years old, my sister and I stood in line for hours to buy bread in one of the few shops that was open. A bomb went off near us." Simi laughed, "It was so funny, there were bodies and blood everywhere, but we did not move because we needed the food and there was no other place to buy it."

Simi's laughter about the traumatic experiences reminded me how my colleagues and I dealt with the atrocities in Sierra Leone and Liberia, humor from a place of shock. I simply listened to Simi so she would know she mattered, and provided friendship.

Knowing the importance of education, Simi was an avid reader and enjoyed going through the books in the basement. It was no surprise that one of her favorite books was Louis Hay's *You Can Heal Your Life*. She also read Mickey's book *Three Essays on Universal Laws — The Laws of Karma, Will, and Love*.

After reading these books, Simi was so excited to discuss them. "Tell me, what is the soul and what is the ego?" She was hungry to explore, and so we sat next to Kwan Yin, discussing the subtle dynamics of the ego, soul, and karma.

Seeing Simi's curiosity in mind-body healing and natural laws, I took her to see Rick Levy, and she came out from the session just nodding her head. On the way home she shared, "He saw what I already knew. There is a lot of old pain in me. I know it. I need to release it."

By this point, Simi was like a young sister, and I wanted to help in any way that I could. I also realized her presence in the house was so in harmony with my writing about my own efforts to come to terms with the harsh realities of deadly conflict and looking for peace.

Simi started to ask questions about how to release the old pain, and she was open to hearing about my own experiences.

We would go in and out of these conversations and then talk about the frogs, trying to figure out which was the male and which was the female. We were tickled when a smaller frog appeared, and we decided it was Lilly and Pad's baby.

Toward the end of Simi's stay, a *Time* magazine arrived with a photo of a young woman from Afghanistan on the cover. She had her nose and ears cut off by the Taliban. I just looked at the cover and thought, "Damn, war is so much easier when you do not know anyone affected by it."

There was much less rage this time than I had experienced years earlier with the photos of women in Sierra Leone with chopped-off limbs. Still, there was an opening of the heart to the human struggles, an impulse to assist, and an awareness of some divine presence available to help.

Simi and I continued our conversations about God, the soul, the ego, and how to release trauma from the conscious and subconscious minds. Of course, we talked about meditation, and I simply encouraged her to explore what felt true for her and her Islamic tradition.

Simi wanted to focus on trauma healing in her graduate studies and was determined to go back to Afghanistan to help women. I mentioned, "You know, to help people heal, you will have to heal yourself."

She replied, "I know, I will need help."

"We all do," I said.

The Summer of Peace

Let Go

The burning finally subsided and opened to a prolonged period of peace and gratitude. I was so grateful not to be slow roasted over an open fire. With the peace and gratitude came joy bubbling up at the end of meditation that permeated throughout the day. Peace was giving way to joy, joy where I would smile and at times giggle and laugh with no prompting.

I went to work at Search for Common Ground each day with a deep sense of gratitude for the organization's mission, for my job and my colleagues. I was grateful for all of the opportunities I had had over the years to return to Africa, to be part of programs that directly helped A.K., the Contehs, and many others in tangible ways. I was grateful to have colleagues who were Democrats and Republicans, Israelis and Palestinians, Hutus and Tutsis, and many other people from various sides of conflicts who were all working side-by-side to create a more peaceful world.

I was simply grateful.

With all the joy and gratitude arising, I channeled energy into writing as a way of exploring the spiritual underpinnings of conflict and peace, while fundraising for Search with renewed passion. I also continued volunteering for the Global Peace Initiative of Women.

Meanwhile, on my wall in my bedroom I posted a list of nine intentions for my next job. The overriding point was to work with visionary leaders looking at the inner and outer aspects of peace. Together, we would explore the peace continuum from inner to international levels, including the spiritual and scientific dimensions of inner peace, along with the practical ways of transforming outer conflict.

In early 2011, I received a nudge to start looking for the next job. Search for Common Ground re-structured the fundraising department, and I was offered a position in San Francisco Bay Area. The terms were not ideal. My colleagues knew about my ambitions to explore spirituality and conflict and yet there were no openings for such a position at Search. Out of loyalty to me, they were trying to keep me in a role that was needed and, out of love for my colleagues, I was trying to see if it would work.

When consulting Rick Levy he agreed neither option — taking the job offer or leaving — was good, and that the situation was perfectly designed by spirit to test my faith and to learn how to surrender. Rick reminded me that we are souls playing roles, and it was time for the next role. His advice was always the same: meditate, tune in, and let Master/Mother guide you. He reminded me that I was working for them, not myself. He said, "Look, Master would not bring you this far and not keep you busy."

When I asked Dena Merriam, the head of the Global Peace Initiative of Women, for advice, she simply said, "Mother wants you someplace else; otherwise the job offer would have been better."

After weighing the options and meditating extensively, I opted to leave Search for Common Ground without another job lined up, which seemed ridiculous in the poor economy. Shortly after making the decision, fear was triggered, and I began to oscillate. I reopened the negotiations, and went back and forth. Each time I approached taking the position, my body would shake with waves of energy going up the spine. My body was saying no, yet my mind was trying to hold onto security.

For over two months I burned, intensely burned, driving myself and a few close friends and colleagues nearly crazy. There was little sleep, just deep burning up and down the spine and throughout my body. I watched as my attachments came up. I was surprised how much I identified with being a Search for Common Ground employee. This had become my identity.

I was reminded of a practice: Take away the job title, take away the name, gender, religion, body. What was left? Who would remember me? I prayed to Mother — when all is taken away, will you be there? I knew the answer.

After excruciating deliberating, I finally decided to listen to my body. With incredible gratitude and love for Search for Common Ground, my colleagues, and the opportunity to return to Sierra Leone to help, I finally let go and entered into not knowing.

The Shift

The first point on the list for the next job was to be recruited by visionary leaders. As I roasted in the BBQ, this seemed like a far-distant possibility.

A few weeks before my final day at Search for Common Ground, I went on a meditation retreat in Los Angeles. While there I received a voice message from Devaa Haley Mitchell. She and her husband, Stephen Dinan, had left IONS and started The Shift Network. They were donors to Search for Common Ground, and Devaa had volunteered for the Search programs in Democratic Republic of Congo and Angola. Having heard I was leaving Search, Devaa asked if I wanted to apply for a job with The Shift Network's Summer of Peace 2012 program. A few days later, I received an email from her husband, Stephen, the founder and CEO, asking me to apply.

After a few interviews with other staff, I was offered a job with The Shift Network, based at the IONS campus north of San Francisco. It was ironic that the job was in the Bay Area, when I had just turned down a position with Search for Common Ground out there.

Flying out for a week of meetings, I realized that all nine points on my job intentions list were met, including working near beautiful nature. The office was located on the IONS 194-acre campus of pristine nature, with rolling hills and stunning large oak trees.

In the first staff meeting, we started with a group meditation, and Stephen Dinan shared the vision of The Shift Network, which came to him in mediation eleven years earlier. The premise was that the world was going through a crisis/transition, that the old infrastructures were falling apart, and that the old mindsets of greed and sense of separation from one another and nature could not be continued. Instead of trying to "fix" what was breaking, The Shift Network was focused on highlighting and accelerating what was emerging that was inspired by higher levels of consciousness. The key was to trust the new was coming, though we would not be able to predict what it would be like from the old consciousness. Still, we could trust it was coming and play our roles in helping facilitate "the shift."

In listening to this vision, I realized how my own experience with BBQ was similar in nature: old ways being stripped away, old identities, old mindsets; preparing for something new to emerge. It was interesting to think of applying lessons learned from personal experience to a larger collective process. I knew that millions, if not billions, of people were concerned about the global situation and could be going through personal and collective crises. It was nice to be with a team of people looking at how to help the birthing process on a global scale.

As a social enterprise, The Shift Network was dedicated to the democratization of access to consciousness-raising information across multiple sectors, including business, peace, health, and women and men's consciousness. The Shift Network sponsored numerous free online telesummits highlighting luminaries from around the world. It offered courses, books, and other products people could purchase to go deeper into the content. It was a collaborative business model where people and organizations from around the world could share insights and best practices on emerging new ways of being.

On my return to Washington, DC after the initial staff meeting, Rick Levy asked if this new job was along my soul purpose and if it was a better match than doing fundraising. Rick asked several questions and then let me have it. "Ye of little faith, you must have more faith in Master and Mother," he said.

As Rick relished in telling me he had told me so, I was reminded of a time in Sierra Leone as a Peace Corps Volunteer when I nearly drowned. I had been fishing with a Peace Corps friend, and a storm caught us by surprise at dusk. With lightening flashing everywhere, we paddled upstream, only to have the canoe be swamped. I grabbed the fishing gear and headed to shore. As I struggled in the water, I was reminded of when my mother had encouraged me to take swimming lessons as a child and I had successfully avoided the lessons. Then I remembered the crocodile that lived in that part of the river and thought it was better to put it out of my mind. My legs then got tangled in a submerged tree, and my head went under. As I thought, "Damn, I'm going to drown in Africa," my body instinctually extended, my feet hit the bottom and I stood up. I was in three feet of water. Moral of the story: when in over the head, stand up.

Our Lady of Peace

On July 1, 2011, the morning after a new moon, I left Arlington, Virginia and started the drive across the country. My grandmother's statue of Mother Mary was my copilot, nestled safely in the backseat of the car. The drive was relaxing and enjoyable, an opportunity to let go of the past and prepare for the new. I visited family in Indiana and attended a Global Peace Initiative of Women gathering at the Fetzer Institute in Michigan. I then visited a brother in Iowa and stayed with him and his family for a week while continuing to work for The Shift Network remotely.

On the drive from Iowa to Colorado to see a sister, I cruised through Nebraska. As I neared the border of Wyoming, I needed gas and decided to take a side road to a small town. The area seemed nice, so I stayed on the back road, the first time in over fifteen hundred miles I had left the main roads. Within a few miles, I saw a white figure in the distance. As I drove toward it I realized it was a statue of Mother Mary.

My heart was flooded with a wave of energy, and tears of joy came to my eyes as I pulled into the parking lot of a shrine to Mother. She was over thirty feet tall, standing on a ten-foot tall base, giving her an impressive presence of over forty feet. There were fourteen other life-size statues of Mother Mary and Christ on the grounds.

A mother and daughter were there visiting the shrine, and we took photos for each other. After they drove off, I was left alone with Mother. At the base of the statue was a sign that read, "Our Lady of Peace." I was engulfed in Her presence.

The tears flowed as I thought back to the Peace Corps, to A.K, Tendy, Josephine and the Contehs and to the war that devastated Sierra Leone. I remembered all of the amazing peacebuilders I met across Africa through Search for Common Ground, and how they and many other people were bringing forth Mother's love and compassion in tangible ways in difficult situations.

For over an hour, I sat at the feet of Mother, feeling Her embrace. In between the tears of joy, I prayed, "Mother, I still don't understand why all the suffering, but thank you for your love and guidance."

I reflected on how Her hand had guided me over the years, most recently in the transition from Search to the next role. I laughed, realizing I could have much deeper trust and faith in Her and told myself to remember this moment the next time I felt confused or overwhelmed. I asked Mother to help me be more in tune and to follow Her guidance with much more grace and ease, at least for the sake of my family and friends so I would not drive them crazy. I also realized that I would not be able to predict what She would have in store, and that I would have to learn to enjoy the show.

As I prepared to leave, I started laughing as I remembered Mickey Singer. Finally, I realized, I was not the one pulling the strings. I just kept laughing and laughing, as it had taken a rather large sign from Mother for me to finally get this point. I left the shrine with a deep sense of peace and joy, as well as humor.

Crestone

After a brief visit with my sister and her family outside Fort Collins, I headed south to Crestone, Colorado to spend a week with James O'Dea. James had left IONS and was the lead faculty for a peace ambassador training program offered by The Shift Network. James had moved to Crestone to be in the beautiful nature and spiritual community. We reflected on how it was auspicious that after knowing each other for twenty years, we finally would be working together, just on the eve of 2012, a year that is the subject of prophecies in many spiritual traditions.

James and I had several conversations about the process of burning off dross and how to surrender to it. James had gone through several rounds of burning himself. He said the last time felt like a swarm of locusts was eating him alive. He laughed merrily with a slight Irish accent. We acknowledged how the burning was a sacred passage, making a person more ready to be a pure channel for spirit to flow. There was no room for attachments or ego aggrandizement to be in the way of service.

While in Crestone, James took me to a temple to Divine Mother, and I immediately felt at home there. It was so nice to meet people of different spiritual traditions who also were devotees of Mother. The resonance was so similar from tradition to tradition.

From Crestone I made a brief visit with cousins in Sedona, Arizona. They also had a Mother Mary statue in their background. I then headed to Encinitas, California where I started a meditation retreat. I found myself melting into the vibrations of the retreat center, ever so aware of the tremendous service that the monks and nuns provided by offering their lives to maintaining the essence of the Kriya Yoga lineage. The monks and nuns, who were the epitome of utter humility, created the space for me and thousands of people to explore a direct relationship with Spirit. They, in my mind, were the real peacebuilders and the wealthiest people on Earth, holding open a portal to remind all of us caught in the delusion of titles, roles, and materialism that there exists a realm vaster than anything on Earth could provide. They held the space for the inner exploration of peace, the foundation upon which outer peace could be built.

During the retreat, I had a clear dream of a Youth Rising for Peace Summit that would highlight how youth were working for peace around the world. The idea was to interview young leaders who were working on peace. The online summit would start near the International Date Line and then move westward, interviewing leaders every hour on the hour for twenty-four hours. The vision felt clear, inspired, and a bit on the ambitious side. (Youth Rising for Peace Summit did take place later. http://youthrisingforpeace.com/)

The Chief of Peace

After forty-four days driving across the country, including two weeks of meditation retreat, I arrived in Northern California. The trip had started on a new moon and ended at midnight under a full moon. At first I stayed with a dear friend in Mill Valley, and would later move to Petaluma. At the office I began working closely with Emily Hine, the Chief of Peace.

Emily had had her own sacred journey that had led her to The Shift Network. Raised in Washington State, Emily came from a family that was very socially active. Her mother had a long political career that included serving as mayor of her town and as majority leader for the state House of Representatives, then, later in her career, overseeing the building of the Seahawks football stadium in Seattle. As the youngest of six, (not the "baby", as Emily would say), Emily was driven to make a difference in the world. She worked for the United Way and was later recruited by Microsoft to head up their employee-giving programs. Emily stayed with Microsoft until, one day, she realized that her soul had left the building. The tragedies of September 11 put more urgency into making a life and career change. So, she made the leap and started her own consulting firm, helping to bridge the gap between nonprofit organizations and corporations. Over the course of her career, Emily helped raise over 150 million dollars for nonprofit efforts.

Emily began to have her own mystical experiences where different spiritual figures began to appear to her in meditation. She would sit and have conversations with them, and each of them told her she needed to work for peace. One such figure was His Holiness the Dalai Lama, so Emily did what she was told. She went to India and found herself with uncanny access to His Holiness. Coincidentally, nine months later, Emily was chosen as senior director for Seeds of Compassion, a five-day event in Seattle featuring the Dalai Lama. Over one hundred fifty thousand people attended events, and compassion curricula were introduced into schools around Washington state. As a member of the executive team, Emily oversaw many aspects of Seeds, including all fundraising and the twelve hundred volunteers who made the event a reality.

I quickly came to admire Emily, who had chosen the title Chief of Peace as an example for corporate cultures. Meanwhile, Emily appreciated my depth of experience in peacebuilding. "I come from the jungles of corporate America," Emily would say, "and Philip from the jungles of Africa."

We developed a seamless working relationship where we would pick up each other's thoughts before the other would say them. I was amazed what it was like to work in an environment where many meetings were started with a meditation and where the goal was to listen and follow the energy to look at what would be the most efficient ways to inspire a shift in consciousness.

Emily and Stephen Dinan loved the idea of a Youth Rising for Peace Summit and we planned on it for February 2012. Ideas informed by deep intuition, that could be implemented in practical ways, were highly valued, as the new would emerge from ideas inspired by Source.

Emily picked up on the idea of the peace continuum from inner to international peace, and we began to introduce it into all the language. Emily and I also had an uncanny ability to find puns out of thin air, and we encouraged the behavior in one another. We quickly deemed ourselves the "peace pundits" and had at it, every chance. Our poor colleagues had to withstand the punishing humor.

Together, Emily and I began outlining a plan for The Summer of Peace 2012, an idea Stephen Dinan, Devaa Haley Mitchell, and several others had developed and were now ready to implement. We set the ambitious goal of having the Summer of Peace 2012 be the largest celebration and call to action for inner and outer peace in one season in the history of humanity. A cornerstone of the Summer of Peace 2012 was to acknowledge and celebrate that there were tremendous efforts going on around the world toward building a culture of peace.

To support this vast vision, we were encouraged to set up our offices as sacred sanctuaries. Needless to say, I made a shrine to Mother Mary, using the statue that was my grandmother's. I also placed on the walls images of Gandhi, Yogananda, and the entire line of gurus from Self-Realization Fellowship. Of course, I placed photos from Sierra Leone as a reminder of my dear friends.

PeaceWeek 2011

In September 2011, Emily and I, along with other colleagues, organized PeaceWeek 2011, a free telesummit with over sixty peacebuilders from around the world. PeaceWeek 2011 was a stepping-stone for the Summer of Peace 2012. The intention of PeaceWeek 2011, as well as the Summer of Peace 2012, was to acknowledge and celebrate that there are thousands if not millions of people around the world working on peace in a wide variety of situations, from inner to international levels.

PeaceWeek 2011 covered the entire Peace Continuum and the Peace Wheel, an integrative mandala system created in 1962 by Avon Mattison, cofounder of Pathways to Peace and one of the inspirations for the United Nations in 1981 to create the International Day of Peace — September 21. "The Peace Wheel consists of eight to twelve sectors, or pathways, that are interconnected and that symbolize the diverse ways that people are building a culture of peace for the benefit of all. These pathways transcend national, ethnic, racial, religious, age, and gender differences. There are many pathways common to every society — governance/law/security, education/media, economics/business, health/relationships, science/technology, religion/spiritual teachings, environment/habitat, and culture — and that form the synthesis of all the diverse pathways." [11]

PeaceWeek 2011 was inspiring and fun, as James O'Dea, Avon, Stephen, Emily, and I, along with a couple of other colleagues, took turns interviewing different peacebuilders.

For the inner dimension, Brother Anilananda, a senior monk from Self-Realization Fellowship, and Sister Jenna, from the Brahma Kumaris, talked about meditation as a personal peace practice. Mirabai Bush, the founding director of the Center for Contemplative Mind in Society, talked about a study she had conducted called *Contemplation Nation: How Ancient Practices are Changing the Way We Live.* Mirabai reported there has been a steady rise in the number of people practicing meditation, yoga, and other forms of contemplation in the United States. She mentioned there are over ten million people practicing meditation in the United States, and that yoga had passed golf as the favorite pastime for lawyers.

Mirabai said many people were drawn to meditation and yoga for their health benefits. She also shared stories about how she is working with Google and other corporations to introduce meditation into their companies.

Daniel Goleman talked about scientific research around emotional intelligence and how he is integrating these findings into his work with companies. Meanwhile, Andy Barker, the social mission specialist from Ben and Jerry's Ice Cream, talked about the importance of being a socially responsible business.

Michael Shipler, from Search for Common Ground, was on a panel discussing peace and the media. Another former colleague from Search for Common Ground, Chip Hauss, was in a dialogue with Captain Richard O'Neill about the evolving role of the military in promoting peace. This dialogue was between unlikely partners, as Chip had been a conscientious objector during the Vietnam War while Captain O'Neill was a retired Navy Officer. After nearly three decades of working on conflict transformation and peacebuilding, Chip was working side-by-side with Captain O'Neill and other military advisors to the Pentagon on how the military could provide security in an increasingly complex world by drawing upon conflict transformation and other tools. Chip was quick to say that much of the forward thinking about peaceful approaches to human security was coming from military professionals.

I especially appreciated the dialogue on peace and the military because of the role the British military, the United Nations, and West African peace-keeping missions played in stopping the violence in Sierra Leone.

Another former Search for Common Ground colleague, Rob Fersh, talked about his work in bridging political divides in Washington, DC. Rob had founded Convergence, a nonprofit organization that he incubated in Search for Common Ground and that successfully brings together a wide range of stakeholders, including Democratic and Republican leaders, to look at creative solutions to difficult national policy issues. Rob was quick to say that there are good people in both political parties. When good people are in bad systems, it is hard to get anything done. When good people are brought into positive, constructive, and practical approaches, a lot of good can get done.

There were several interviews about preventing youth violence in the United States, including a panel with a U.S. congressman. I also was pleased to hear two different speakers talk about the economics of peace, including David Korten, author of *Agenda for a New Economy: From Phantom Wealth to Real Wealth*, and Steve Killelea, the creator of the Global Peace Index, a means of measuring the economic impact of peace and/or lack of it. Both Dan and Steve brought the hard science of economics into the realm of peacebuilding. I was moved when Steve Killelea pointed out there were fourteen words in Japanese for beauty, and that we only had one word for peace. Steve said humanity was only at the beginning of understanding peace, and that we needed to develop the language to describe peace in different contexts.

Michael Furdyk spoke passionately about TakingITGlobal, a nonprofit he cofounded that is working to educate and empower young people around the world to constructively address critical issues. TakingITGlobal is using the power of social media to inspire hundreds of thousands of young people per year to take action in their communities.

Arun Gandhi spoke about nonviolence through inspiring stories about what he learned from his grandfather, Mahatma Gandhi. Jane Goodall talked eloquently about the relationship between peace and the environment. Jane Goodall's Roots and Shoots program is working with youth in 120 countries around the world. Jane was passionate that youth were the future for peace and the environment.

What was most impressive about Arun Gandhi and Jane Goodall was their humility. Even though they had impressive accomplishments, they spoke with utter humility, which allowed their wisdom to penetrate deeply and quickly.

Rick Levy joined Pooran Pandey from *The Times of India* in a conversation about the coming together of East and West. Minutes before the call with Rick and Pooran, an Indian woman walked into The Shift Network office to say hello. She was one of the students of the Peace Ambassador Training program. She was on campus attending a workshop and wanted to introduce herself. She said her name was Ambika. When I asked what it meant, she replied, "Mother of the Universe," at which point I just laughed. Of course, the Mother of the Universe would walk in just before a conversation bridging East and West.

One of my favorite PeaceWeek 2011 sessions was with Kimmie Weeks, the young man who, at the age of sixteen, had walked into Talking Drum Studio in Monrovia, Liberia with the idea of creating a children's radio program. Kimmie produced *Golden Kids News*, which inspired children's radio programs in Sierra Leone and at least ten other countries. I had heard of Kimmie, and yet we had never met. Here Kimmie was, fourteen years later, having created a nonprofit organization called Youth Action International. Kimmie and I had so much fun talking with each other and, I must admit, we got a bit carried away with ourselves. Kimmie impressed me with his positive attitude. Even though he had nearly died in a refugee camp as a child and he had seen horrific suffering in his home country, Kimmie was joyous, grateful, and optimistic.

PeaceWeek 2011 left me energized and excited. All the PeaceWeek 2011 interviews were made available free online. We had over 23,000 people from 152 countries listening, including a school in Burundi that reportedly played some of the recordings for the classrooms. (To listen to the PeaceWeek 2011 recordings, go to: peaceweek2011.com)

The New Peace Movement

PeaceWeek 2011 was only a sampling of the numerous ways that millions of people are exploring and expressing peace across the peace continuum from inner to international levels. During PeaceWeek 2011 and following the Peace Ambassador Training program, James O'Dea frequently spoke about a "wave of peace" emerging around the world. James loved to say, "This is not your parent's war protest," rather, this is a movement that is naturally arising from the hearts and souls of people around the world looking at how we can live peacefully together and in harmony with the environment.

Another quality about this wave of peace emerging is that there are many people looking at how "to be the change" while taking action. The idea of being angry protesters against something is giving way to millions of people who are manifesting peace in the world while also maintaining their own personal peace practices to inform their actions. There is a wide range of personal peace practices being used, including interpersonal skills, such as Nonviolent Communication (NVC) taught by Marshall Rosenberg, as well as tools to cultivate inner peace, such as meditation, yoga, and/or martial arts.

This new peace movement is also the result of a convergence of several fields that have grown exponentially and simultaneously the past few decades. Meditation and yoga have become mainstream practices; meanwhile scientific research is documenting the positive impact of these ancient methods on mind-body health. The number of colleges offering conflict resolution, mediation, and peacebuilding programs has grown from a handful in 1984 to several hundred today. Also, a vast majority of high schools in the United States have peer-mediation programs, and the same is true in New Zealand, Japan, and many other countries. Combine these emerging fields with the growth of the internet and social media, and there is an exponential growth of people striving to embody peace while working for peace in the world.

For instance, after a Global Peace Initiative of Women dialogue in Cairo, Egypt, Dena Merriam said she was surprised to find that there were many young people in Egypt who were meditating while also participating in the Arab Spring activities. Dena said there was a strong spiritual essence flowing through the young people in nonviolent actions. Dena also said the young people in Egypt were closely watching what young people in the United States were doing in the Occupy Movement; thus, young people around the world were learning from one another. Youth rising for peace is taking on new meaning in this information and communication age.

The blending of the inner and outer has been organically and quietly growing as millions of people are looking to address the pains of their lives, communities, and the world. For instance, Aqeela Sherrills shared during a Peace Ambassador

Training class about how he brokered a peace treaty between the longtime rival gangs the Bloods and the Crips in Los Angeles. He openly talked about how the death of his own son through gang violence sent him into an intensive period of soul-searching. Aqeela spoke powerfully about his own inner work that included daily mind-body-spirit techniques.

Another peacebuilder that inspired me in her ability to bridge the inner and outer was Louise Diamond. Louise has been a forward thinker about "whole systems" approaches to peacebuilding. During a Peace Ambassador Training class, Louise talked about how she successfully organized large dialogues in Washington, DC with people from the U.S. State Department, Defense Department, and various nonprofit organizations. When asked how she learned about whole systems approaches, Louise surprised all of us with her answer — she tunes in with "the Spirit of Peace," which she says is a real energy, consciousness, and being.

Prior to writing this book, I had been shy about openly sharing how there is an invisible hand that has guided me through the pains of personal and global crisis. In seeing the wave of peace arising around the world, I have to believe that there is a hidden hand, or a Spirit of Peace, that is manifesting through the hearts, minds, and souls of millions of people. For some people, the language that will appeal to them is that we are all part of a quantum field of energy and consciousness, and as more and more people become conscious, the collective benefits.

I like to think the crisis in the world, individual and collective, is driving each of us to seek a deeper peace and, ultimately, that which we are seeking is causing us to seek. Peace is a hidden treasure, and as we move toward it we must share it with others, as we see ourselves in the other and we recognize that we are all connected. In this way, compassion is a gift of the soul, and it compels each of us to reach out to help one another in a time of crisis. As we answer the call of our own souls, we outwardly express our own unique gifts guided by our soul's wisdom. In essence, we all become instruments of Her peace in a grand symphony of peace that is emerging around the world.

Notes

1. *Self-Realization*, Fall 2000, Self Realization Fellowship, Los Angeles, CA
2. Black Elk in *The Sacred Pipe: Black Elk's Account of the Seven Rites of the Oglala Sioux* (1953)
3. *In the Sanctuary of the Soul*, Self-Realization Fellowship, Los Angeles, CA
4. *Man's Eternal Quest*, Self-Realization Fellowship, Los Angeles, CA
5. Mariatu Kamara, after enduring the RUF atrocities in Sierra Leone, has since dedicated her life to the freedom and well-being of all children and youth in her native Sierra Leone and beyond. Even as a young woman, Mariatu has influenced our world deeply toward peace and understanding. Her website, www.mariatufoundation.com, includes more of her story as well as ordering information for her award-winning book, *The Bite of the Mango*.
6. *A Human Approach to World Peace*, The Dalai Lama, Wisdom Publications, London, England
7. *Where There is Light*, Self-Realization Fellowship, Los Angeles, CA
8. Spiral Dynamics; Wikipedia: http://en.wikipedia.org/wiki/Spiral_Dynamics
9. *Where There is Light*, Self-Realization Fellowship, Los Angeles, CA
10. *Man's Eternal Quest*, Self-Realization Fellowship, Los Angeles, CA
11. Pathways to Peace; http://pathwaystopeace.org

Appendix One

The Peace Continuum

Sanskrit has 108 words for love.
Islam has 99 names for God.
Japanese has 14 words for beauty.

We've got one word for Peace.... We don't have enough words
to accurately describe all the different types of peace.
I think it was Socrates who once said if you don't have a word to describe something,
then how can you think about it?
— Steve Killelea (PeaceWeek 2011)

The Peace Continuum is a framework for viewing the ways that peace and peacebuilding are emerging in the world, from inner to international levels. It brings to life the age-old idea that peace starts within and then spreads outward from there. It also offers ways of seeing how peace and peacebuilding can mean something different to people in various situations.

The Peace Continuum can be visualized as concentric circles, with inner peace (pure consciousness and then mind-body-spirit relationship) being in the center and then expanding outward from there. The inner affects the outer, and the outer affects the inner. The Peace Continuum is complemented by the Peace Wheel (http://pathwaystopeace.org/pw/overview.html), which has eight components or sectors contributing to a culture of peace, along with the Global Peace Index (http://www.visionofhumanity.org/gpi-data/#/2011/scor), the Structures of Peace (http://www.visionofhumanity.org/info-center/structures-of-peace-2/), and Spiral Dynamics (http://www.spiraldynamics.net/). Together, these frameworks offer a comprehensive means of viewing the various ways that peace is being approached in the world today.

A special thanks to Emily Hine, Jennifer Wood, and others for their encouragement and contribution in developing the Peace Continuum.

The Peace Continuum includes:

1. Inner Peace

a. Pure Consciousness (or Spirit)

Science and spirituality are finding common ground around the idea that physical reality arises from consciousness. Meanwhile, mystical traditions for centuries have taught scientific methods of working with energy and consciousness to help people to directly experience and identify with higher states of consciousness. Language becomes tricky as the states of consciousness experienced are more subtle than thought, and each mystical tradition has its own cultural nuances and vocabulary to describe the indescribable. Such words as essence, soul, spirit, and universal consciousness are often used for what scientists might call "quantum field."

Peace is often experienced in higher states of consciousness. Some mystics say one of the first signs of contacting one's true essence or soul is an experience of negative peace, or absence of stimulation. Negative peace then opens to a positive peace that can lead to profound experiences of bliss, joy, ecstasy, and love as one unites his/her soul or essence with the larger universal consciousness. In this sense, peace is like a hidden treasure that exists in the soul of each individual and is a quality of universal consciousness or the quantum field; therefore peace is in the very fabric of the universe and is who we are at the deepest level.

The path of the peacebuilder starts by learning how to tap into and identify with this deeper essence for a sense of inner peace, as well as inspiration and guidance for expressing her/his unique gifts in the world. A natural result of connecting with essence can be a sense of oneness with and compassion for all life.

b. Mind-Body-Spirit Relationship

Consciousness gives rise to the body and mind. Science and spirituality are again finding common ground around the relationship between body, mind, and spirit (or consciousness). There are multiple areas being explored from how cells respond to thoughts and environment, to how a person's behavior is influenced by subconscious memories, to how what we eat affects our physical well-being and moods. A person's ability to tap into essence or spirit, and to relate harmoniously with other people, is often influenced by his body-mind-spirit well-being, both on conscious and unconscious levels.

Meanwhile, ancient spiritual disciplines, such as yoga, meditation, and prayer, along with modern modalities such as psychotherapy and Heartmath (http://www.heartmath.com/) technologies, have become popular in spiritual and secular settings alike to help people deal with stress, improve their health, and tap into an inner sense of peace, strength, and wisdom. Scientific research is documenting the positive impact of ancient traditions such as mindfulness meditation on people's health, including how such practices can reshape brain cells and activate innate capacity for compassion.

c. The Individual Pursuit of Happiness: Where Inner Meets Outer

While many spiritual traditions and scientists agree that each person is part of a larger universal consciousness or spirit, we often experience ourselves as separate from one another. Albert Einstein called this "an optical delusion of ... consciousness." This separation delusion is a result of becoming identified with our thoughts, bodies, emotions, families, races, cultures, nationalities, etc. This sense of separation is at the root of most conflicts in the world, and overcoming it lies at the heart of inner and outer peacebuilding.

For instance, a sense of separation can lead to fear, which gives rise to the "wanting self" — I want to be happy and want to avoid suffering. Every human being has this basic operating system; this is our common humanity — we are all pursuing happiness and trying to avoid suffering for ourselves and loved ones. Meanwhile, the physical universe is based on duality (light/darkness, pleasure/pain, birth/death, etc.); change, as everything rises and passes away; and natural laws such as the law of cause and effect, or karma. Duality, change, and natural laws drive motion and govern each of our lives. As a result, conflict is a natural part of being human as we eventually bump into each other, as well as reap what we sow, while pursuing happiness, avoiding suffering, and expressing our unique gifts in the ebbs and flows of life.

How we pursue happiness, avoid suffering, and deal with conflict greatly impacts the people and natural environment around us, as well as the rest of the world.

2. Interpersonal Relationships

The cornerstone of all outer peacebuilding starts with one-on-one, interpersonal relationships — overcoming our perceived separation while appreciating our individuality. How we are with each other sets into motion a series of cause-and-effect circumstances that can potentially impact the lives of dozens, if not hundreds, thousands, and even millions of people.

How we are with another person is influenced by our inner state of being — when more at peace within, it is easier to be patient, understanding, and compassionate. When restless, angry, or fearful, it is easy to project our frustrations onto others. Add into the mix cultural, language, gender, religious, political, or economic differences, and there is fertile ground for creativity and/or misunderstanding. (For a sophisticated mapping of biopsychosocial systems in the world and how they affect conflict and peacebuilding between individuals, communities, and nations, please see Don Beck's Spiral Dynamics.)

"Peace" takes on new meaning as it goes from an inner state of being to looking at how to promote harmony and cooperation between people in the midst of their individual pursuit of happiness. In the past few decades, there has been an exponential growth in the fields of conflict resolution, mediation, and nonviolent communication, all aimed at helping people deal with their differences constructively. Meanwhile, emerging scientific disciplines such emotional intelligence, Heartmath technologies, and others are offering means of improving human relations through developing mind-body-spirit capacities. Also, spiritual disciplines, such as mindfulness meditation and the ability to read and transmute energies, are slowly being integrated into one-on-one peacebuilding practices.

A key component of one-on-one peacebuilding is helping people to go beyond their perceived separation to focus on their common ground or common humanity. A natural result of rediscovering common humanity is often the awakening of innate human capacity for compassion, tolerance, and forgiveness. (This is similar to what happens in a meditation practice when a person expands her/his sense of identity and feels a connection with all of life.). When experiencing compassion, it easier for people to go from attacking each other to standing side-by-side in order to address shared problems.

3. Family

The family unit is at the heart of social structures. How a family deals with the challenges of daily life shapes each individual who then goes out into the world carrying forth many of the values, habits, beliefs, and even traumas learned from the family.

Cultivating peace and harmony in the home and learning constructive ways of dealing with differences is crucial to developing societies at peace. There is a wide range of factors that contribute to a family's well-being, such as spiritual upbringing, economic conditions, and learned means of communication, as well as how to deal with conflict.

4. Education and Livelihood — Schools and Workplaces

Access to quality education and gainful livelihood are two factors that greatly contribute to a stable and peaceful society. When education, livelihood, or both are missing or deficient, there can be considerable social unrest. The range of education in the world varies greatly, from informal education in indigenous societies, to one-room schools, to vast public education systems, to private universities such as Harvard. Likewise, livelihoods can be anything from subsistence farming to small-scale businesses, to factory jobs, to investment banking, to teaching, to medical professions, etc.

People fortunate to have access to formal education and gainful livelihoods can spend considerable amounts of their lives in schools and at workplaces. These settings are where people act out, for better or worse, what they learned in their families. They also are environments that affect our ability to experience peace both within and in relation to other people.

Schools in many countries, such as the United States, have been picking up the burdens of dealing with social problems that have exceeded the capacities of families. Schools also have seen an exponential growth of peace, conflict resolution, and mediation education as they try to help students learn nonviolent means of dealing with conflicts.

While many businesses look at only a bottom line of profits earned, there are many companies putting into place socially responsible practices that look at the well-being of employees, community, and the environment. For example, Google has introduced mindfulness meditation as a means of helping employees cultivate inner peace and innovation, while Ben and Jerry's contributes a percentage of its profits to peace efforts. Emotional intelligence and other emerging, one-on-one toolsets are finding receptive audiences in businesses that want to improve innovation and productivity through better human relations.

5. Community

A community can be based on geography, such as a village, town or city, or it can be formed by identity, such as religious, ethnic, racial, political, economic, or gang affiliation. Communities have traditionally taken on responsibility for promoting the well-being of its members, thus the saying "it takes a village to raise a child."

In recent years, communities around the world are facing new challenges and opportunities brought about by new technologies and an interconnected and interdependent global economy. An extreme example: once-isolated rural farming villages in West Africa have experienced incredible violence, some at the hands of child soldiers armed with automatic weapons from former Soviet Union countries, financed in part by the international diamond trade and trained by watching *Rambo* and other violent films.

Likewise, cities in many Western countries are dealing with a rise in youth violence as well as downturns in the global economy. Meanwhile, there are a wide variety of grassroots creative efforts emerging in response to these new challenges. There also are a plethora of examples where communities are celebrating diversity and/or promoting local agriculture and alternative energy sources, all aimed at contributing to more peaceful and environmentally sustainable ways of life.

6. National

The Global Peace Index has developed a sophisticated system for measuring the level of peace in a country based on twenty-three indicators, including level of organized conflict, jailed population, deaths from internal conflicts, levels of violent crime, political instability, disrespect for human rights, etc. Vision for Humanity, which produces the Global Peace Index, also publishes The Structures of Peace, a report similar in nature to The Peace Wheel. The Structures of Peace identifies elements that lead to peaceful societies, such as well-functioning government, sound business environment, equitable distribution of resources, acceptance of the rights of others, good relations with neighbors, free flow of information, high levels of education, and low levels of corruption.

Just as there are several factors contributing to the state of peace in a country, there are many innovative efforts emerging in each of these areas to help a country become more peaceful.

7. International

It is on the international level that we see the collective impact of the individual pursuit of happiness. For instance, the advancement of new technologies has accelerated the pursuit of happiness through massive consumerism. Humanity is now bound together by a global economy that is creating problems far more complex than our current mindset can handle, including climate change, unpredictable economic downturns, and geopolitical conflicts.

Scientist Ervin Laszlo has said humanity is sitting at a bifurcation point, where we could have a complete breakdown through economic and/or environmental disasters that threaten human survival, or we could have a breakthrough to a new level of consciousness. He goes on to say that this global challenge is not a technological, but rather a spiritual, crisis. We must learn to expand our circle of compassion to embrace all people and life on Earth and learn to meet inner spiritual hunger in more sustainable ways. We also must learn how to collaborate with one another at an unprecedented level to find solutions to these complex problems. We are being forced to find peaceful means of dealing with our differences and to turn diversity into a source of creativity.

With that said, there is a "blessed unrest" as thousands of grassroots organizations are emerging to work on peacebuilding, environmental degradation, and a range of other issues. Also, international groups such as the United Nations, International Criminal Court, and others are making strides to coordinate international efforts.

8. Earth — Relationship with Environment

Included in each of the stages above is a person's relationship with the Earth or environment. The Earth, and all of life on it, emerge out of consciousness. Yet, human's bodies, like all life forms, come from, are sustained by, and eventually return to the Earth. Many spiritual traditions, especially indigenous ones, recognize how living in balance and sacred relationship with the Earth can help a person shift her/his consciousness to experience her/his own spiritual essence and thereby a deeper sense of inner peace.

However, the modern pursuit of happiness through massive consumerism depicts the Earth as a commodity instead of being sacred. Natural resources are extracted, consumed, and then disposed back into the Earth at an accelerated rate. Humanity is literally at war with the Earth and thereby threatening our very existence.

It is clear that how we find and cultivate peace within ourselves, with others, and with the Earth is a question that our lives and those of our children depend on. Fortunately, there are many efforts underway to stem the tide of environmental degradation and to "awaken the dreamer and change the dream" — i.e., examine how we pursue happiness and seek more sustainable means.

(Note: Scientists claim the Earth is in a solar system that is in a galaxy with hundreds of millions of stars, that is in a universe with billions of galaxies, each with hundreds of millions of stars. This sense of expansion is similar to what happens when a mystic takes his/her consciousness inward and expands it to universal consciousness. However, many mystics have said that the inner domain is vaster than the physical universe, as all matter arises out of consciousness. Again, peace is experienced when going into these expanded states of consciousness; thus, peace is in the very fabric of the universe.)

Appendix Two

Tools for Cultivating Inner and Outer Peace

In writing *God and Conflict: A Search for Peace in a Time of Crisis* I have sought to bridge the worlds of inner and outer peacebuilding. I am grateful for the many wonderful friends, colleagues, and other teachers who have shared a number of tools along the way.

Below are a few of the tools I find helpful. This is only a sampling of what is available, as there is an abundance of conflict resolution, mediation, mind-body health, and other tools available that can help a person cultivate inner and outer peace.

Embrace Conflict as Natural — Peace as our Birthright

Conflict is a natural part of the human experience and an integral part of a spiritual path.

As described throughout the book, there are several levels to see how conflict is natural. On a basic level, conflict is a result of differences — opinions, positions, and the myriad forms of human expressions.

On a deeper level, conflict stems from a person's identification with his/her thoughts, emotions, and body and, as a result, feeling separate from her/his own soul and God. (See Appendix One's section on The Individual Pursuit of Happiness: Where Inner Meets Outer)

By accepting conflict as natural, we can relax and choose how to approach it in the moment. How we deal with conflict determines if it is destructive or constructive, or something in between. Constructive approaches to conflict can deepen personal relationships and serve as a driving force in helping families, communities, and entire societies evolve over time.

Meanwhile, peace is the very essence of the soul. By going inward and attuning with our soul, we can tap into a sense of peace that can open to a deepening experience of bliss and love and eventually into oneness with God/Universe/Spirit (whatever word works for you). Peace and bliss are our birthright, as they exist in our own souls. They can be experienced as we seek our own divinity. It is not so much a matter of discovering as remembering our soul essence.

Religious Rules and Natural Laws

Every major religion has its list of do's and don'ts. For Abrahamic religions — Christianity, Judaism, and Islam — it is the Ten Commandments. For yoga, it is Yama and Niyama — Yama are rules that are prohibitive, such as avoiding injury to others, untruthfulness, stealing, incontinence, etc; and, Niyama are ones that a person should do, such as purity of body and mind, contentment, self-discipline, self-study (contemplation), and devotion to God.

Such rules are the very foundation of building a spiritual life, as it is scientifically impossible to reach higher states of consciousness when breaking them. Such guidelines also serve as the underpinnings for a peaceful society.

When obeying these rules, relationships are more likely to be harmonious. The Golden Rule is especially useful to follow: *do unto others as you would have them do unto you;* and *love thy neighbor as thyself.*

Meanwhile, the Ten Commandments are backed up by natural laws. Almost every culture has expressions for natural laws, such as "what goes around comes around." By remembering there are natural laws, such as karma, or cause and effect, we can be more mindful before acting. Once we act, then we reap what we sow, in this life or another.

Meditation

Meditation is an important tool for directly experiencing the soul, or higher states of consciousness, and tapping into a deep sense of peace. Meditation also can be helpful for learning how to deal with inner and outer conflicts constructively.

Choosing a meditation practice

Choosing a meditation practice is very personal. Some people are drawn to meditation for its scientifically proven mental, emotional, and physical benefits, and want to keep away from the spiritual aspects. Other people look to meditation to deepen their spiritual practices and will blend Eastern meditation techniques with a Western religion. I know many Christians, Jews, and Muslims who practice Kriya Yoga or Buddhist meditation traditions while still being loyal to and observing their religious traditions.

When first starting with meditation, it can be helpful to experiment with different traditions to see what works for you. I tried several spiritual and meditation traditions before seeking just one. Mickey Singer's advice was very helpful: *set the intention of being drawn to one tradition and let go of trying to figure it out.*

Other advice I found helpful: *once finding a tradition that satisfies both your mind and heart, stay with it and go deep.* I love the metaphor told at many meditation retreats: If digging for water, you want to find a good location and then dig deeply. You do not want to jump around from spot to spot digging shallow wells — chasing pleasant experiences or avoiding the tough inner work. Meditation, as shown in my own story, can take a person through many layers of inner delusion, which can be uncomfortable at times. It is by riding through the dry or dark periods that we get to deeper states of peace and self-realization.

Habit: If you can make meditation a daily habit — whether first thing in the morning, at noon, and/or before going to bed — you will find it is easy to meditate longer.

Fellowship: I find it helpful to be in a meditation tradition that has a community of people that offer regular opportunities to meditate together. Group meditations can create a powerful energy field that can deepen and reinforce your daily meditation practice. I also find meditating with people of other traditions to be an uplifting experience when we all go into silence together.

Retreats: If you can afford the time and money, a several-day- or week-long meditation retreat during the year can reinforce a practice.

Guidance: It is very helpful to be in a tradition where you have access to guidance from teachers on a regular basis, whether by phone or in person.

Introductory method

There are many resources available online that provide a basic introduction to meditation, including recorded guided meditations. If you Google "meditation," you will find a profusion of resources; look for a tradition that appeals to you and give it a try.

If you do not have access to meditation resources and want to get started while researching options, here is a simple technique:

Sit comfortably in a chair with your eyes closed. (You want to turn your eyes slightly upward toward the "third eye" — a point between the eyebrows. When your eyes are turned downward, it is easy to go to sleep or into subconscious mind; straight ahead, conscious mind; and, upward into superconsciousness.)

Take a deep breath in while tensing all the muscles in the body, hold the breath for a few seconds and then exhale slowly while relaxing the body. Repeat this a few times. The tensing and relaxing will relieve tension, preparing you to meditate.

With your eyes still closed, focus your attention on your breath. You notice the breath coming in and then going out, without trying to control the breath. You are simply "witnessing" the breath. More than likely, you will have a lot of thoughts come up. Simply bring your attention back to your breath, allowing the thoughts to rise and pass away. The breath helps bring you back to the present. Sit for five minutes or longer if you have time, witnessing your breath. Be sure to be gentle on yourself when the mind wanders, because it will! This is called "monkey mind" and we all have it. Just let go of judgments and bring your attention back to your breath.

Again, this is only an introductory technique and is not a substitute for getting established in a tradition.

The Witness: Doorway to the Soul

Meditation helps a person to develop the witness —the part of oneself that is witnessing thoughts, emotions, and physical sensations. The witness is pure consciousness or, as some would say, the soul itself.

The more a person meditates, the more he or she can calm the restless mind and go into deeper states of communion with the soul, which is the doorway to universal superconsciousness (God/Spirit). Peace is often one of the first experiences of the soul. By meditating on the peace that arises in meditation, a person can eventually go into states of bliss and other impersonal aspects of God. The peace experienced in meditation can be carried into daily life and can be remembered whenever we feel restless.

It is important not to be looking for experiences while meditating. The goal is not experiences, as they can be a distraction.

There are numerous health benefits to meditating; more and more scientific studies are showing how meditation can relieve stress. Another benefit of meditation is to access wisdom from your own soul as well as from other parts of superconsciousness. Wisdom is more subtle in vibration than thought and will arise in the form of intuition. The more you meditate and tune in with the witness by going deep into silence, the more wisdom will flow through you in the form of intuition.

The Witness: Responding Instead of Reacting — Breaking Cycles

Developing the witness is critical for being able to consciously respond to situations instead of unconsciously reacting. As one yogi said, "we perceive, interpret, and react, just like that." If we overly identify with our thoughts and emotions, we can instantly react from a place of habit when someone does something that provokes us. When you develop the witness, you can perceive, interpret, pause and observe your thoughts and emotions. During the pause, you can invoke feelings of peace experienced in meditation (close the eyes just for a second, breathe deeply, focus on the third eye and remember the peace you felt while meditating) and then more calmly choose how you wish to respond by drawing upon soul wisdom.

By pausing and tuning in with your soul, you can take responsibility for your reactions and separate them out from the person triggering you. This way, you can break any cycle of habitual reactive patterns that set into motion cause-and-effect dynamics, or, negative karmic seeds. Instead, you can create positive karmic seeds based on wise responses and, over time, reduce the power of your reactions that get triggered.

In this way, you actually develop free will instead of being a puppet of unconscious habits.

Dissolving karma

Meditation helps dissolve karma in several ways. As just mentioned, meditation can help us break patterns of unconscious reactions that perpetuate creating new karmic seeds (see above — responding instead of reacting.) Meditation also can help us relax when we are triggered, allowing the stored-up negative energies to rise and pass away without feeding them.

There are more scientific aspects of dissolving karma that are specific to each tradition, where the energetic karmic seeds melt away over time. You will want to explore with your meditation teachers how that specific tradition works with karma.

Walking Meditation — Everyone acts for reasons

There is the old Native American saying, do not judge another person until you've walked a mile in their moccasins. This old saying has deep wisdom. Everyone acts for reasons, whether conscious or unconscious. The reasons could be intentional or they could be the patterns from cultural, family, or other environmental influences or habits brought in from another life; you just do not know why.

A walking meditation is to be aware that everyone does act for reasons. One way to do the meditation is to remind yourself: everyone wants to be happy and to avoid suffering. This person is doing what he thinks, or has learned, will bring himself happiness and avoid suffering. If a person is angry or mean, there is a good chance they are acting out from a place of pain.

This simple practice helps us to remember the humanity in each person and to develop compassion, even if we never fully understand why they act the way they do.

Walking Meditation — We are all connected

As highlighted in a few chapters, the global economy and modern technology has made the world more connected today than ever before. One walking meditation is to be aware that the food on the table comes from many parts of the world and from many different people. (Hopefully, we all buy as much locally as we can.) Stop to think where each item comes from, imagine the people who handled it… think about their families. Remember that each person wants to be happy and wants to avoid suffering, that each person wants the best for their family, friends, and other loved ones.

Listening

As a Meditation

Another positive effect of meditation is learning to concentrate. I have found that my ability to listen dramatically improved after starting to meditate because of my ability to focus my attention.

The reason is simple: in meditation you learn to witness your thoughts and bring your focus back to your breath or a mantra. In listening, you can do the same thing by letting go of your thoughts and bringing your attention back to the person who is speaking.

When in conversations, most of us are thinking about how to respond to what the other person is saying, or, we can be distracted by thinking about something totally unrelated — whether going off on a tangent from something they said, or thinking about something else we have to do later. By becoming aware of our thoughts, we can choose to fully give another person our attention. Wherever we place our focus, that is where our energy and consciousness go. When fully focused on someone, we energetically and consciously connect with them on many levels.

When a person is fully heard, they often feel more valued and are more likely to deal with conflict constructively.

Attentively listening is a way of connecting more profoundly with another person, as we take the time and energy to fully understand what their mind, heart, and soul are trying to relay. This type of listening also allows us to hear with other parts of ourselves that go beyond our mind. It allows us to hear with our intuitive self or soul.

Active Listening

Active listening is a tool commonly taught in meditation, communications, and other classes. It is a powerful way to fully hear what another person is hearing and to navigate difficult conversations.

Actively listening is done by periodically repeating back to the other person what you heard them say and to ask if it is what they meant. While simple, it can be surprising to learn that our interpretations of what others say is not always what they were trying to communicate.

The purpose of actively listening is for the person speaking to be acknowledged and understood. When two people practice active listening, it can create deeper understanding between each other.

As if They Matter

Another aspect of listening is being aware of our judgments of the person speaking. As highlighted by Dean Radin in *Entangled Minds*, our thoughts do travel and can be picked up by other people, whether intuitively or through our expressions.

You can try an experiment: witness your thoughts, especially your judgments, of the person(s) speaking. See what happens if you change negative judgments to positive ones. Listen as if that person matters! You could listen as if that person is a soul playing a human role, or that person is a child of God, or that person is beautiful and whole. Choose whatever works for you and see what happens; the key is to keep it positive. This does not mean you have to agree with everything they say; you simply acknowledge their humanity and divinity!

As shown throughout this book, this same dynamic in listening can be played out in interpersonal situations as well as national and international affairs. Imagine if Democratic and Republican politicians on Capitol Hill listened to one another with deep, mutual respect. Consider how the discussions about national issues would change. Also, think about how each country would respond if they knew other countries valued and respected them!

What is nice about these listening exercises is that you can apply them in your daily life. You can be the change you want to see in the world!

Namaste — greet people

The namaste technique is a variation of "listening as if they matter" and an easy meditation-like habit to develop. When greeting someone, slow down and look at them. In your mind, mentally acknowledge they are a soul, that they have a spark of divinity in them that is also in you. (Again, use whatever words/concepts work for you — soul, divinity, consciousness, humanity…). When they respond, listen and acknowledge them and their response. Eye contact and a smile can be great, if it is culturally appropriate.

The namaste greeting is a way of letting someone know they matter and it only takes a minute or two to do. You can do it with people you see every day as well as with strangers. It is a simple way to connect with someone and the result can be a building of trust over time. What I like about this technique is it reminds me of Sierra Leone and Nepal. In both countries, people valued connecting with one another when greeting.

Ground Rules for Relationships

Ground rules are agreements that we can make with someone, whether a loved one, family member, or work colleague. The ground rules provide a framework for the relationships and serve as a reference point to return to if needed.

Ground rules can be simple and agreed-upon by all parties. Four ground rules I learned from a mentor/supervisor that I found helpful were:

1. Open, honest communication.
2. Give the benefit of the doubt: before jumping to conclusions or assumptions, give the other person the benefit of the doubt. You can then inquire what motivated their actions.
3. Go gently on mistakes: everyone will make mistakes. If your friend or colleague makes one, go easy on them.
4. Focus on lessons learned: when a mistake does happen, together look to see what the lessons are and how both of you can learn from them.

You may want to develop other ground rules for special friendships or work relationships. You can have the ground rules printed in a place where you can both see them or refer to them periodically, until they become second nature. The intention is to maximize the positive potential of the relationship.

Tools when in conflict

Conflict happens. When it does, here are some tools you can try. (Note: please use common sense, and do not put yourself in physical or emotional danger. There are times when it is necessary to be cautious.)

Awareness: Stereotypes & Dehumanizing

One of the first steps to approaching conflict constructively is awareness — how do you react or respond to conflict? Do you avoid conflict, or do you thrive on it? Do you approach conflict differently with family and loved ones than you do with people at work or with strangers? By watching how you are in conflict, you can become conscious of your own style in different situations and then choose if you would like to change it over time.

It is helpful to be aware of when stereotyping, demonizing, or dehumanizing. While it can be fun to go off on a political party or person from "the other" group, we have to remember we are caught in a mindset that ultimately does not serve anyone. The reason is: when we dehumanize someone, we make it easier to attack them or treat them inhumanely. When we are attacking the other we are not focused on the real issues.

Looking for Common Humanity

Many of the techniques mentioned in this appendix help us to see the humanity and divinity in other people. The natural result can be the awakening of "soul qualities" such as compassion, tolerance, and forgiveness.

A fun thing to do when you catch yourself stereotyping another person is to look for your commonalities with him or her. Do you both love the same sports teams? Do you enjoy the same type of music? Do you both have children? There are always many more things that we have in common than we do not have in common. By learning to focus on the commonalities, and engaging people with those commonalities, we create the conditions for positive human qualities to come forth.

Positions & Interests

When in a conflict situation, there is a simple tool you can use to find common ground: distinguish between positions and interests. This is a very simple technique that you can apply at home and that is used by professional mediators and people addressing international conflicts.

The basic idea is that we often develop positions around issues that are important to us. We get firmly planted in those positions and are not willing to budge, especially if we have a lot of fear or anxiety around them. We can go into a slippery slope of dehumanizing the other and attacking them and their positions.

The idea is to look deeper than the positions. You can ask why. Why do I have this position? Why do they have their position? Positions are like trees — the branches may never meet — but interests are like roots — they often overlap. The interests can be basic needs like security and dignity, and the positions are the way we seek to meet those needs.

One example: Every spring for nine years, my housemate and I argued over whether to use the air conditioning. She wanted to use it and I, having lived in the bush of West Africa, did not want to use it. We had the same argument each spring when the weather started to get warmer. When looking deeper, I could see we both had the same interest: a household where we could find comfort and relax after a hard day at work. She could not sleep with the house too hot, and she also got allergies. I wanted to reduce our energy usage, which was something she wanted too. We agreed to use the air conditioning over a certain temperature, and to find other ways to reduce our energy consumption, such as energy-efficient light bulbs.

Face Problems Together

This concept is simple and easy to apply. When in a conflict, we often identify the other person as the problem and attack them; somehow we believe that if we get rid of them or beat them, we get rid of the problem.

If you can rehumanize the other, this awakens your own soul qualities of compassion and tolerance, making it is easier to stand side by side and address the problems together.

The next time you are in a conflict, apply several of the techniques outlined in this appendix — listen as if they matter, try active listening, try understanding why — and then see if you can separate out the issues from the other person. You can physically stand next to the other person and then figuratively place the problem in front of you. How are you going to address it together?

Think about it: Democrats and Republicans are not the problem; the problems are complex issues such as health care, national debt, and environmental degradation. The time, energy, and money going into attacking the other could be used to research, understand, and address the problems. When we stand side by side, we free up energy and open to new levels of creativity to flow through us.

Remember: the American bald eagle flies because the right and left wing work together. Democrats and Republicans have a lot to learn from the national symbol.

Forgiveness and Apologies

Forgiveness is a fundamental part of humanity being able to evolve over time. Forgiveness does not mean condoning what someone may have done. However, it can free a person from carrying around the anger and resentment in response to what happened to them. Forgiveness also creates the possibility of having a positive and constructive relationship again. Another way to think of it: you start to dissolve the karmic bonds with another person so you do not have to come back again to release them!

Apologies also go a long way to help make amends. Being able to say "I am sorry for what I have done" is a tool in peacebuilding.

Praying for "the Other"

Scientific studies are starting to prove that prayers can have a positive effect on people's behaviors and well-being, as well with helping people heal. Prayer also can be used to help improve relationships, especially when in a conflict.

There is a technique I learned from a monk, which I have applied several times. It is very simple: at the end of a meditation, or at another time, sit quietly and visualize the person in your third eye (eyes closed and turned slightly upward). Imagine this person surrounded by golden light. Pray inwardly, Heavenly Father, Divine Mother (or whatever words work for you), fill this person with peace and harmony, peace and harmony.... Repeat the "peace and harmony" line for a full minute, the entire time seeing this person surrounded by light.

Then, say the same prayer for yourself for fifteen seconds, visualizing yourself surrounded by light and being filled with peace and harmony.

Repeat both prayers — the one for him or her for one minute, then you for fifteen seconds — several times.

Do this prayer two or three times a day without any attachment to outcome or desire to change that person. You are simply praying for you and the other person, asking for God's blessings.

See what happens. My experience is that I find my own attitude starts to change by praying for the well-being of the other person; and, often, our relationship will improve.

Praying for Assistance

Why go it alone when there is help available? Praying is a wonderful practice all of its own. One of my favorite prayers I learned from a nun is: "Heavenly father, change no circumstances in my life, change me."

The Power of Positive Thinking

Most folks are about as happy as they
make up their minds to be.
— Abraham Lincoln

A popular technique for helping to relax and overcome stress is the power of positive thinking. This tool has been taught for thousands of years by yogis and others. It became popular in the United States in 1952 with the publication of *The Power of Positive Thinking* by Norman Vincent Peale. The book has sold over twenty million copies in forty-one languages. The technique is very simple: think positive thoughts.

Scientists estimate the average person has over sixty thousand thoughts per day. Most of us just let our thoughts run wild without being aware we have a choice in what we think. Thoughts create patterns, which then create moods, which then create personalities. Have you met people who have very similar circumstances in life yet one is very bright and optimistic while another person seems depressing and negative? These personalities are due in part to patterns in thinking.

The first step in using the power of positive thinking is to become aware of your thoughts. You want to learn to witness your thoughts throughout the day. The mere process of witnessing helps bring about a calming effect, as it helps keep you present and also realize: "I am not my thoughts." Many spiritual traditions would say the one witnessing the thoughts is pure consciousness or our true Self. The mind, which generates thoughts, is simply a tool of our consciousness.

So try an experiment: for a few days, just watch your thoughts without overly identifying with them. Take note how many of your thoughts are positive, neutral, or negative. What kind of thoughts do you dwell on? Some scientific studies estimate the average person has 80 percent negative thoughts. Once you become aware of the patterns of your thoughts, then you can begin to make a conscious choice on which thoughts preoccupy your mind. You can start by catching yourself when you are thinking negatively to stop and change your thoughts to something more positive and uplifting. This does not mean going through life as a Pollyanna and ignoring difficult situations. You can still address difficulties straight on, and then shift your thoughts to parts of life that give you joy.

The power of positive thinking has become so popular in sports psychology, alternative medicine, corporate trainings, self-help books, spiritual teachings, and other venues, that there are many resources online that go into details on how to apply the technique. If you google "the power of positive thinking" you will find a lot of resources.

Attitude of Gratitude

As mentioned in the book, the attitude of gratitude is an excellent mindset to develop.

On a very simple level, being grateful for everything in life brings one closer to God, in that we are focused on the giver instead of the gifts. Praying before eating is a nice time to practice gratitude, at least being grateful for the people who brought the food to the table and for all the animals and plants that contributed to it.

It is also nice to lie in bed in the morning or night and mentally think of all the positive things in one's life and to give thanks. Gratitude tends to inspire positive feelings and can magnetically attract more abundance. The idea is: what we appreciate appreciates; it grows.

The deeper level is what happens when totally trusting and surrendering to God in a deeply personal relationship, one developed in years of practice. A person begins to trust that God is bringing everything into his or her life for spiritual advancement. The burning-off of karma can be terribly unpleasant and to do so hand in hand with a spiritual tradition, with God, makes it not only more bearable, but with a sense of peace.

Media Fasts

One of the biggest gifts from living four years in Sierra Leone was being on a media fast — not watching TV or movies, not reading newspapers, and not listening to much radio. It can be helpful to take a media fast every once in a while for a week or even a month.

It is a balance to stay aware of events taking place in the world and also not to get addicted to violent and/or negative news. By taking periodic media fasts, we more consciously choose which media we want to enter our minds and consciousness.

Experiments in Collective Consciousness

As mentioned in the book, a frontier being explored by many people is the phenomenon of "collective consciousness." You can start to explore this area in your own life.

Self-Awareness in Groups

The first thing to be aware of is your own consciousness and to watch how it is influenced by different environments. As you practice to meditate more and more, it will be easier to witness your thoughts, emotions, and physical responses in different situations. For instance, focus your attention on a subject, such as an NFL football game (or local news) and see what your experience is. Then, later, disconnect from football and go for a walk in nature, and see how you feel then.

Everything has a specific rate of vibration, and we are all influenced by our environments. Remember, we are all consciousness, giving rise to energy that vibrates. When you are tuned in with an NFL football game, you are tuned into that frequency. When in nature, it will have a different vibration, depending whether it is a waterfall, woods, ocean, mountain, etc.

As you become aware of your own experience in these situations, you can explore what happens when you are in group situations. Collective consciousness is happening all the time; it is a matter of becoming aware of its dynamics and how to intentionally work with it.

One experiment you can try is to watch your thoughts when you are in a meeting. See if anyone says any of the thoughts that pass through your mind. You can start to see that thoughts do travel from person to person and that we can become entangled with one another's thoughts and energies. When you remain calm, you can pick up and witness the flow of thoughts in a group.

Group Meditations

One of my favorite experiences of collective consciousness is in group meditations, especially the all-day Christmas meditations our centers hold every year. It is such a strong experience to have anywhere from 50 to 150 people all coming together to meditate, chant and pray on Jesus Christ for six to eight hours. Each of us practices meditation techniques and brings our deep faith to tune in with that specific frequency. The deep peace and even bliss is powerfully transforming.

If you do develop a meditation practice with a particular tradition, you will want to participate in group meditations and observe your own experience. You also can host meditations with friends around special holidays or themes such as Christmas, Easter, Ramadan, Passover, etc.

One thing to remember is that consciousness and thoughts are universal. When meditating on Christ around Christmas or Easter, or God around Ramadan or Passover, you are tuning in with literally millions, if not billions, of people who also are aware of these special holidays. Many spiritual teachers claim there are also celebrations happening with souls on the astral planes or other dimensions of existence.

At these special times of year, those particular saints are also broadcasting their love to humanity. You can start to experience the human capacity to broadcast and receive like a radio, boosted by the amplification of the group collective consciousness and deep devotion. The call and response relationship with the Divine becomes a deeply loving experience. The invisible becomes so much more real through the intuitive abilities developed in deep meditation.

Creating a Collective Consciousness Container

You also can experiment with a small group of people to intentionally create collective consciousness containers to explore new ideas. You and your friends or colleagues can start with the understanding that collective consciousness exists and that it is possible to create an environment together where you can raise the frequency of your vibration and focus it on an intention or question.

Here are some simple techniques you can apply:

1. When inviting people to participate, be sure they are clear on the nature of the gathering and are willing to following basic ground rules or agreements that can help create a conscious container.
2. You can choose to create a container to explore a specific topic or to see what topics arise out of the field on its own.
3. Find a place where you can be together and not disturbed. Colleagues and I have found that places with strong spiritual vibrations, such as monasteries in nature, are especially good. Granted, this can be a luxury, so work with what you have and prepare the space in ways that are special for your group. You can bring as much or little of spiritual significance to it as you like.
4. Sit in a circle, chairs, or on pillows; whatever is comfortable.

5. Depending on your group, you can open with a prayer. Prayers are a good way to create a protective field and to invite in the love and wisdom of guides and saints.
6. Review ground rules or guidelines for the dialogue, making sure everyone is aligned. Here are a few guidelines that were used in the Aspen Grove Project:
    a. Speak only when you feel moved. — "Can you remain unmoving until the right action arises of itself?" —Lao Tzu
    b. Take one long, deep breath before speaking.
    c. When speaking, always use "I" statements when expressing your own experience.
    d. Each person deeply listens to the one person speaking without interrupting. Practice listening as if that person matters.
    e. Have a moment of silence after each person speaks.
    f. Speak to the middle (instead of any specific individuals).
    g. Anyone can invite silence (tap the bell/chime).
7. After reviewing the agreements, go into a period of silence and meditation — each person practice whatever meditation technique they know. If anyone does not know a technique, invite them to watch their breath coming in and going out without controlling it. After the meditation, you can open with an inspiring reading or quote relevant to the group and/or topic.
8. Take breaks periodically from talking to go back into silence together.
9. If each person is able to calm their inner world and open to their highest wisdom, together the group can create a field that is tapping into individual and universal superconsciousness. Such a field can be a powerful way to deepen connections between people and to inspire creativity. By keeping the conversation aimed in the center, it keeps the focus on what is emerging from the group container instead of any one personality.
10. Keep in mind that consciousness and thoughts are universal. When we are vibrating at certain frequencies — whether love, fear, anger, compassion, desire… — we are tapping into a larger field at the same frequency. A collective consciousness container can leverage this phenomenon to draw upon and give expression to ideas/creativity associated with a particular frequency.

Things to be aware of: the energy from a collective field can trigger people's unconscious reactions. You want to make sure you establish a lot of trust, and that each person feels safe. If someone starts to speak from a place of fear or pain, it will affect the magnetism of the field. It could be helpful to have someone work with these people during the breaks to process what is arising for them.

General Reflections

As you try these different experiments, you can see firsthand that collective consciousness is happening all the time, whether we are aware of it or not.

It can become overwhelming to think of the impact that mass media has on entire societies and how millions and even billions of people are swayed into certain mindsets and states of consciousness. As mentioned several chapters above, mass media and collective consciousness can fuel societal violence and can inspire entire nations to reconcile and become more compassionate. Media also can fuel consumerism by creating cravings, keeping people focused on individual consumption and looking for happiness outside of themselves.

With technology bringing humanity closer and closer together through travel and mass communications, it is important that we begin to understand the power of collective consciousness. Each of us can do our part by taking responsibility for our inner world and what we allow into our consciousness. Developing habits and practicing tools that help us to stay centered in a rapidly changing world are becoming increasingly more important on a global level. In a sense, inner peace is a global responsibility.

Philip Hellmich is Director of Peace at The Shift Network, an international social enterprise mobilizing educational tools and cultivating alliances worldwide. Philip's passion is exploring peace along the Peace Continuum, from inner to international levels, and his framing purpose coincides with the key questions: *How is inner peace a global responsibility? How does the world affect inner peace?* A long-time meditation practitioner, Philip enjoys studying and teaching about the parallels between inner and outer peace.

Philip has dedicated most of his life to global and local peacebuilding initiatives, including fourteen years with Search for Common Ground, an international conflict transformation and peacebuilding nongovernmental organization. He also served for four years as a Peace Corps Volunteer in Sierra Leone, where he lived and worked in small remote bush villages. He serves as adviser to The Global Peace Initiative of Women.

Philip is director of the Summer of Peace 2012, a collaborative global celebration of and call to action for inner and outer peace. Produced by The Shift Network, the Summer of Peace is a groundbreaking series of events that bring together some of the world's foremost peacebuilders and social architects while serving to illuminate practical actions for both personal and planetary peace.

Please visit Philip on the web:
www.philiphellmich.com and www.godandconflict.com